The Illustrator's Guide to PROCREATE

How to create digital art on your iPad

Ruth Burrows

DAVID & CHARLES

www.davidandcharles.com

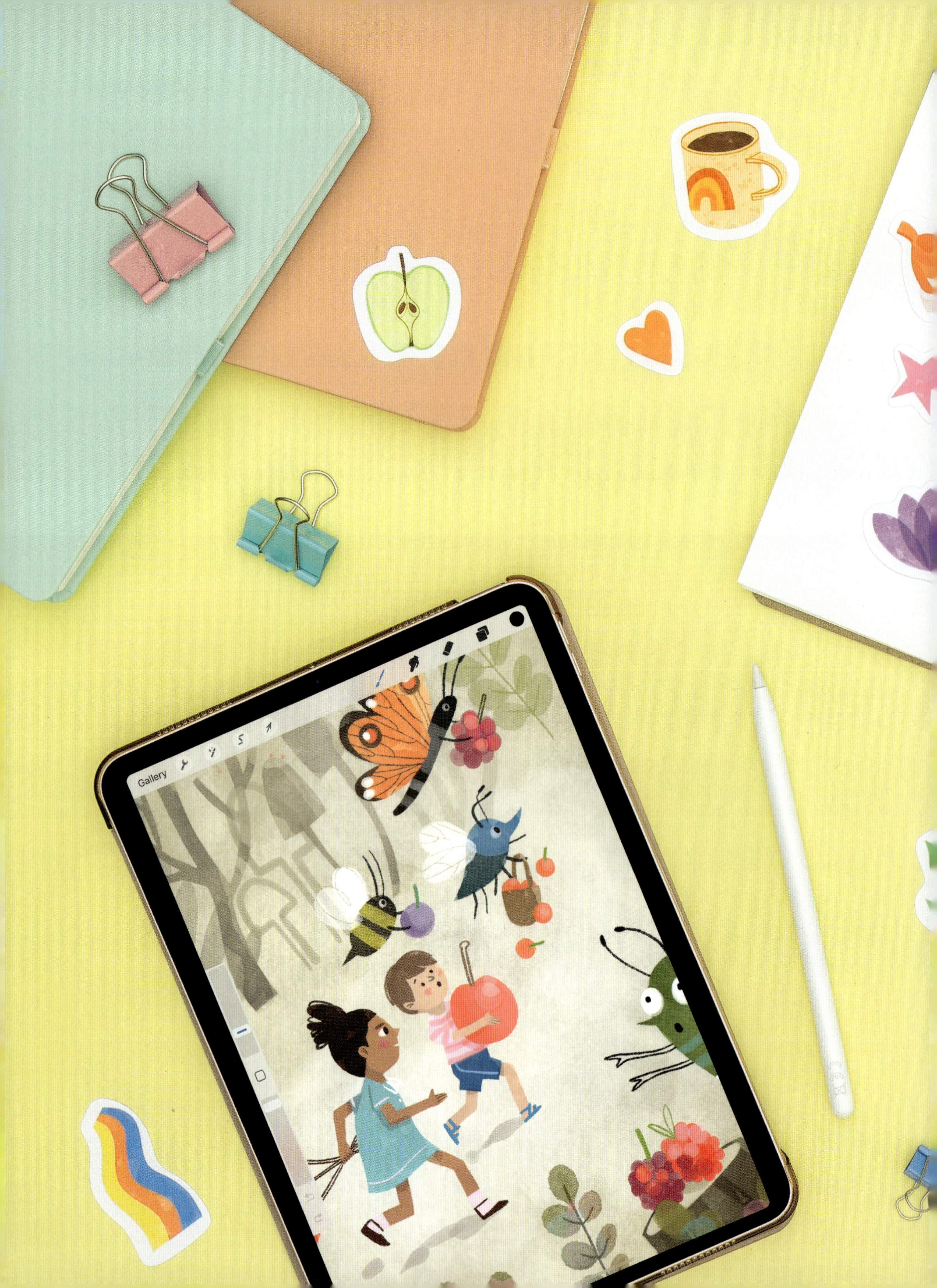
Gallery

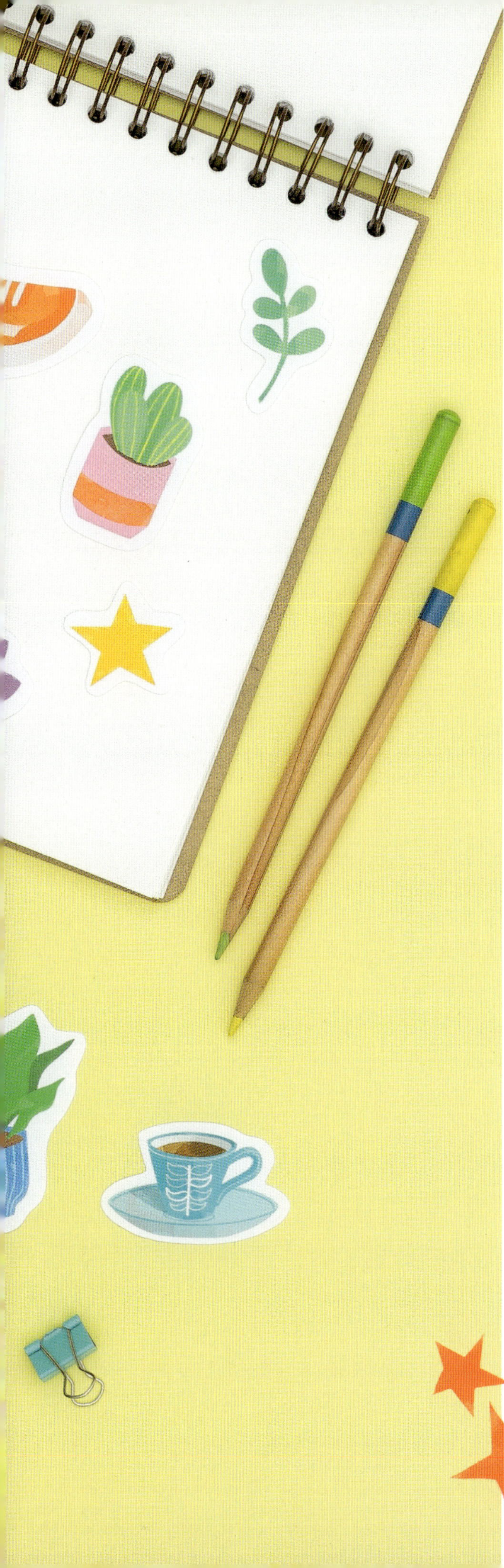

CONTENTS

INTRODUCTION

Procreate is my small-but-mighty friend! It's a powerful tool for creative people, condensed down to the size of a slim notebook. The interface is simple to use. However, behind every light tap or swipe of the screen is a vast library of resources designed to help you make art intuitively.

I bought my first iPad Pro nearly six years ago. The single reason for the purchase was to download and install Procreate, a program I'd just started hearing about and was desperate to try for myself. I distinctly remember using it for the first time to draw a snowman, and how I wowed my handful of Instagram followers with the resulting Time-lapse video showing the process!

Since then, I have used Procreate consistently for both personal, fun work and for professional design and illustration jobs. That's why I call it my friend! It's an app that is reliable, complex but easy to understand, travels by your side with the minimum of fuss, and helps you solve problems by constantly providing simple solutions.

INSPIRATION AND PLAY!

In this book, I would like to introduce you to the way I make my art and illustration using Procreate. It's a "how-to" book, but it's also a "how you might want to" guide. By this, I mean to say, feel free to follow the steps included within these pages, but I encourage you to experiment and explore other ways of working with the app.

What this book is not, is a technical book. I'm a creative person – I often work spontaneously, without much of a plan. I use Procreate to help me create both impulsive, quick sketches, and also complex, meandering illustrations with many elements and layers. In short, I use it to solve problems in my work.

With this in mind, I would like to pass on to you not a heavy technical manual, but rather, an inspirational workbook that encourages you to play, make mistakes and seek out your own way of using the app.

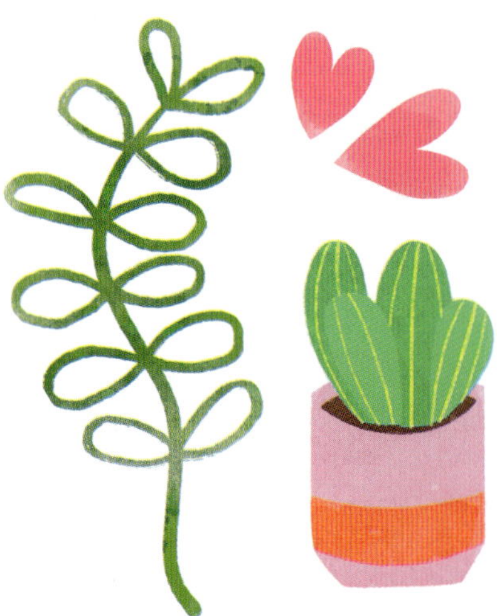

HOW TO USE THIS BOOK

If you're new to digital illustration and are using this book to learn how to use Procreate, I'll first guide you through the basic tools and share tips on how I use the app. The projects that follow are designed to help you understand how you can use the app as part of your illustration journey.

More advanced users may enjoy this book and use it to enhance and refresh their skills by dipping into the projects to try something new.

While putting this book together, I have tried to keep in mind advancements in technology and how the software may be updated in the near future. The interface may change, new tools will be added and updates will improve workflow, but your creative impulse will stay the same. I would like to inspire and encourage you to develop your own set of skills that can keep pace with technology whenever it may decide to take a leap!

The **Getting Started** section of this book will take you on a quick tour of Procreate, introducing essential features. You'll be learning by doing, and if you're unsure of anything later on, you can dip back into this section to refresh your memory.

The **Projects** section will take you a bit further on your learning-by-doing journey. The first few projects will explain techniques step by step. There are screenshots of the actual interface so you can see exactly how different tools work and where they are. The later projects are more art-based, and look in detail at how I personally use Procreate to make my illustrations.

The **Next Steps** section is packed with tips and ideas for developing your style and joining the online art community. There's even advice on monetizing your art when you're ready to take that next step.

I'm happy to share my process and hope that, by doing so, I'll inspire you to use and enjoy Procreate in your own wonderful way!

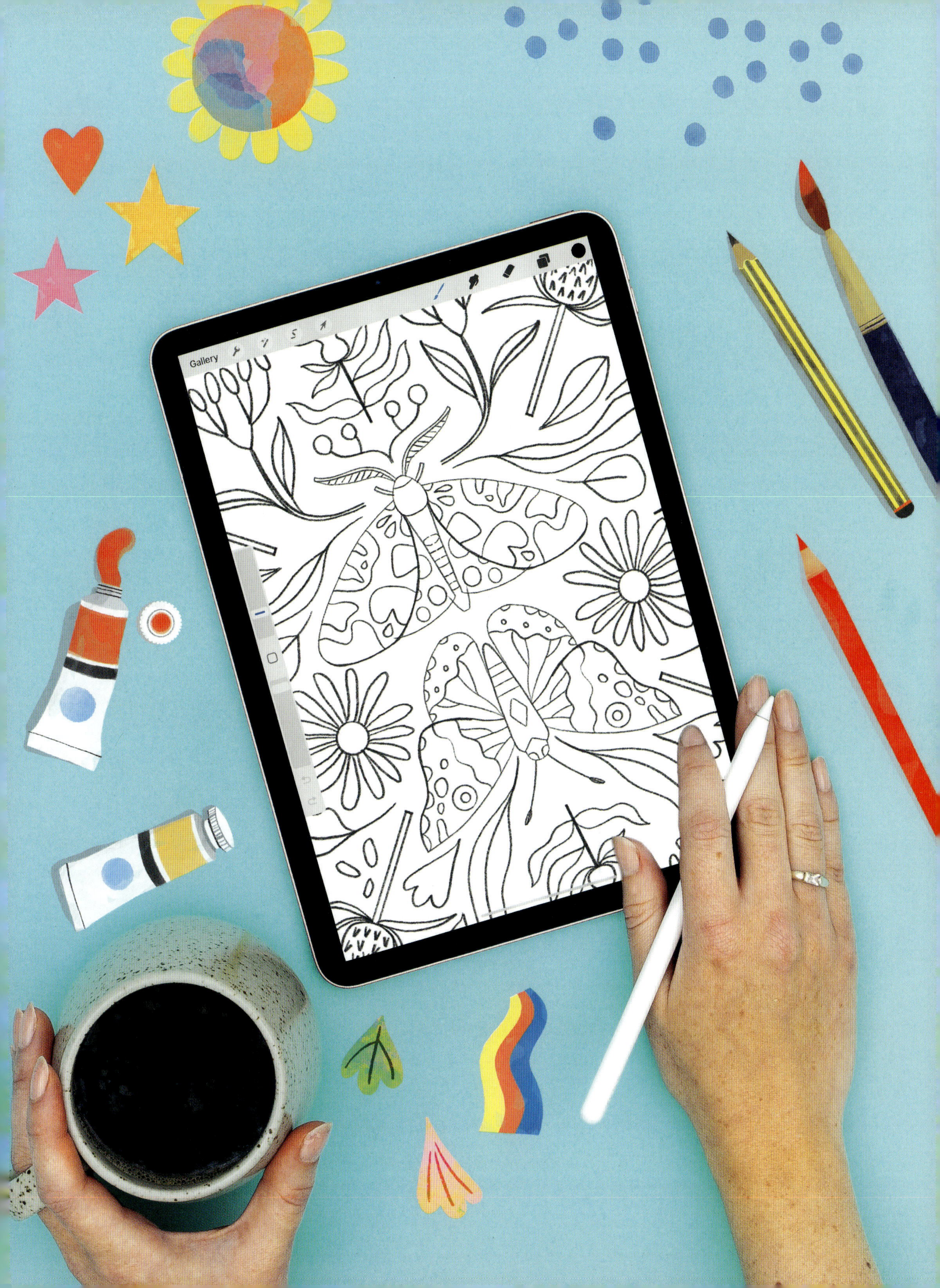
Gallery

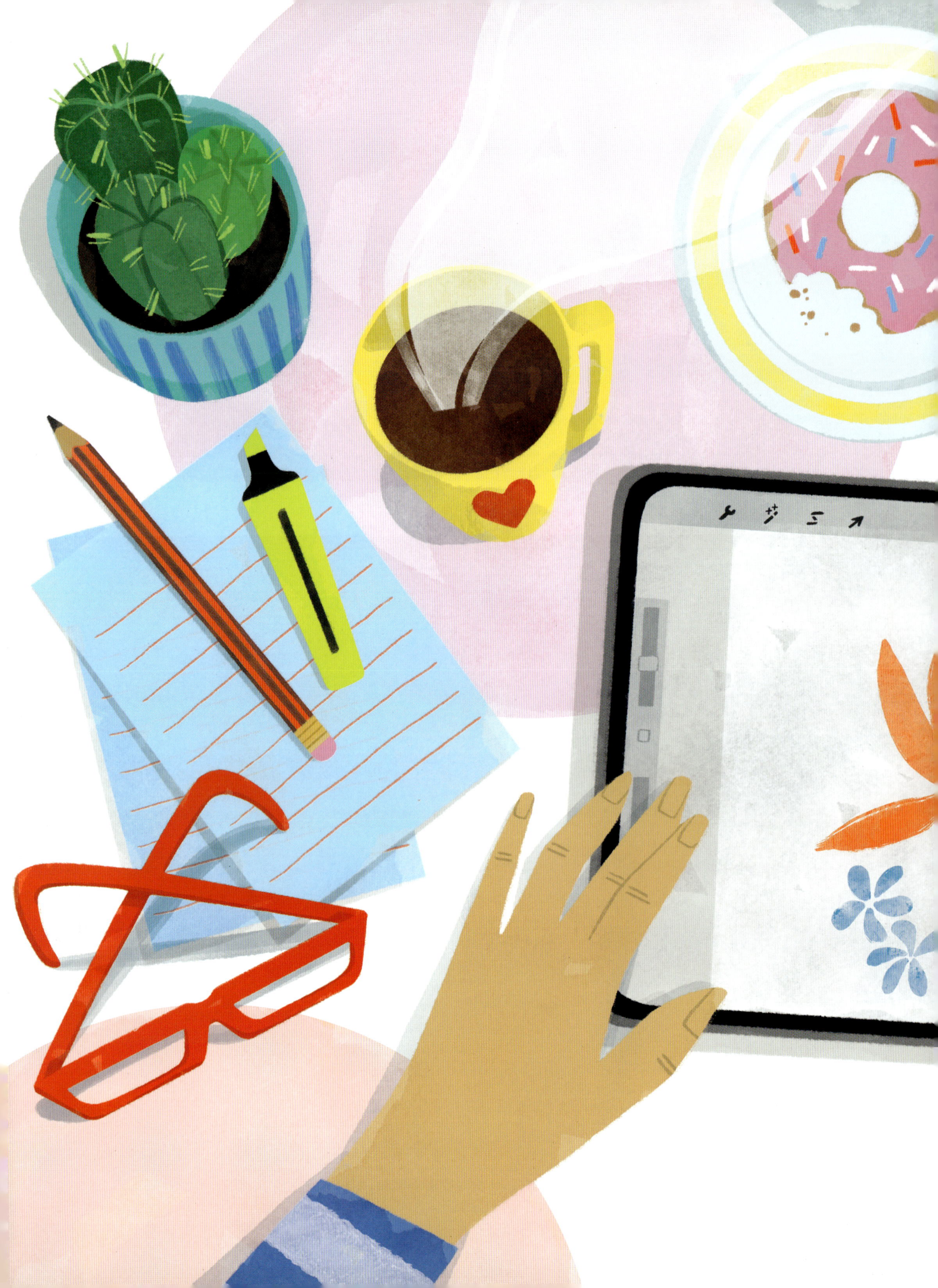

GETTING STARTED

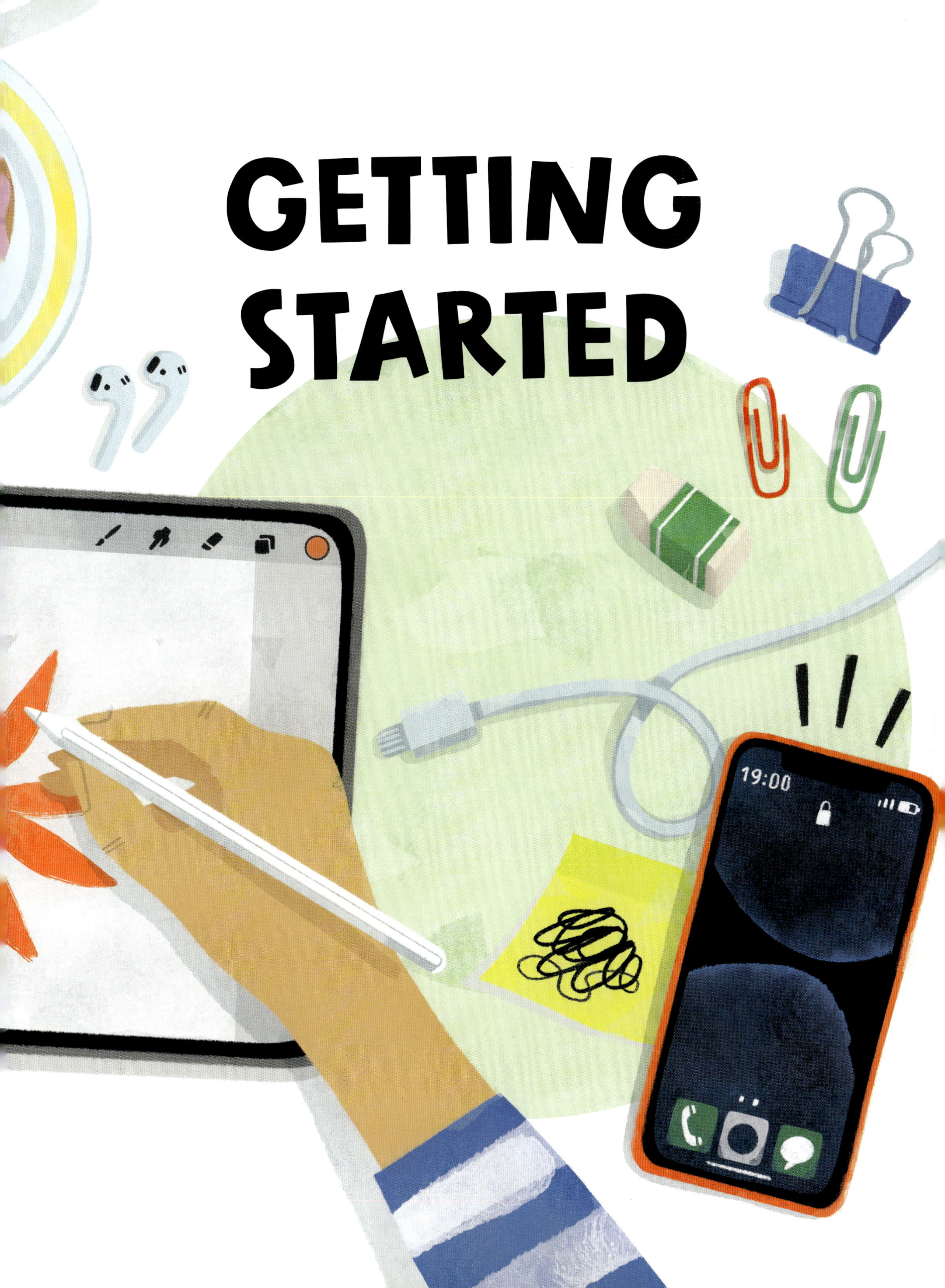

MATERIALS & EQUIPMENT

You really need very little to get started with Procreate, but we'll go through the essentials, and some optional extras, that will help you set up a comfortable workspace.

Procreate App

You'll need to buy and download the app, of course. If you already have an iPad and Apple Pencil, check their compatibility with the latest version of Procreate, and ensure that version will download and run on your iPad. You can check the latest version and compatibility by searching the Procreate website: www.procreate.com.

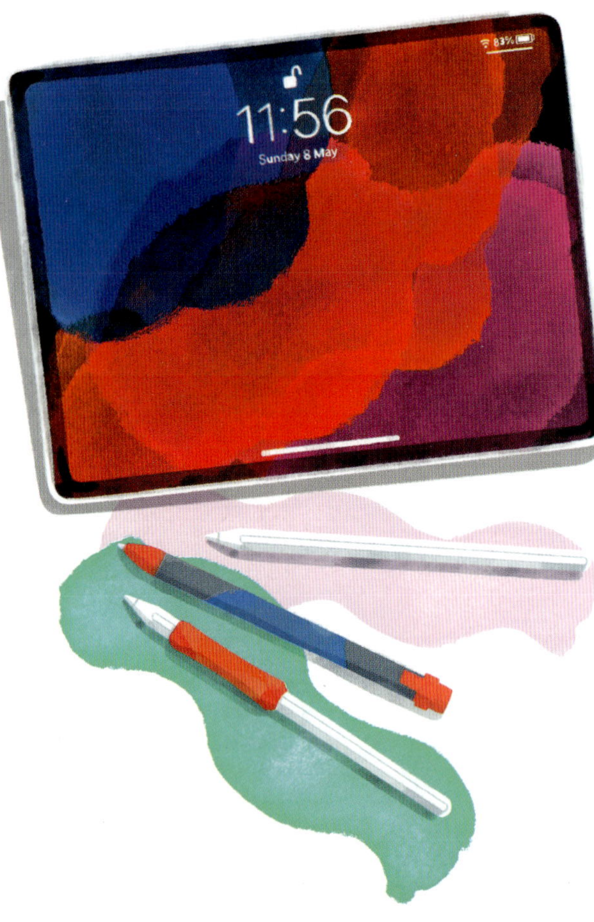

iPad and Stylus/Pencil

You don't need the most expensive technology, but whatever you purchase will be an investment in your illustration career! Do some research and buy the best you can afford.

I use the Apple Pencil, but there are other brands on the market that do the job – it's down to personal preference. However, make sure the pencil or stylus you choose has pressure and tilt sensitivity. This means it will behave like a traditional pencil – by tilting the nib, you can achieve natural looking pencil strokes for shading, while using more pressure will make the strokes bolder.

I'll refer to this tool as a pencil throughout the book.

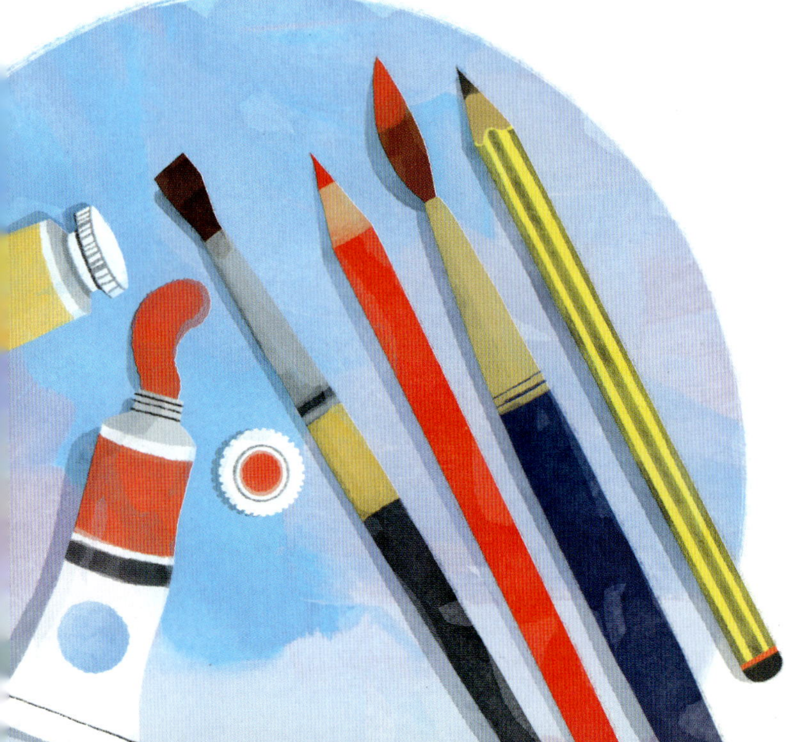

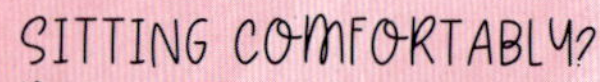

SITTING COMFORTABLY?
Make sure you're sitting or standing comfortably when working through this book. Take regular breaks to stretch and dance a little. Nice weather? Pop out for a breath of fresh air before we begin!

Other Useful Equipment

In addition to the essentials, let's look at a few optional extras that I find useful and you might want to try for yourself.

iPAD STAND

A stand doesn't need to be expensive – I use a cheap one from a well-known Swedish furniture store! It just elevates the iPad at a slight angle, which is good for drawing and prevents leaning over too far, which may cause back and neck strain.

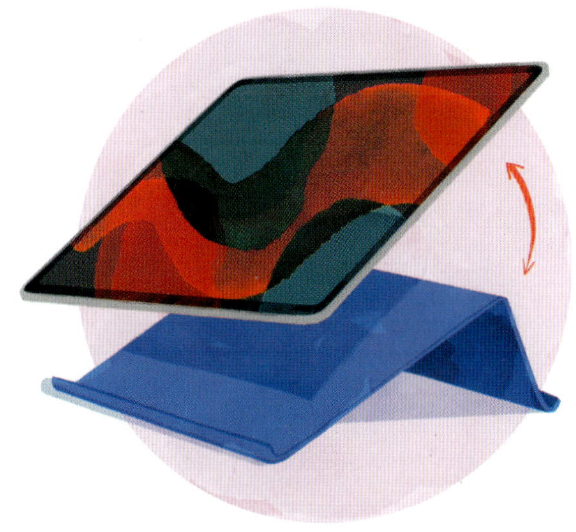

ARTIST'S GLOVE

This is something I can't live without. It is basically half a glove, made from shiny, stretchy fabric. Wearing one helps your drawing hand glide over the surface of the iPad, and helps to reduce fingermarks on the screen.

PENCIL GRIP

Adding a small "grip" to your pencil may help with drawing more naturally. Sometimes I find myself tensing up and holding the pencil too tightly. The grip helps to soften the way you hold your pencil and may ease your drawing posture.

TRADITIONAL MEDIA

I have a notebook for jotting down ideas, plus traditional materials, such as paint and brushes, to hand. You'll undoubtedly learn to create natural looking art and illustration on your iPad, but scanning in drawn elements and painted textures adds another dimension to your work. Later in this book, I'll show you how to successfully incorporate traditional media into your digital drawings.

CAMERA AND PRINTER

When you come to "scan in" or insert a photo of your sketches or hand-painted textures, you can use the camera on the iPad itself. However, I generally find my phone's camera easier to use.

Some of these projects also require a printer, but if you don't have one, you can print online or at your local printshop.

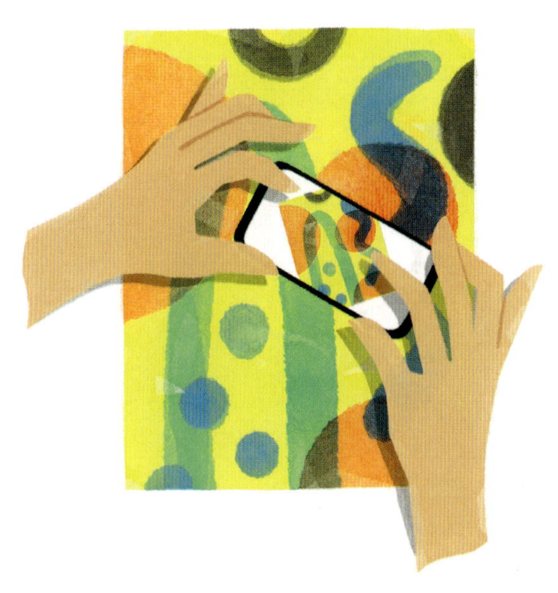

SCREEN PROTECTOR

A lot of artists use is a matte screen protector that creates a bit of friction, mimicking the sensation of drawing on paper versus a shiny glass screen. This is not necessary and is down to personal preference. My advice is to watch a few reviews online and if you think it's for you, try it out.

EXPLORING THE APP

Let's open Procreate and get started. If you're not familiar with the app, follow the steps on the next couple of pages to get you up and running. If you already know your way around Procreate, feel free to go straight to the Projects section, and use this section as a refresher when needed.

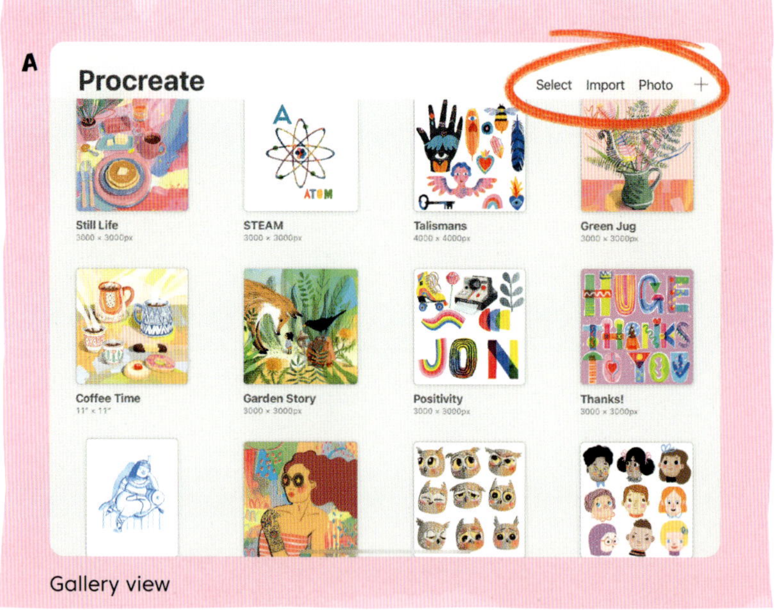

Gallery view

Gallery

The first thing we see is the Gallery where all our artworks are stored and organized. You can create, name, stack and view canvases in the Gallery, and easily scroll through to find and view previous work. You can also share, duplicate and delete artworks here, as well as importing files from outside the app and sharing your artwork to other devices.

GALLERY TOOLBAR

The Procreate interface is clean and simple. In Gallery view, we have only four toolbar items on the right-hand side (**A**).

We'll use the Select, Import and Photo options later, but first tap on the + icon to create a new canvas. A drop-down menu offers different canvas shapes and sizes (**B**). Choose an existing option from the list, or create your own custom canvas by tapping on the + icon at the top right-hand side of the drop-down.

New Canvas

Click on the + icon and select Pixels from the measurement options. Type in 3000px by 3000px at 300 DPI (**C**). This will give you a good size canvas to try out a few things and help familiarize yourself with the workspace. You will also see a number for Maximum Layers. I'll explain the importance of this later on! Tap Create and the new canvas will open.

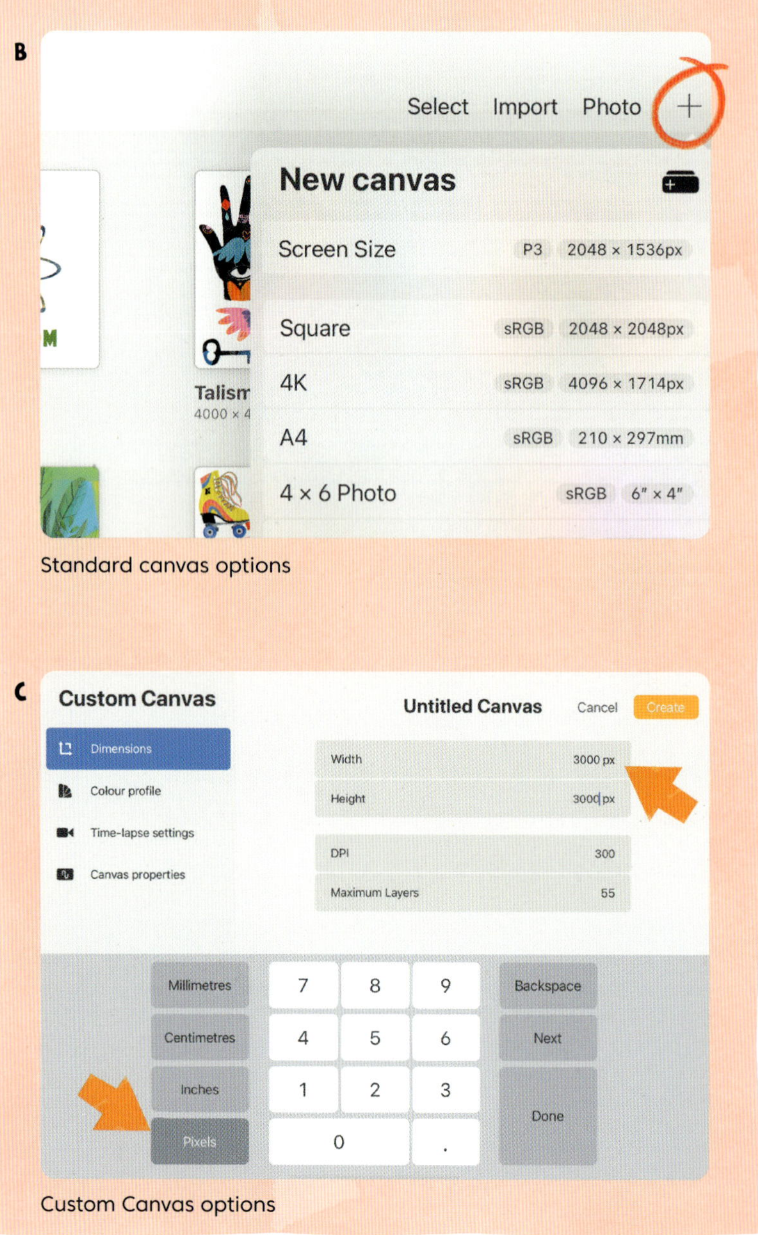

Standard canvas options

Custom Canvas options

Tools Overview

The workspace is just like a new, blank sketchbook page or fresh canvas. Again, you'll see a toolbar across the top of the screen. We'll concentrate for now on the basic tools for mark making – these are found on the right-hand side of the top toolbar (**D**).

In this section I'll introduce the basic functions of these tools, then we'll learn more throughout the book by doing and creating. I encourage you to explore and experiment with everything on the toolbar now, in preparation for the projects.

BRUSH LIBRARY

Tap on the brush icon to open the Brush Library (**E**) – a large selection of brushes that replicate just about every medium, painting and drawing tool you can think of. Add to that the ability to edit and change the settings for each brush, and you have an endless combination of tools at your fingertips! You can also create your own brushes or import brushes and effects created by other artists. More on this later! For now, select a few brushes and just make some marks on the canvas (**F**).

SMUDGE AND ERASER TOOL

The Smudge and Eraser tools, located to the right of the brush icon, both share the Brush Library, allowing you to smudge and erase with the same brush you're using to paint or draw. This can help to keep your work more natural looking. You can also try contrasting tools to create different effects.

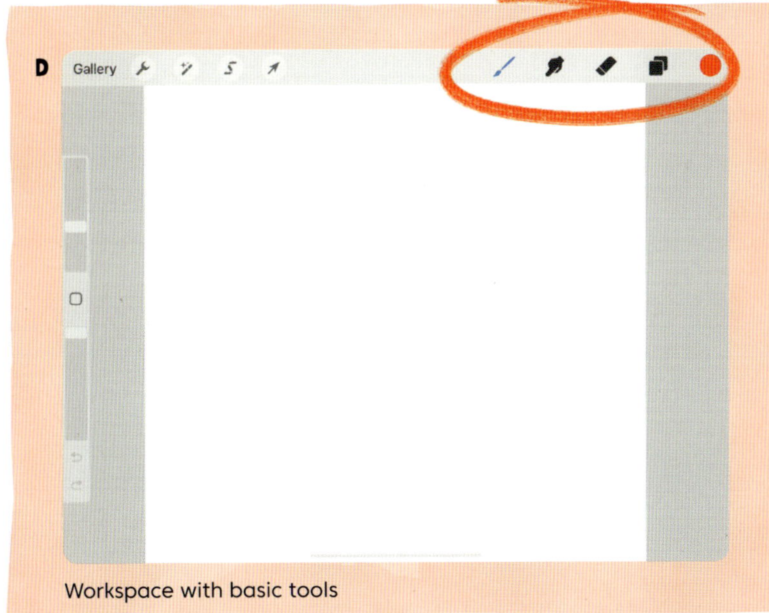

Workspace with basic tools

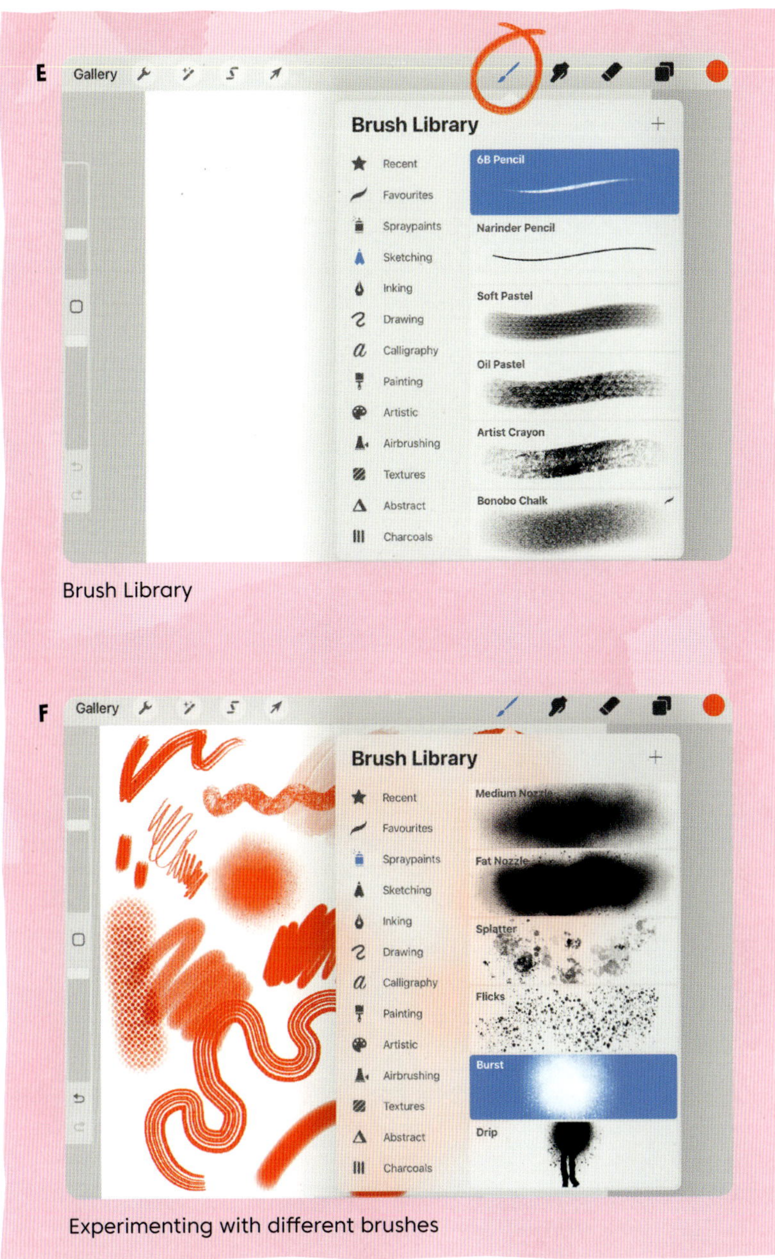

Brush Library

Experimenting with different brushes

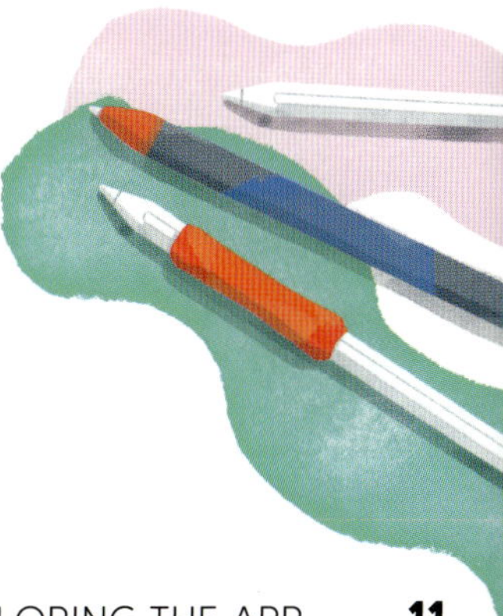

VERTICAL TOOLBAR

Let's look quickly at the vertical toolbar on the left of the screen (**G**). Have a play!

- Control the **Size** of your brush with the top slider.
- Control the **Opacity** of the paint you're laying down with the bottom slider.
- Our best friends **Undo** and **Redo** are below the sliders.

COLOURS PANEL

I'm sure you're ahead of me and have already tapped the Colours icon, top right (**H**)! If not, tap now. The Colours panel is where we can create, mix and select every colour we'll need. We can also store colours in custom palettes or type in values to create exact shades and hues.

Explore the ways you can choose, save and edit colours, familiarizing yourself with the tool ready to learn more about colour later on.

LAYERS PANEL

The Layers panel (**I**) is where the magic really happens. Working with layers is the key to creating stunning digital art and illustrations. The Layers panel will help us organize our drawing and painting. It also helps us to apply different effects.

AND THERE'S MORE!

On the top left of the toolbar are four drop-down menus for Actions, Adjustments, Selections and Transform. We'll learn about these and how to use them throughout the projects in this book.

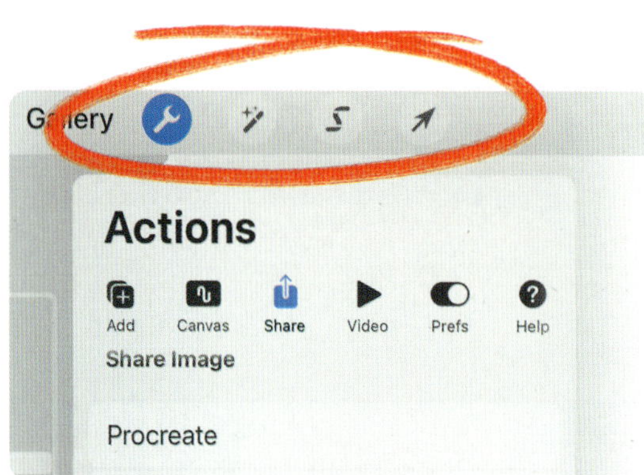

From left to right: the Actions, Adjustments, Selections and Transform menus

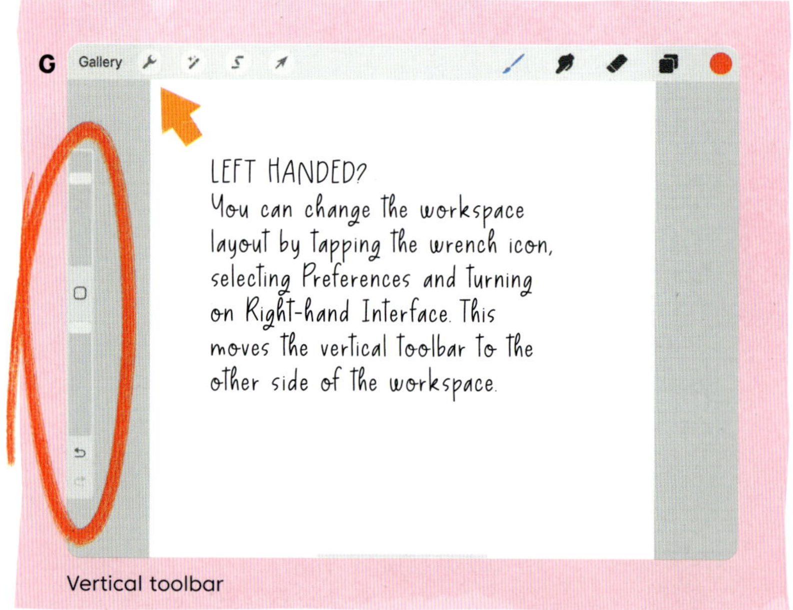

Vertical toolbar

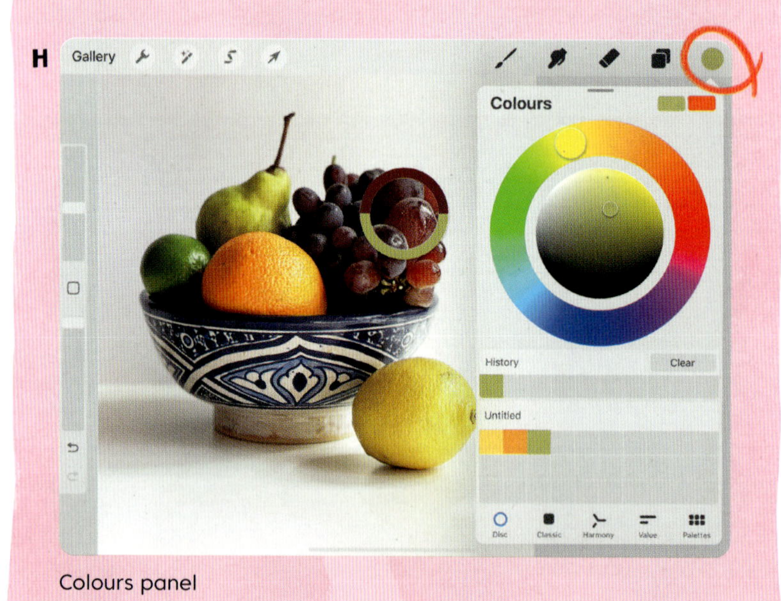

Colours panel

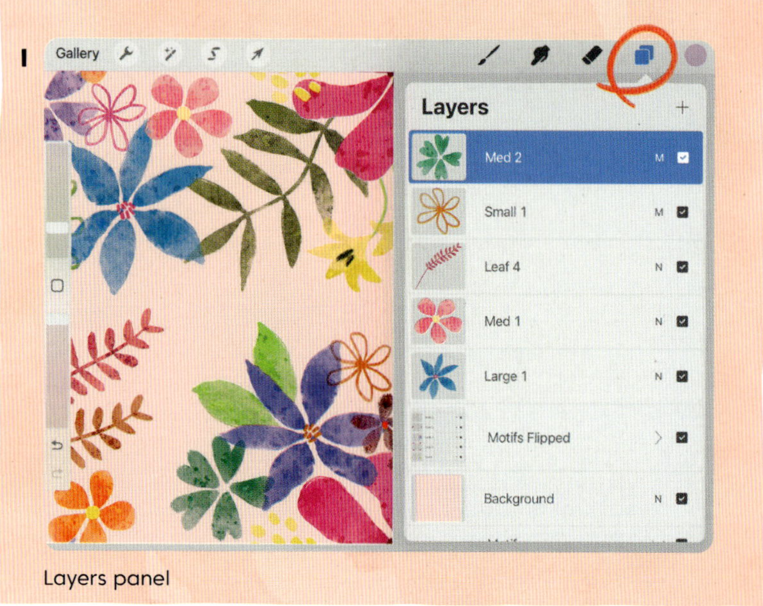

Layers panel

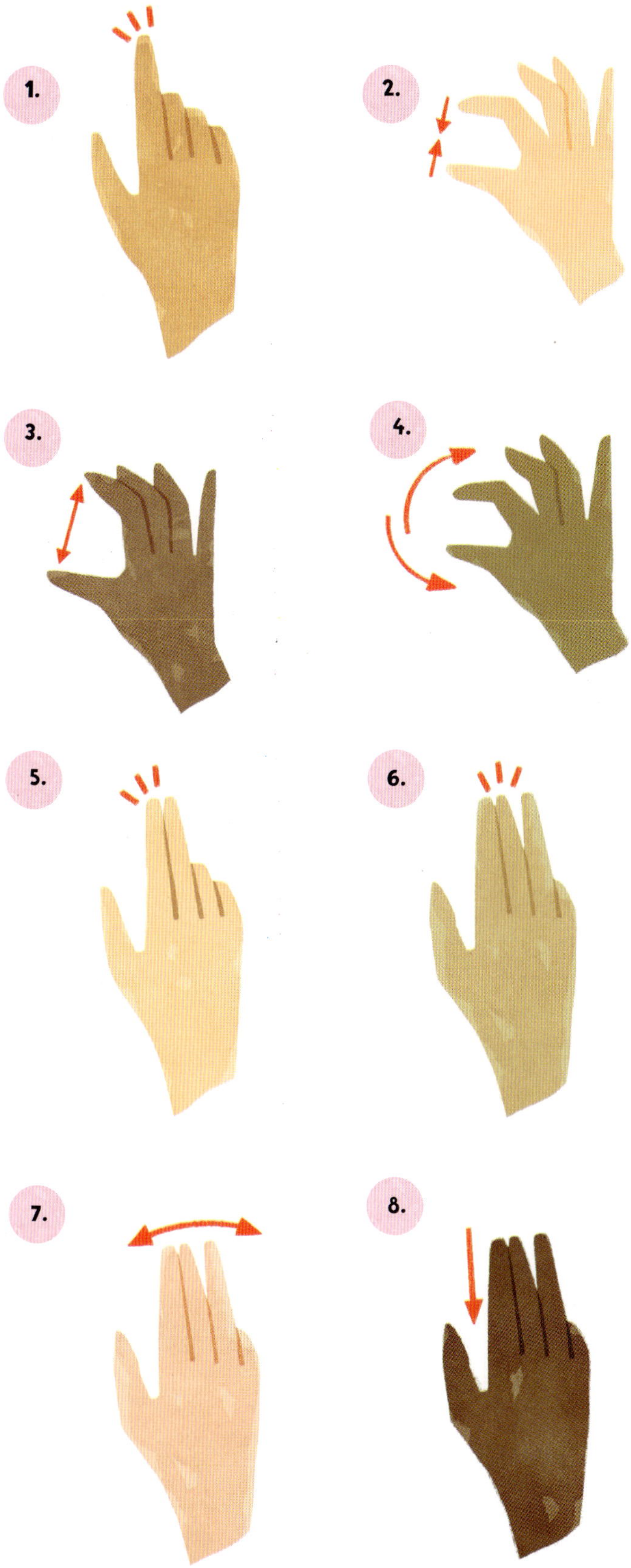

1.

2.

3.

4.

5.

6.

7.

8.

Hand Gestures

Now we'll look at how we move around the canvas and perform tasks. Most people are familiar with tapping and swiping on their phones and this is much the same, but there are a few extra motions that can help us speed up the workflow. Practise the gestures shown here and described below.

1. **One finger tap** – use this to select, open and close all the functions.
2. **Two fingers pinch in** – this basically zooms out and makes your artwork smaller on the screen. You can also twist the canvas using two fingers to change the orientation of your artwork. A quick pinch will return the canvas to fit the screen.
3. **Two fingers stretch** – the opposite of pinch, this will zoom in and make your artwork bigger. Great for getting down to the details of your drawing.
4. **Two fingers twist** – this will rotate your canvas.
5. **Two fingers tap** – use this to Undo.
6. **Three fingers tap** – this is the gesture to Redo.
7. **Three finger scrub** – use this to erase everything from the layer.
8. **Three finger swipe down** – this brings up the Copy & Paste panel, which also includes Cut.

... and Breathe!

There's a lot to take in and some of the terms may be unfamiliar to those starting their digital-art journey. Try not to feel overwhelmed – we'll learn by doing! The projects are designed to help you explore the app in your own time, teach you the basics, and encourage experimentation and exploration.

Most of all, I want you to feel confident using the app and your iPad. Illustrating in Procreate can be a joyful experience. Being able to make art with all the tools and none of the mess is one of the great advantages of this program.

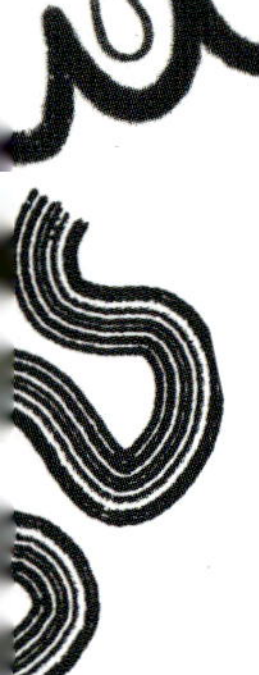

BRUSH LIBRARY

All your mark-making tools – every brush, pencil, crayon, oil pastel and pen you can think of – are kept in this vast storeroom. I'll touch on ways to experiment with its endless possibilities. Just take your time and keep things organized.

Brush Studio

Tap on the brush icon to open the Brush Library. On the left-hand side, the brushes are sorted into categories called sets. I think of these sets as folders that store individual brushes. On the right-hand side you'll see the list of brushes within a selected folder (**A**).

Tap once on a brush to select it. Tap again to open the Brush Studio, where you can play with settings such as Shape or Grain. You can alter things like spacing, colour and dynamics but before you play with anything, I want to show you a couple of ways to make sure you do not lose the original settings.

RESET BRUSHES

Scroll down the left-hand list and tap on About this brush. You may see an option to Reset Brush, which you can use to revert the brush to its original settings (**B**). If that option is not there, you'll see Create New Reset Point. Click on this before proceeding to ensure you can revert to the original.

DUPLICATE BRUSHES

Another foolproof way to ensure you don't lose your favourite brush settings is to swipe left on your chosen brush in the Brush Library and tap Duplicate (**C**). You can play with the settings on the duplicate, then rename it by going into Brush Studio and tapping About this brush. Tap on the name – the keyboard will pop up for you to type in the new name.

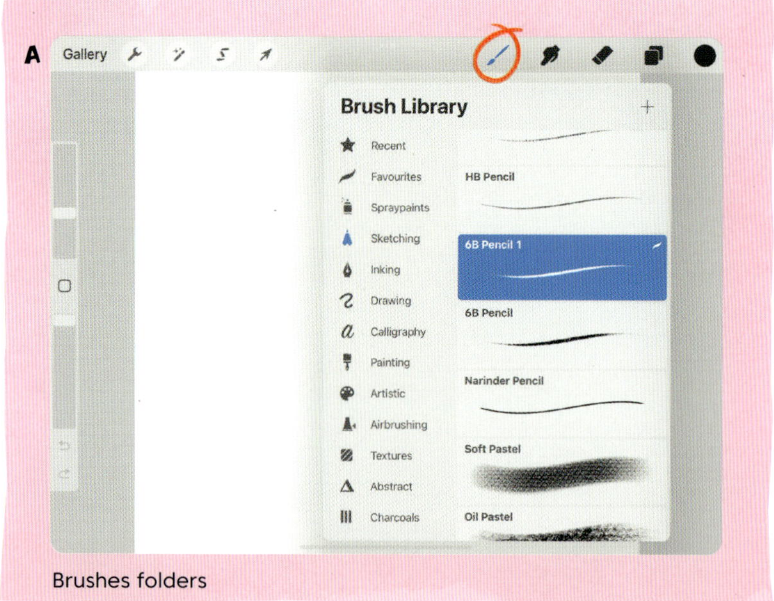

Brushes folders

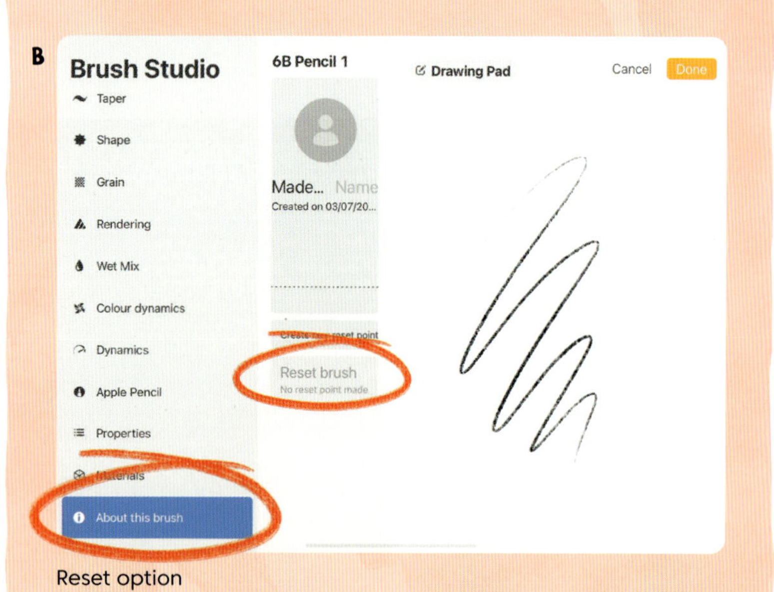

Reset option

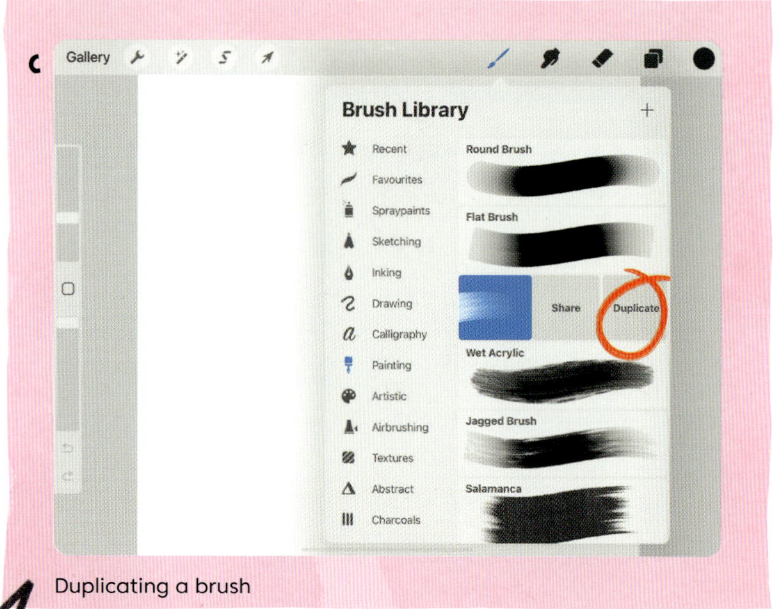

Duplicating a brush

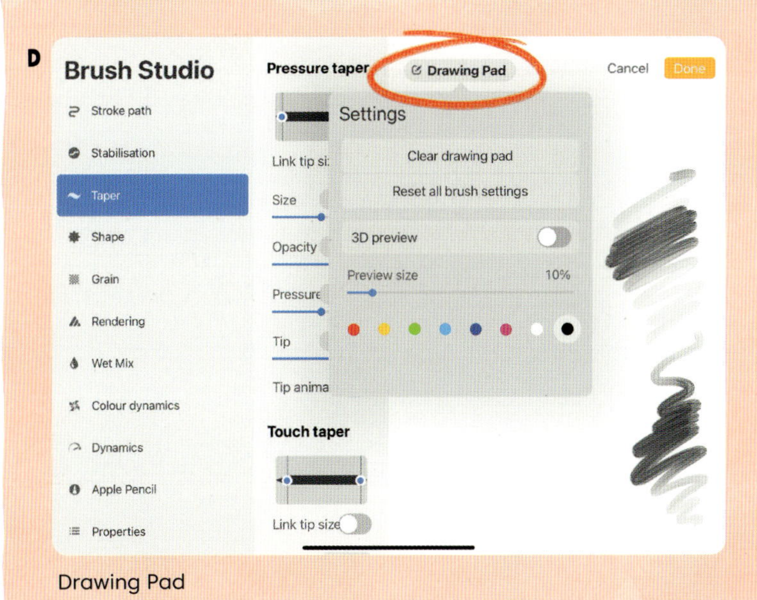

Drawing Pad

Drawing Pad

On the right-hand side of the Brush Studio is the Drawing Pad where you can try out the brush and test the changes you're making. Tap on the Drawing Pad button at the top to open the settings – this allows you to clear the pad if necessary (**D**). You can also reset the brush from here. To save altered settings, tap on Done. If you change your mind and want to keep the original settings, tap Cancel to return to the Brush Library with no changes.

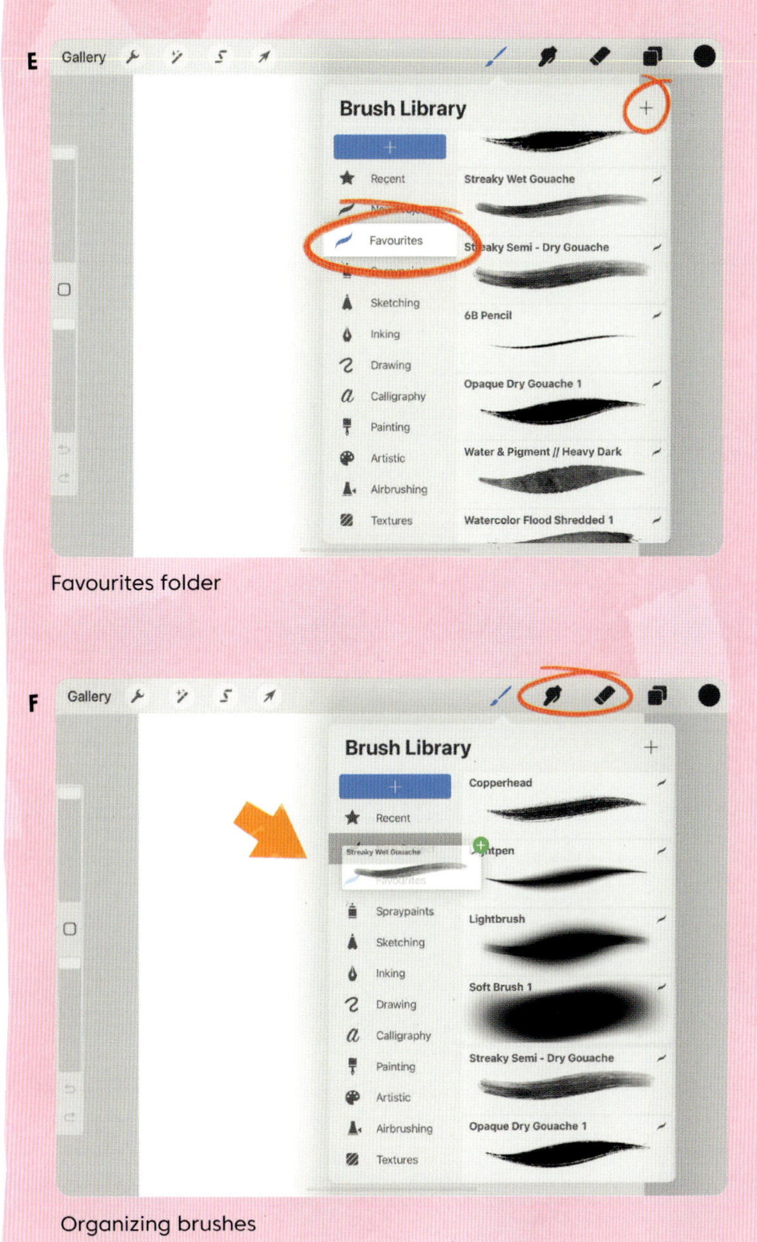

Favourites folder

Organizing brushes

Organizing Brushes

Brushes can be organized into folders, then re-ordered *within* a folder.

CREATE A NEW FOLDER

Tap on the + icon at the top of the Brush Library palette. This creates a new folder for duplicate or modified brushes, handy when using certain brushes you need to find quickly and easily. I always have a "Favourites" folder for frequently used brushes (**E**).

MOVE BRUSHES BETWEEN FOLDERS

Tap, hold and drag brushes to the destination folder. The folder will highlight and a green + icon will appear, then you can drop the brush into it (**F**).

SMUDGE & ERASER TOOLS

This information also applies to the Smudge and Eraser tools (next to the Brush tool) as both open the same Brush Library.

Exploring Brushes

You can tweak existing brushes, create your own, and import brushes created by other artists – we'll try those later. For now, set your colour to black and choose existing brushes from the Sketching, Inking and Drawing folders. Create a page of simple doodles – mine will be an A4-size canvas as I may print them out to make a physical colouring page. Use whatever size you want, and don't worry about how you lay out your doodles – we'll cut them up and move them around in the next section.

ERASE OR UNDO

If you want to clear anything, simply use the Eraser or Undo function with a two-finger tap.

SELECTIONS, TRANSFORM & LAYERS

In this section we'll look at some of the tools most useful to digital artists. Learning to cut, copy, paste and transform sections of your work means you can build really effective compositions. You'll also be able to rearrange, alter and adapt your work at any stage.

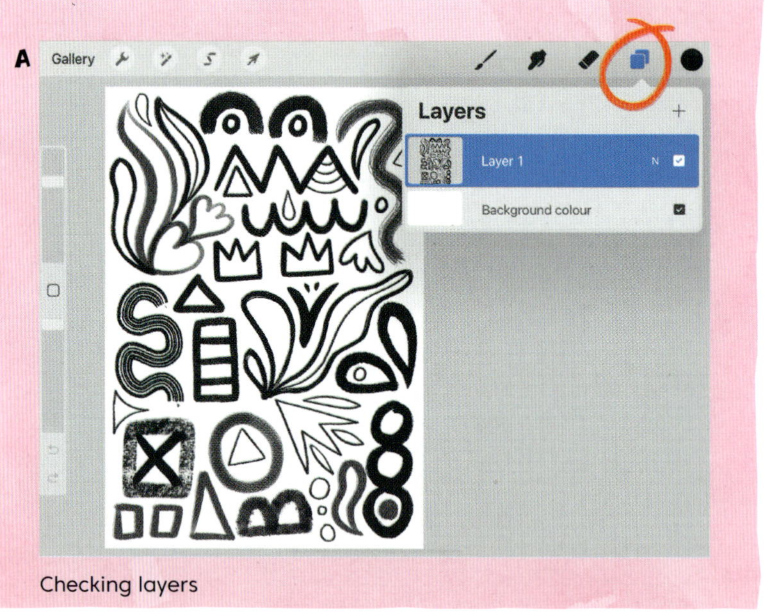

Checking layers

PREPARE YOUR PAGE

We'll use the doodle page you created in the previous section to help us explore the Selections and Transform tools and Layers.

Open the app, find your page of doodles in the Gallery and tap to open. If you're new to Procreate, you probably created all your doodles on the same layer, which is great for this section. Tap on the Layers panel to check (**A**).

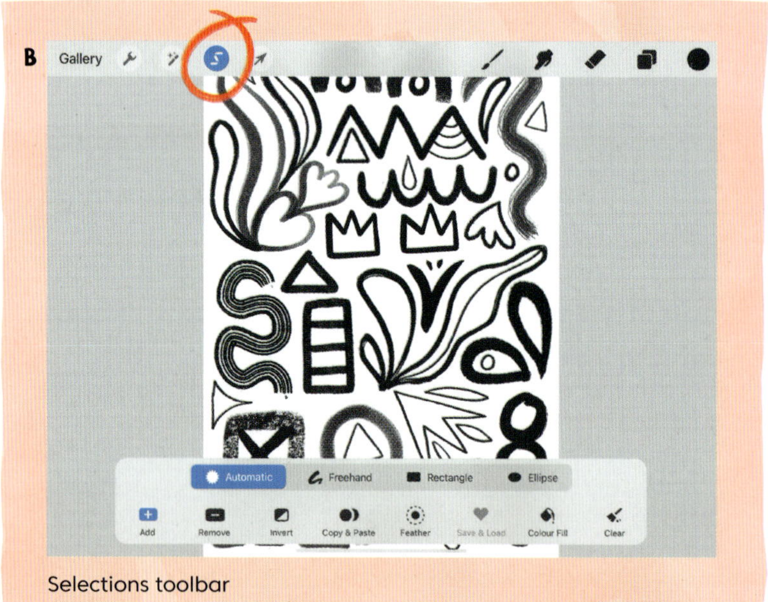

Selections toolbar

Selections

Let's have a look at how Selections works first. Tap the Selections icon on the left-hand side of the top toolbar (**B**). A horizontal menu will slide up from the bottom of the screen. There are a lot of options here, so we'll have a quick look at each one.

AUTOMATIC

Automatic Selection (**C**) will select the area of the canvas you tap on. You can hold your finger down and slide it across the screen to increase the threshold of what is being selected. This is great for quickly selecting simple, solid shapes.

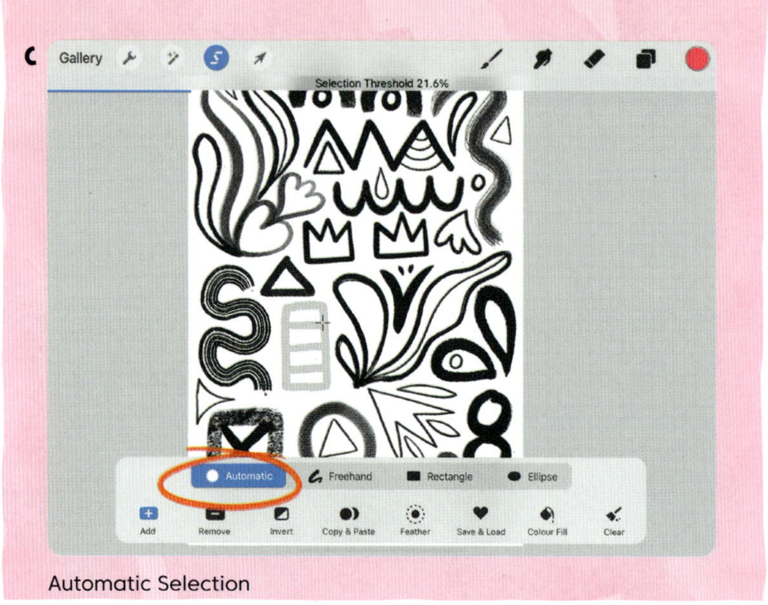

Automatic Selection

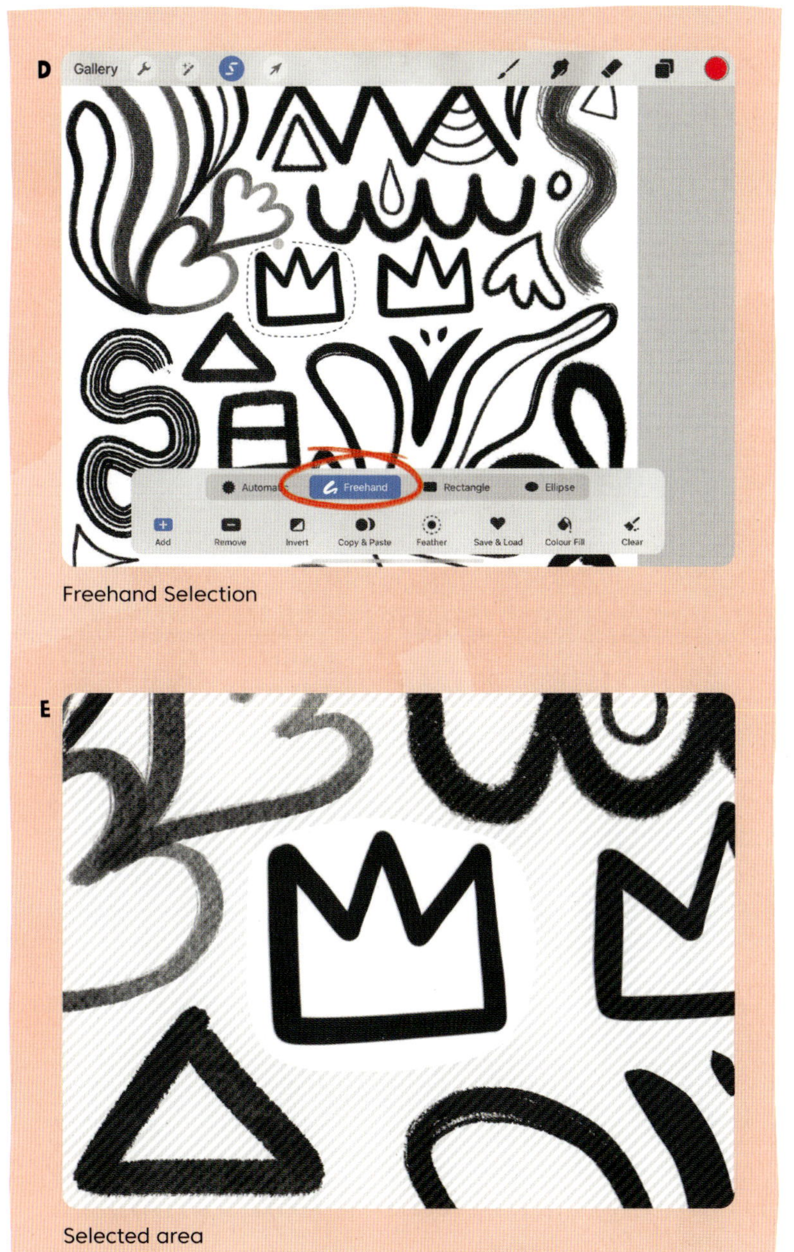

Freehand Selection

Selected area

FREEHAND

Freehand Selection (**D**) is the one I use most as you can accurately draw around elements on the page. It's good for more complicated shapes and when you want to isolate just part of a layer. Let's try it out now:

First, tap on the Freehand tab, then use your pencil to draw around one of your doodles, this will create a dotted line with a grey spot at the beginning. Complete the selection by tapping on the spot.

Diagonal lines will appear on all the parts of the canvas that haven't been selected (**E**). Selected areas remain clear.

RECTANGLE AND ELLIPSE

There are two other useful Selections items here you might want to try out. Rectangle will allow you to drag and select around an object in that shape. Likewise for Ellipse.

PERFECT CIRCLES

To draw a perfect circle using Ellipse mode, tap and hold with your finger at the same time as dragging with your pencil.

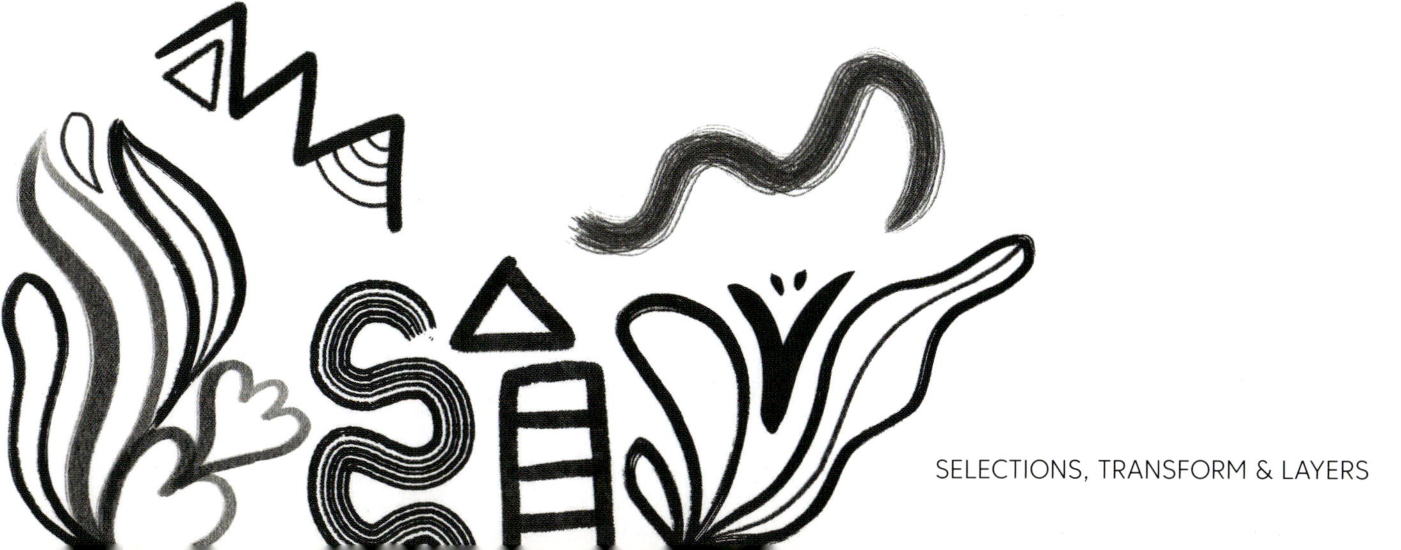

ADDITIONAL OPTIONS

Once you have finished selecting the items you need, you may want to use the options at the bottom of the toolbar.

- **Add** is selected as default. It allows you to keep adding to your selection. You can also tap on it again to close any open selections.
- **Remove** option is useful for correcting selections you may have made by mistake.
- **Invert** will flip the selection (**F**).
- **Copy & Paste** will automatically copy your selection and paste it on a new layer (**G**).
- **Feather** will soften the edges of a selection – you can control this using the pop-up slider.
- **Save & Load** will allow you to save an action if you use it frequently.
- **Colour Fill** will fill the selected area with the current colour. You would need to be on a layer underneath your doodle if you wanted to colour in a line drawing this way (**H**). More on this later.
- **Clear** will, of course, clear all your selections with a simple tap.

We'll constantly use the Selections tools in different ways throughout this book, so it's a good idea to play around and make yourself familiar with all the different ways they can be used.

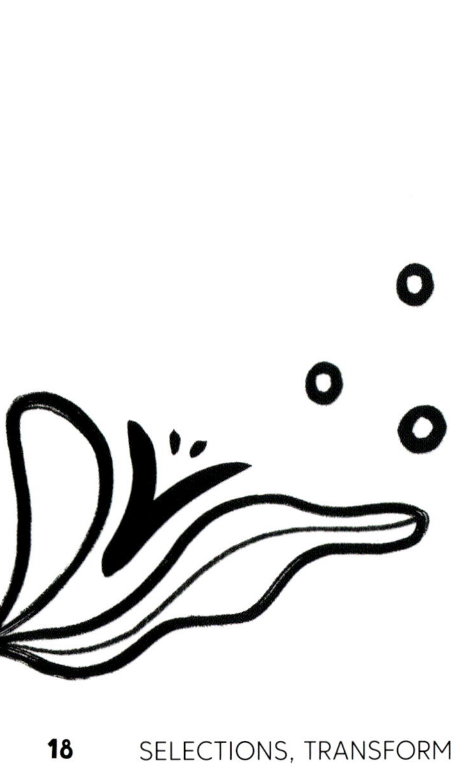

F

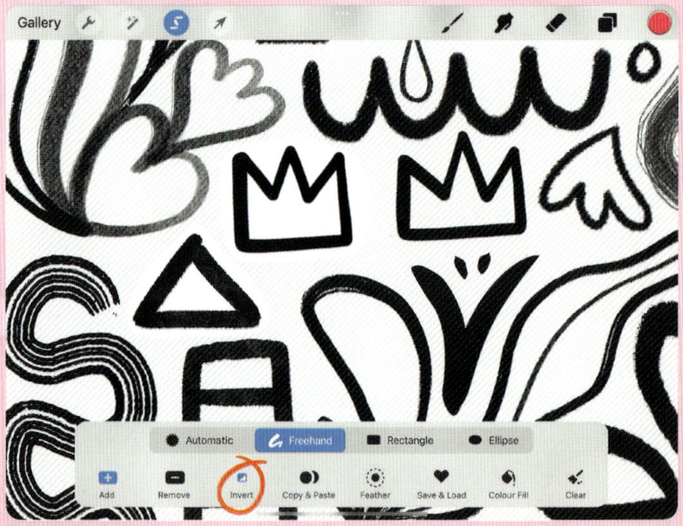

Invert tool

G

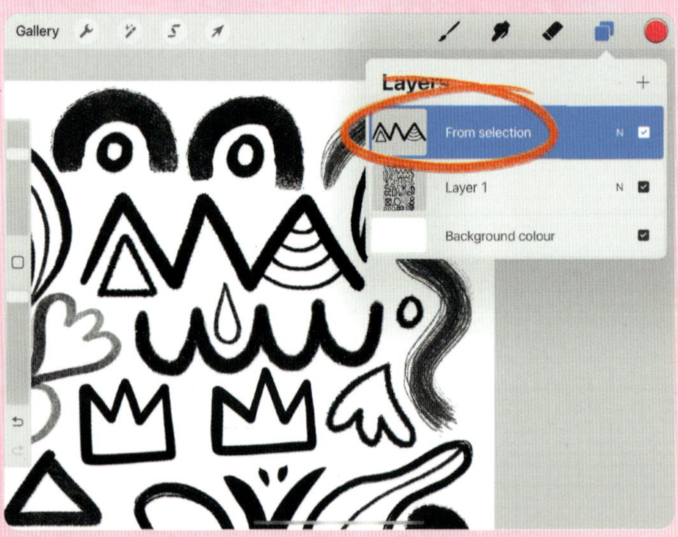

Copy & Paste tool

H

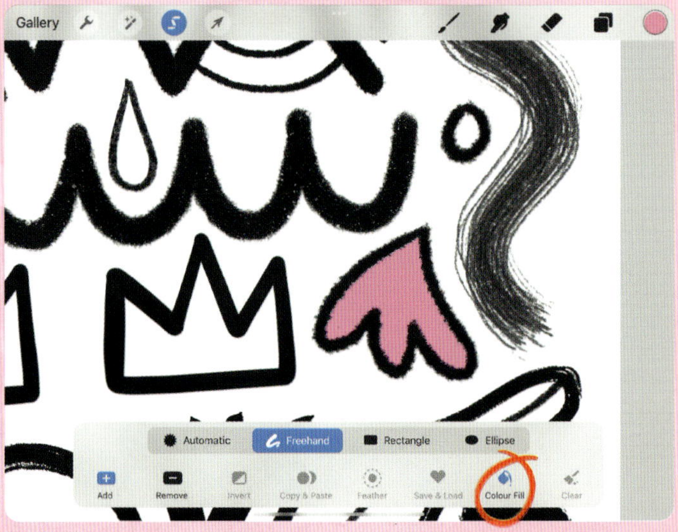

Colour Fill tool

A

Bounding box applied

B

Selection moved

C

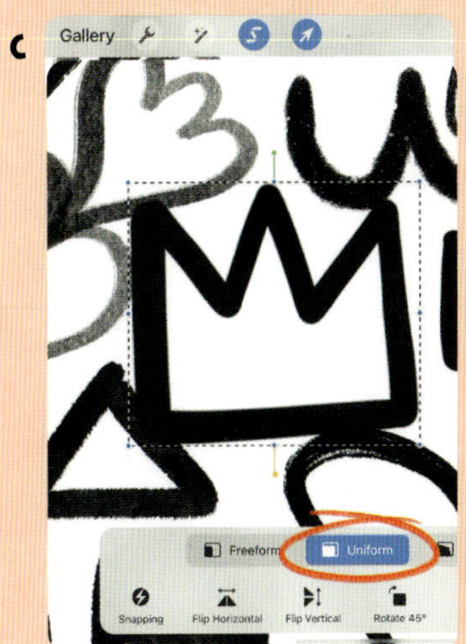

Uniform

D

Freeform

E

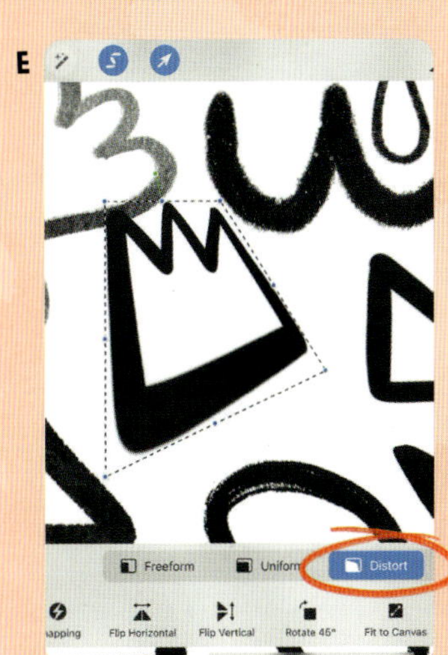

Distort

F

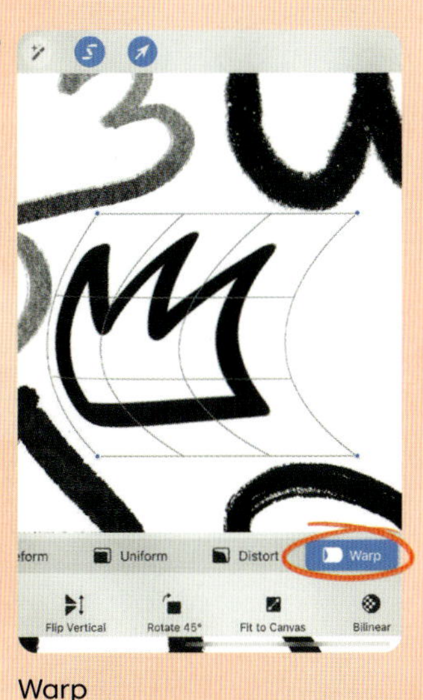

Warp

Transform

Now let's see how Transform works.

1. **Use the Freehand Selection option** to draw around one of your shapes. Close the selection.
2. **Tap on the Transform icon** (**A**) to contain your selection within a "bounding box".
3. **Move the selection** with your pencil. Drag well outside the box to avoid accidentally resizing or rotating it. Try it – you'll notice your shape can be placed precisely where you want it (**B**).
4. **Move the selection only very slightly** by tapping outside the bounding box in the direction you want it to go. This action will very gently nudge it.

Remember, everything is still on the same layer, so be careful not to overlap your shapes too much.

TRANSFORM OPTIONS

The blue spots on the bounding box allow us to manipulate the shape and size of our item, depending on which Transform option is selected.

- **Uniform** allows you to change the size of the shape, but *not* the proportions. Tap and hold one of the corner spots and drag to resize (**C**).
- **Freeform** lets you resize by stretching or squeezing the shape disproportionately (**D**).
- **Distort** allows you to resize each corner independently (**E**).
- **Warp** brings up a grid that can be moved around to create curved and wavy effects (**F**). You can further edit in this mode by tapping on **Advanced Mesh** (found on the far left-hand side of the toolbar). This will give you extra blue spots you can move around.

Tap **Flip Horizontal** and **Flip Vertical** too, to see how your shape looks upside down and back to front!

Tap **Rotate 45°** to turn your shape in increments of 45-degrees clockwise. Alternatively, to rotate the shape in any direction or increment, tap and drag it round using the green handle.

SIZING UP

Try not to enlarge the shapes too much as you'll lose some of the resolution.

Layers

In my opinion, this panel is where the real magic happens! The ability to separate and organize your artwork into layers is invaluable.

BASIC COMMANDS

- **Create a new layer** by tapping on the + icon.
- **View options** by tapping on a selected layer to bring up a useful menu.
- **Lock**, **Duplicate** or **Delete** a layer by swiping left on it.
- **Hide a layer** by tapping on the tick box to uncheck it.
- **Choose a background colour** by tapping on the background layer. You can't draw directly on this layer. Instead, you have to select a layer above for your artwork.

As we work through the projects, we'll use layers at every stage to build up the artwork and create effects. Layers also ensure your work is organized and it's easy to edit every aspect.

PREPARE YOUR DOODLES PAGE

1. **Tap on the Layers icon**, then on your doodle layer. A menu will pop out to the side with a list of options. Rename the layer by tapping on the option to bring up the keyboard (**A**).
2. **Duplicate this layer** before you edit it. Swipe left on the layer and tap Duplicate (**B**).

   Warning! I'm going to move some of my doodles to bleed off the edge of the page. If you do this, the doodles will be cropped and you'll lose whatever is hanging off the canvas. Be sure to duplicate first!
3. **Rename the copied layer** and hide the layer underneath by unchecking the tick box (**C**).

CONVERT TO TYPE

If you tap Rename with your pencil, you can handwrite the new name with your pencil and it will convert to type.

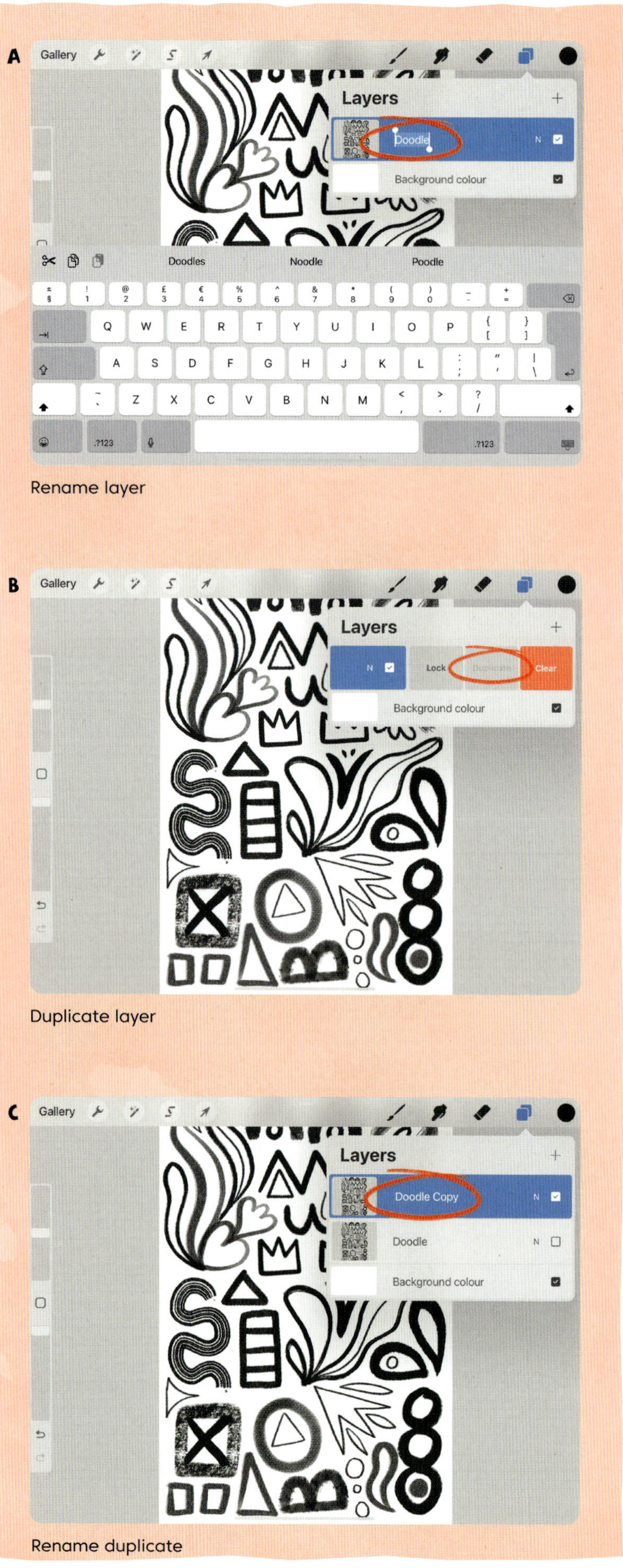

Rename layer

Duplicate layer

Rename duplicate

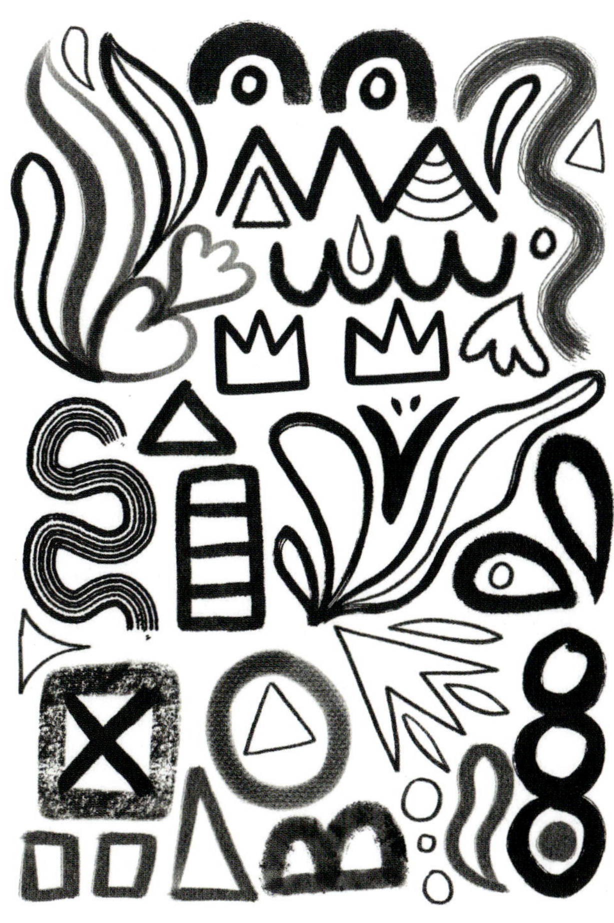

Try It Now

Let's have fun using the techniques you've just learnt by exploring these tools. We're going to create a colouring page of joined up shapes from your brush doodles.

1. **Select, cut and copy** the shapes and motifs you like onto new layers.
2. **Cut and copy** those you don't need onto a new hidden layer. Don't delete them – they may be useful later.
3. **Move, resize and reshape** your doodles using the Transform tools.

TRIAL AND ERROR

Beginners may find this exercise hard at first, but you can really learn by solving problems that arise through mistakes. You may overlap lines and find you can't move a shape independently without cutting a part of the drawing you want to keep intact. You might cut but not paste, losing a motif, or forget to duplicate a layer and lose a favourite graphic. Embrace this way of working for now – you'll soon develop your own creative flow!

Get to Know Your Layers

As you work your way through the projects, you'll pick up techniques for using layers in a number of ways. Here's some useful advice and information to get you started.

REMEMBER YOUR ORIGINAL

Always keep your original-art layer duplicated and safely hidden in case you want to start over.

LAYER ALLOWANCE

The number of layers available for any canvas depends on the dimensions and dpi of your canvas. In short, the larger your canvas, the fewer layers it will have. The amount of memory your iPad has also affects this.

KEEP COUNT

Keep an eye on the number of layers you're using by tapping on Actions, Canvas, Canvas Information, Layers.

MERGING LAYERS

To help manage the number of layers you have available, you can merge two layers. Do this by tapping once on the layer and selecting Merge Down, or by pinching multiple layers together with two fingers in the layers panel. Once layers are merged, it will be difficult to separate overlapping objects, so it's a great idea to keep a copy of your layers (or even a duplicate of the whole canvas) before merging.

LAYERS IN ACTION
Here's an example of how my layers look while I'm working. As you can see, it's important to keep everything organized. Select or hide the layers as required.

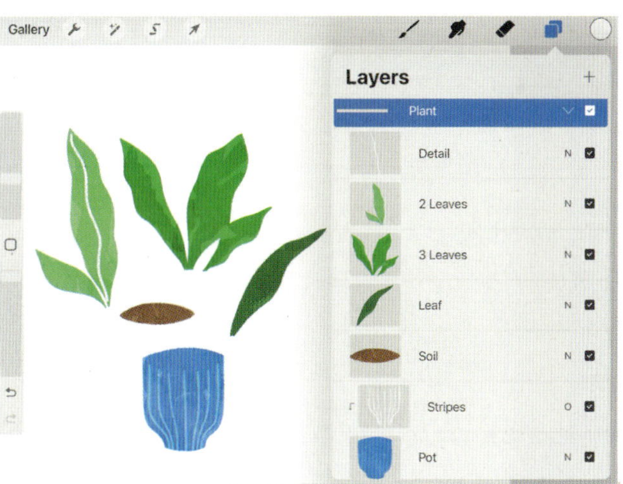

COLOUR

Using colour in Procreate is easy, with tools to help us create organized palettes that work. We'll use the Disc and Palettes options to make a custom palette for our doodle page.

USING DISC VIEW

This shows your default palette, your history and a disc where you can adjust your chosen colours to suit.

- **Hue** is adjusted with the outer ring.
- **Lightness**, **Darkness** and **Saturation** are adjusted with the inner circle.

1. Hide the doodle layer and create a new layer to try out colour.
2. Next, tap the Colours icon and go to Palettes (bottom right). We want to start with an empty palette, so tap on the + icon, top right, and choose Create New Palette (**A**). Rename it if you want, and make sure it has a blue tick next to the name (this means it's set as default).
3. Return to the Disc view to start filling the palette. Choose your first colour by tapping somewhere around blue on the outer ring. You can hold and drag the circle around the ring. When you're happy with the colour, do the same on the inner circle to lighten or darken the blue (**B**). Tap a square in the empty palette to save your colour.
4. Go to the Inking or Sketching section of the Brush Library and choose something to test your colour with. The Syrup brush (in the Inking folder) is good as it has opacity, and the tapering goes from fine to thick in a smooth motion. Colour a blob on your canvas for reference.

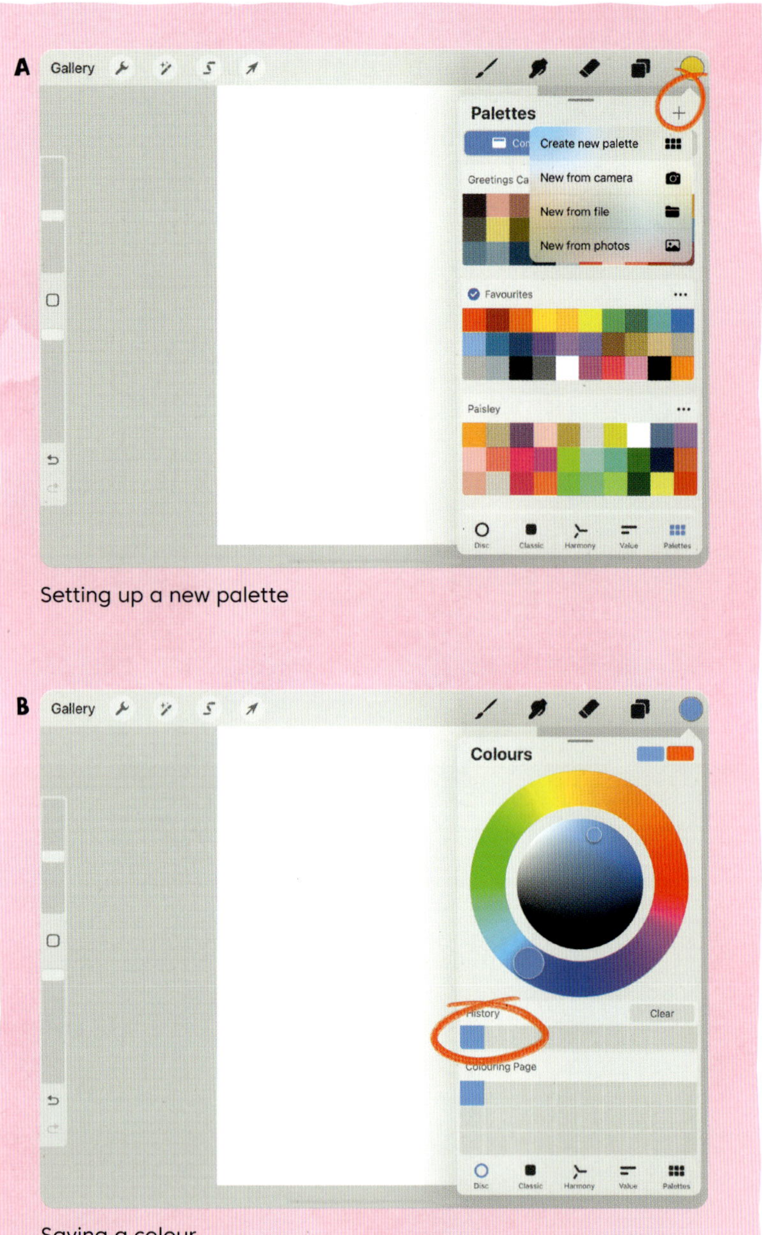

Setting up a new palette

Saving a colour

Use a bold, expressive brush such as Syrup to test your colours and create swatches.

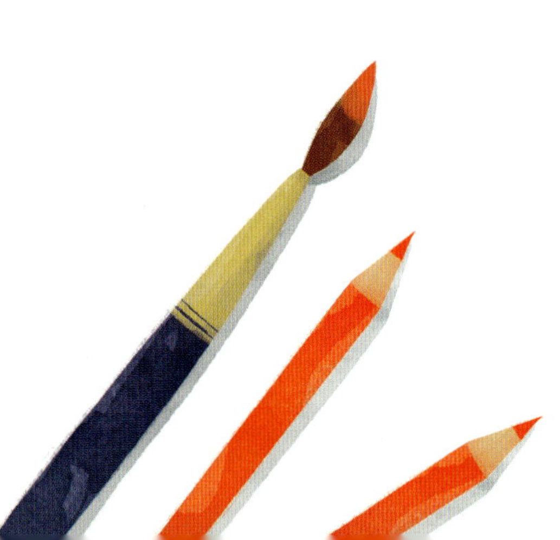

Using the Colour Picker

Deleting a swatch

USING THE COLOUR PICKER

Let's reverse this process by adding a colour to your custom palette with the Colour Picker.

1. Return to the Disc and drag the circles to select a green colour. Colour a blob with the green, then tap and hold your finger on the blob. A magnifier will pop up showing the previous blue colour and the green you have just selected (**C**).
2. You can now tap in an empty square on your custom palette and it will save the colour.

Play around with selecting, picking and saving colours to the palette. If you want to delete anything, just tap and hold to bring up the Delete Swatch option (**D**).

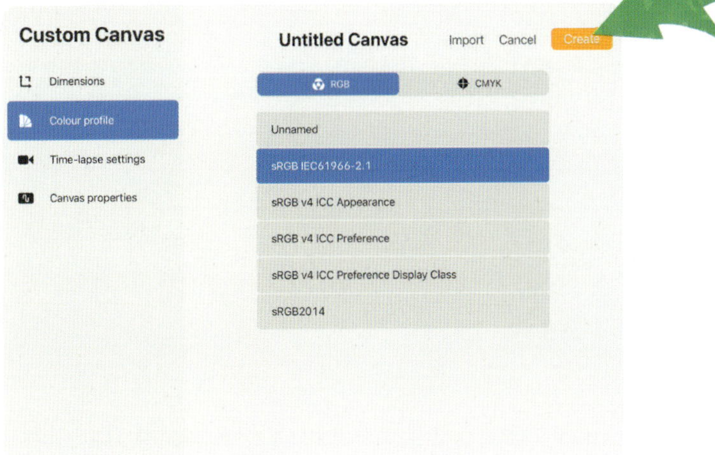

Working with colour profiles

COLOUR PROFILES

When you create a new canvas, tap on the Colour Profile option. Typically, files for print should be created in CMYK, and for screen in RGB. If working for a client, check with them which format they require. I've found working in RGB in Procreate to be the best option as I use a lot of vibrant colour and blend modes that are not so successful in CMYK mode. I flatten the final image and convert to CMYK in Photoshop if necessary.

Colouring Our Doodle Page

Now you know the basics of building a custom palette, let's look at a couple of different ways to colour in the doodle page.

Before you start, delete or hide the colour blob layer and unhide your doodles. Create a new layer under the doodles and rename it. We'll use this layer to colour in some shapes.

TRADITIONAL COLOURING

The first way to colour is by using the pencil as you would a regular pen or crayon on paper.

USING COLOUR DROP

On larger shapes, you can colour around the inside edge, then simply Colour Drop by dragging the selected colour from the circular colour icon in the top right of the screen, or swatch, to fill the centre of the shape. Take care to close the shape before colour dropping to avoid flooding the whole canvas.

FREEHAND SELECTION TOOL

You can also use the Freehand Selection tool to trace the shape you want to colour (**E**). Then colour within the selection (the area with the diagonal lines will be "masked off" to keep the colour within the shape). I find this a quick way to colour more complex shapes. It's also useful if you want to select multiple shapes and Colour Drop them altogether.

MAKE USE OF LAYERS

I would recommend using a different layer for each colour, allowing you to go back and tweak colours more easily. To change a colour, select, drag and drop from the colour icon, or from the swatch itself.

Spend time playing with ways of colouring. Working through the page, you'll find yourself using layers, selection and colour. We're not too worried about the end result – relax and enjoy the process. Learn by doing and you'll end up with a funky all-over pattern something like mine!

MIX IT UP

Experiment with different brushes and remember you can change the size and opacity of the brushes using the sliders on the left-hand side.

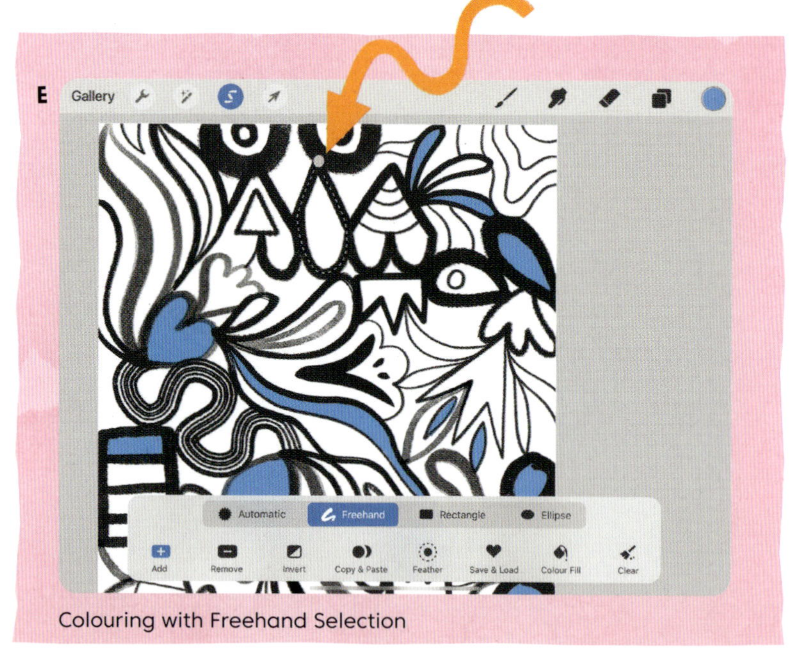

Colouring with Freehand Selection

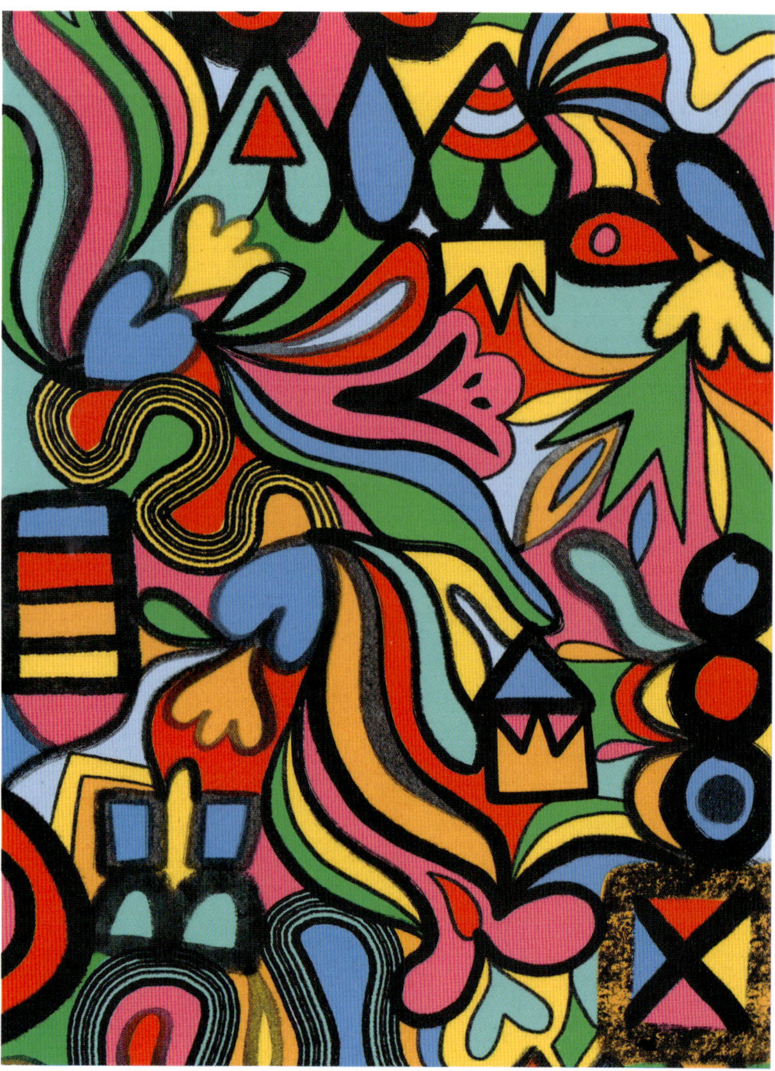

The final result! Subtle variations in line weight and texture add to the overall dynamic effect.

ADDING FILES & PHOTOS

Adding photos and other types of image to your canvas is a useful option. You may want a photo on the canvas as reference, or to make it part of the art itself.

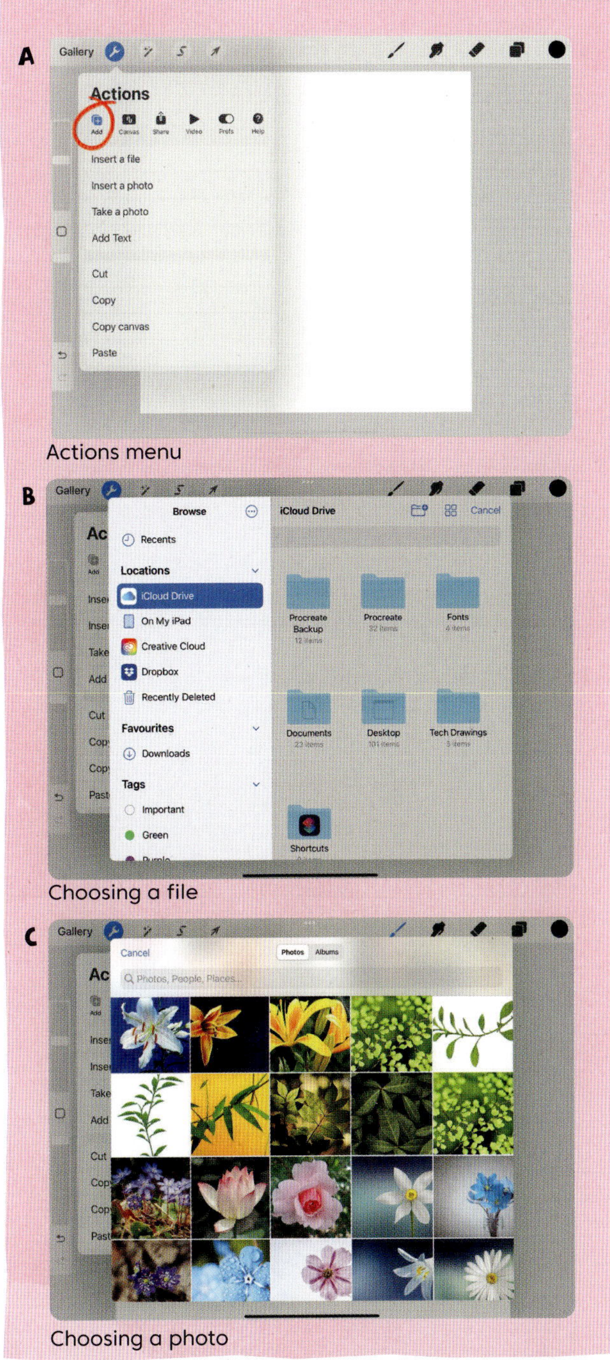

Actions menu

Choosing a file

Choosing a photo

IMPORTING AN IMAGE

Creating collage-type artwork in Procreate is easy and fun – we'll look at this in detail in the Projects section. For now, let's have a quick look at how we can import images easily from different sources. Tap on the wrench top left, to open the Actions menu, then Add, to view the options (**A**).

- **Insert a file** will take you directly to the Files browser of your iPad. You can then choose a saved file from your iPad or any cloud-based application you use for storing and transferring your files (**B**). You can insert a JPEG, PNG or PSD file from here.

  Side note: If you add a PSD file from Photoshop in this way, Procreate will flatten the image – the layers will not be preserved. You can import a layered file by using the Import option from the Gallery view. It will open the file browser in the same way.

- **Insert a photo** will take you to your Photo Library where you can scroll through and select anything stored there (**C**).
- **Take a photo** opens your iPad's camera.

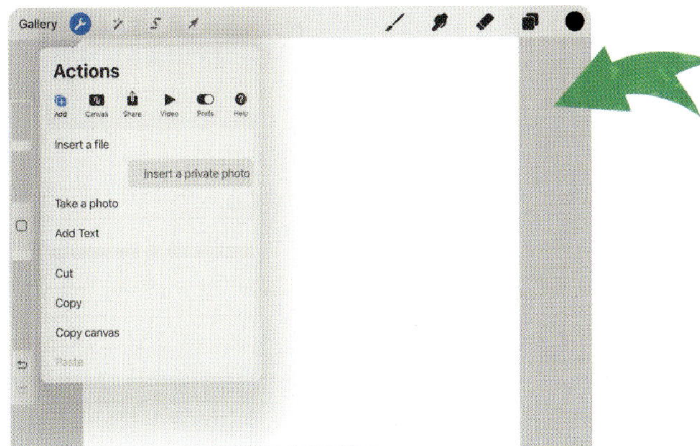

TIME-LAPSE PROTECTED

Did you know, by swiping left on Insert File, Insert a Photo or Take a Photo you'll see an option to Insert a Private Photo. This is great if you want to trace a rough drawing from your sketchbook. It will act like a normal layer but will not show up in a Time-lapse Recording playback (read more about Time-lapse videos at the end of this section).

TRY IT NOW

Let's go ahead and insert a photo from the Photo Library. I'm using an image of a flower from a royalty-free website.

1. As you can see, the image is dropped automatically onto its own layer (**D**). You can now use this image as part of your artwork.
2. I use the Freehand Selection to copy (**E**) and paste (**F**) the flower. I've flipped the flower horizontally and scaled it down a bit.

You can add another layer and draw on top of the images (**G**).

D

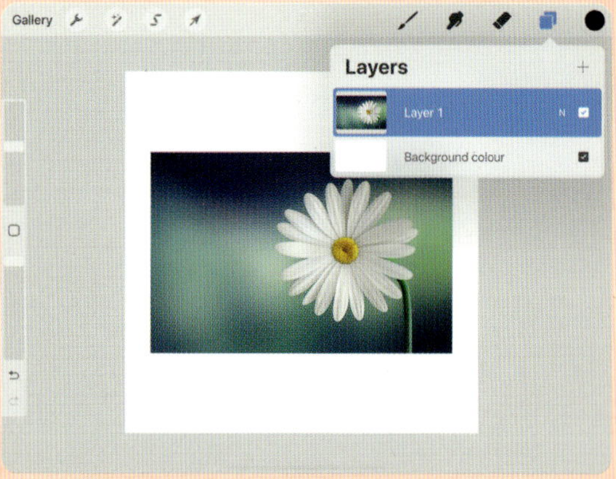

Imported image

E

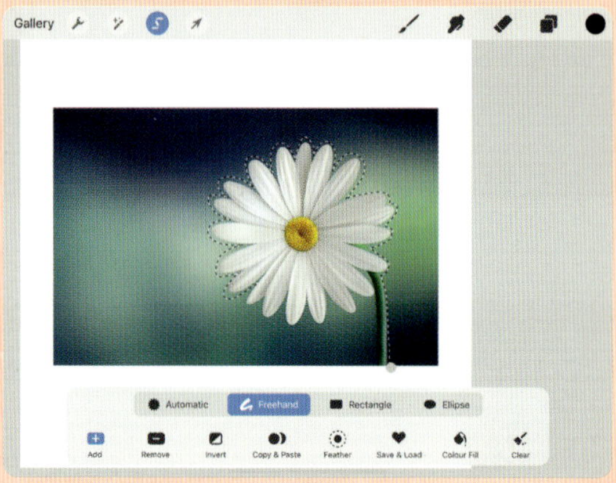

Copy

F

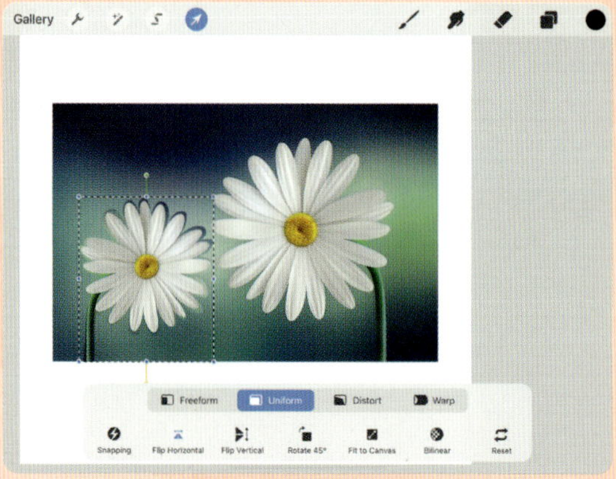

Flip and resize

G

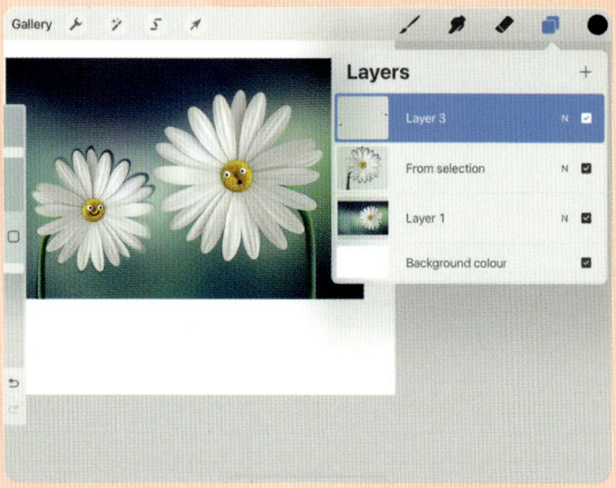

Illustrated layer

MOTION BLUR

There are also a lot of editing tools in the Adjustments menu. Try a few out on the photo layer. Motion Blur is a favourite of mine! Just slide your finger up or down to adjust the strength of the blur.

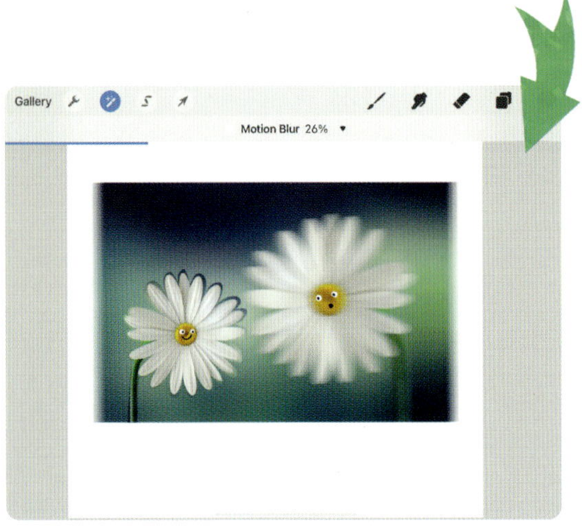

SHARING IMAGES

Send your work to your laptop for additional editing, or send a JPEG to your phone to share on social media.

In the Actions menu, under Share (**A**), is a foolproof system for sharing different files and formats.

- **Share as a Procreate file:** This will preserve all the layers, effects and blend modes. It will be fully editable but can only be opened in the Procreate app. Good for sending to someone who has Procreate and needs to edit in the same app.
- **Share as a PSD:** This is my most used option. Tapping on this will prepare the file for export (it may take a few seconds if the file is large). Once ready, a box with more options will open. From here, I use AirDrop to send it to my laptop to continue editing in Photoshop if necessary (**B**).
- **Share as a PDF:** This format will flatten the image but give you three options for the quality (**C**).
- **Share as a JPEG:** A great option if you don't need to edit, you just need a good quality image to send to a client or share on social media.
- **Share as a PNG or TIFF:** Both options are good if you want a high quality export with the added option of preserving a transparent background.

SHARING LAYERS OPTIONS

These will mostly be used for animation files, but you might want to use the PDF option (**D**) to save each layer as a different page in a combined PDF file – great for presentations and slideshows.

Try all the options. Practise sending and moving files to help you develop an efficient workflow.

A

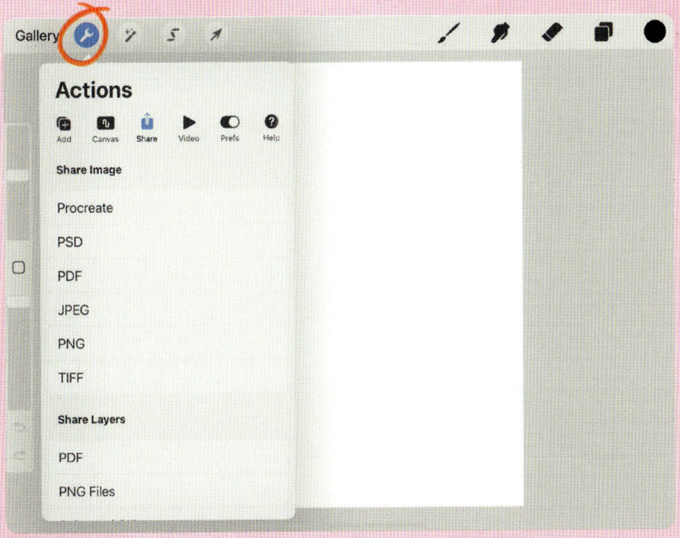

Sharing options

B

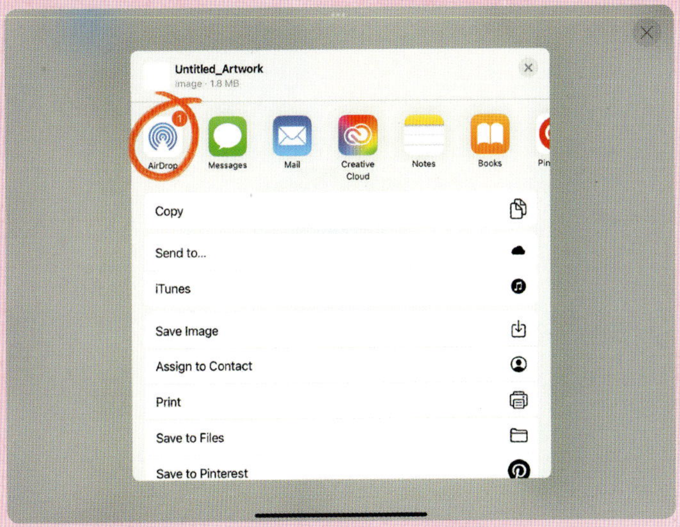

Sharing with AirDrop

C

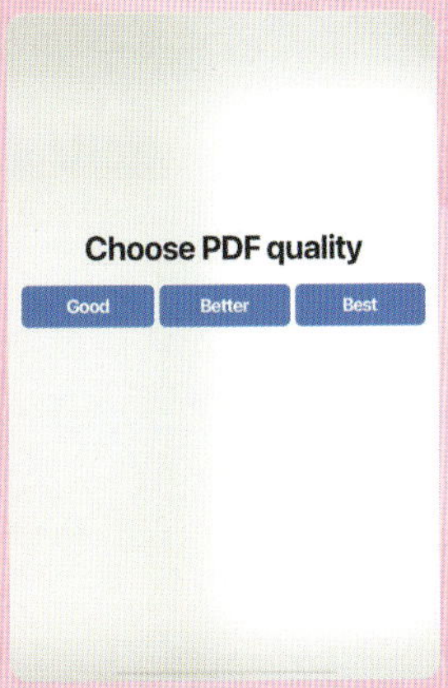

PDF options

D

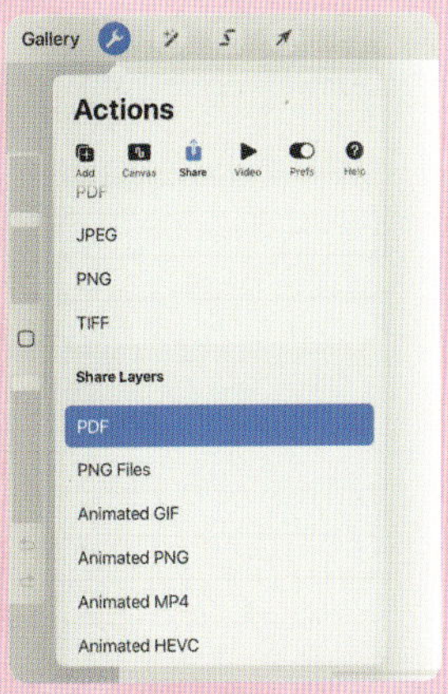

Sharing layers

Time-lapse Videos

The ability to create a Time-lapse video of your workflow is a useful (and fun!) feature, unique to Procreate. You may have watched videos of other artists at work, but you can also make your own. This feature is set to "on" by default, but if you want to check before you start drawing, go to the Actions menu, Video, and Time-lapse Recording. When you've finished, go back to the same menu and choose Time-lapse Replay – here, you'll also find the option to export the video. Play around with this feature to find out how you can get the best from it.

PROJECTS

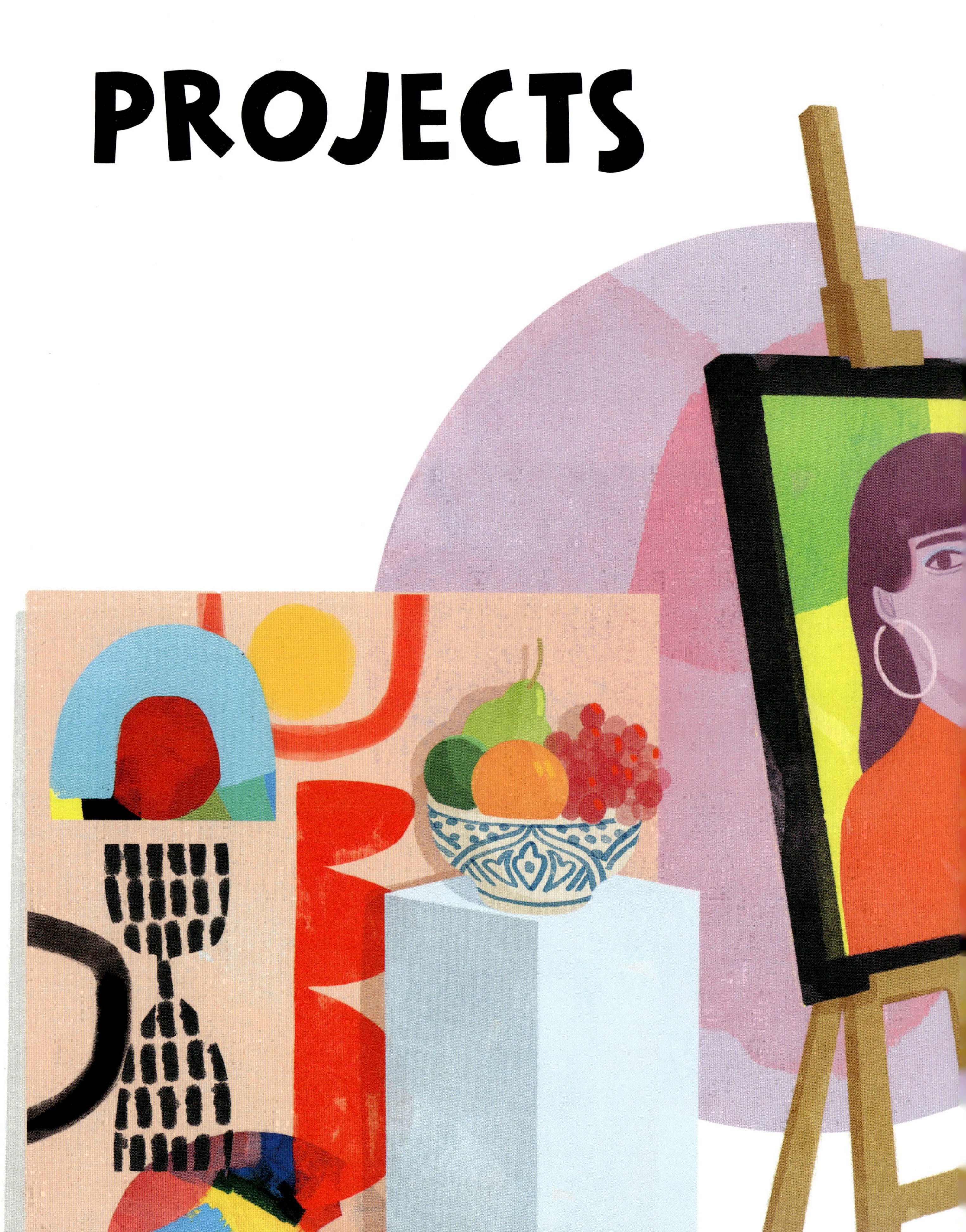

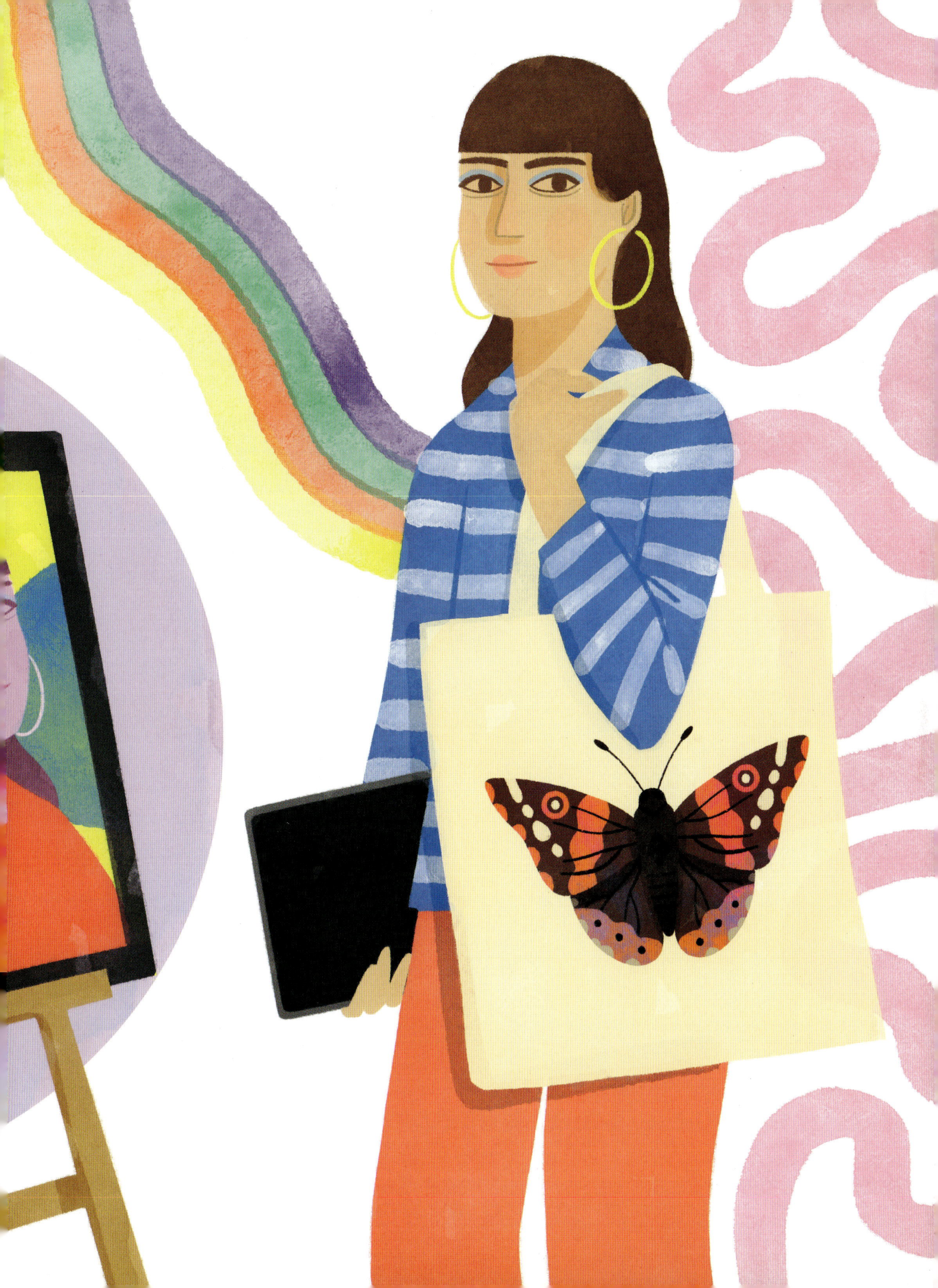

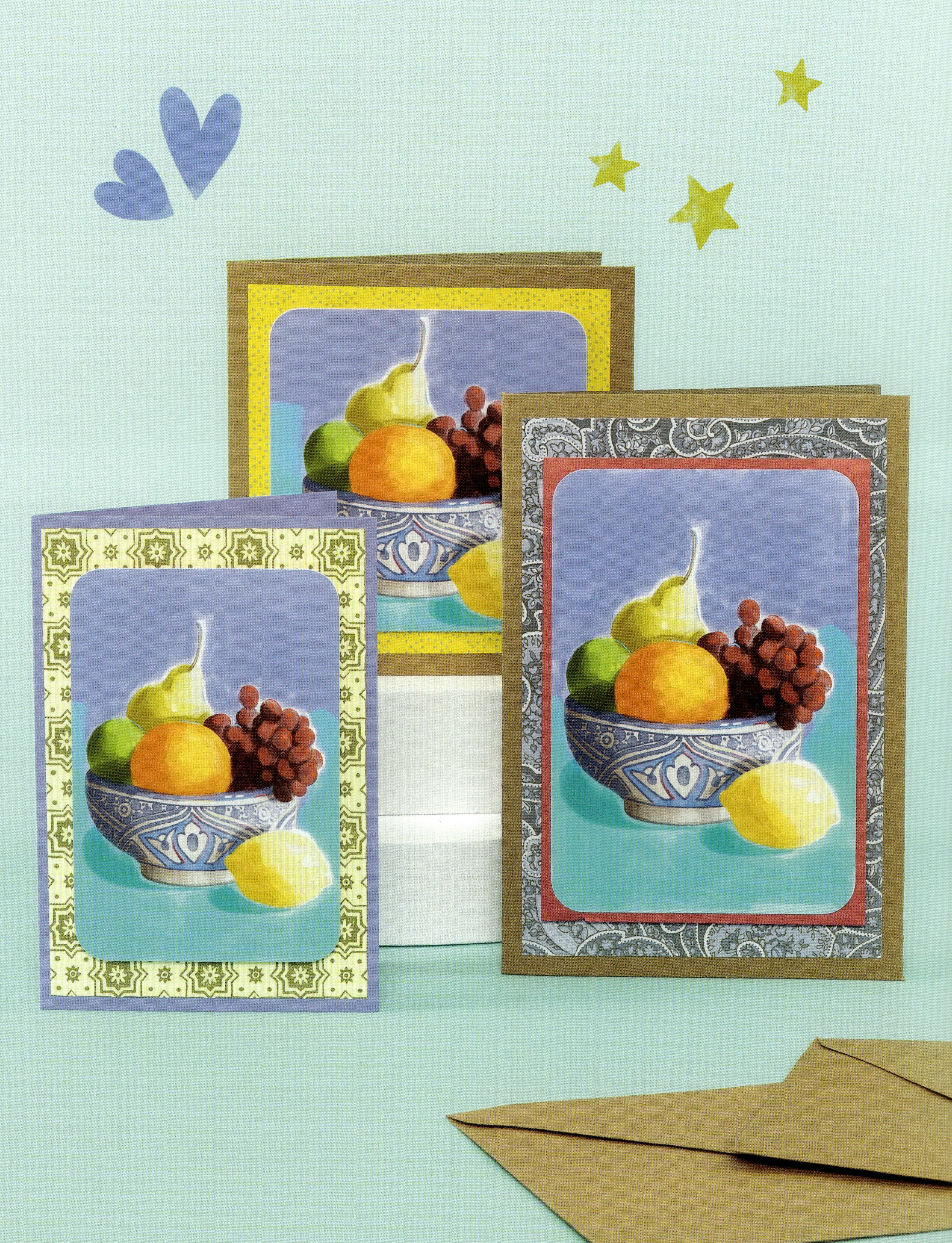

Still Life Greetings Card

When you open an instructional art book or go to a beginner's class, very often the first project is a still life. It is a chance for the artist to show their skills in composition, light, shade, texture and colour. It is also a great subject to start with – simply pick up objects from around the home and get started straight away. In this first project, we'll touch on everything you have learned so far to create a colourful still life that can then be made into a greetings card.

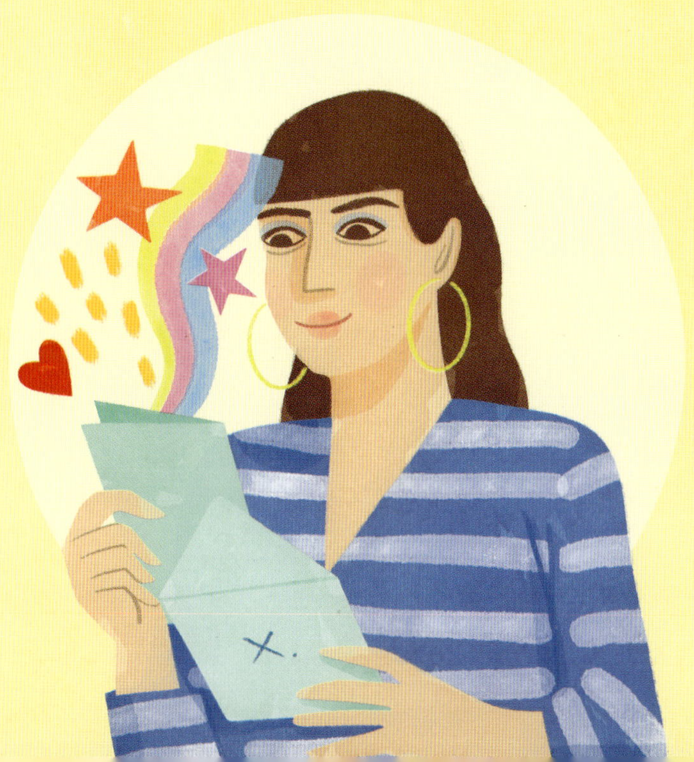

Put Your Skills to the Test

If you have used Procreate before, or have worked your way through the first few chapters of this book, you'll have a good idea of how basic tools and techniques work. This project will give you a chance to put your skills to the test!

1. Creating your composition

A fruit bowl composition is a favourite of mine, as it offers the chance to incorporate simple shapes, bold colours and some decorative elements. You can play around with how realistic or stylized you want your work to look. Simple, stylized flat shapes and block colours will work just as well as more realistic, dimensional images with lots of light and shade.

GATHERING OBJECTS

Have a look around for an interesting vessel and maybe pop to your local store for some fresh, colourful fruit. You can then start to set up your composition. Try to look at the set up as a series of shapes and colours. See how well they fit together and what looks good to you. We're not going to get into the technicalities of composition here, but are instead aiming to find an arrangement that is pleasing to *your* eye.

WORKING FROM PHOTOS VERSUS LIFE

If you have space to work, time to spend and good light, you can work from life. If not, I recommend taking a series of photos. If you don't have a dedicated art-making space or you work on your projects when there is little or no natural light, it's probably best to work from photos.

It's a good idea to take photos regardless, as they will give you reference to work from if the light changes or your fruit goes mouldy before you finish!

If you're short of time, you can use my photo reference instead. You'll see that my image is light and bright with a little contrast, allowing us to experiment with shading and shadow in the artwork.

2. Setting up the colour palette

Let's create the canvas using a standard greetings-card size. In this case, 12.7cm by 17.8cm (5in by 7in).

ADJUSTING THE PHOTO

To help me make a basic palette, I'm going to insert my photo on the canvas. You can make adjustments to the photo, including brightness and contrast, using the options in the Adjustments panel. During Adjustments, you can tap anywhere on the screen to bring up the panel to Cancel, Reset or Apply your changes (**A**). You can also Undo from here, and even tap and hold the Preview icon to switch between the original and the adjusted image. Tap Apply to commit to the changes.

CREATING COLOUR SWATCHES

The next stage is to gather a few swatches using the Colour Picker. Exit Adjustments and open Colours. Tap and hold to bring up the magnifier, and move around the screen to pick up a few mid-tones from each fruit and the bowl (**B**). You can then go back in and create lighter and darker versions, maybe some with more saturation (**C**). This is an easy way to set up a basic palette to get you started.

USING THE PHOTO AS A REFERENCE

Let's delete the photo layer for now to avoid the temptation to trace it. We've learnt a lot of technical things so far – now it's time to start developing our artistic muscles. If you're using a photo versus still life, bring it up on a separate laptop or print it out for reference. This will replicate drawing from life more closely, meaning you have to keep looking up at the reference to compare shape and colour from a distance, resulting in more alive and original results. It will also help you to work on your style, and make judgments and decisions about your work which will also impact on the finished piece.

USING A LAYER AS REFERENCE

If you only have your iPad to hand, resize the photo to fit in a corner of your canvas. Keep it on a separate layer to turn on and off throughout.

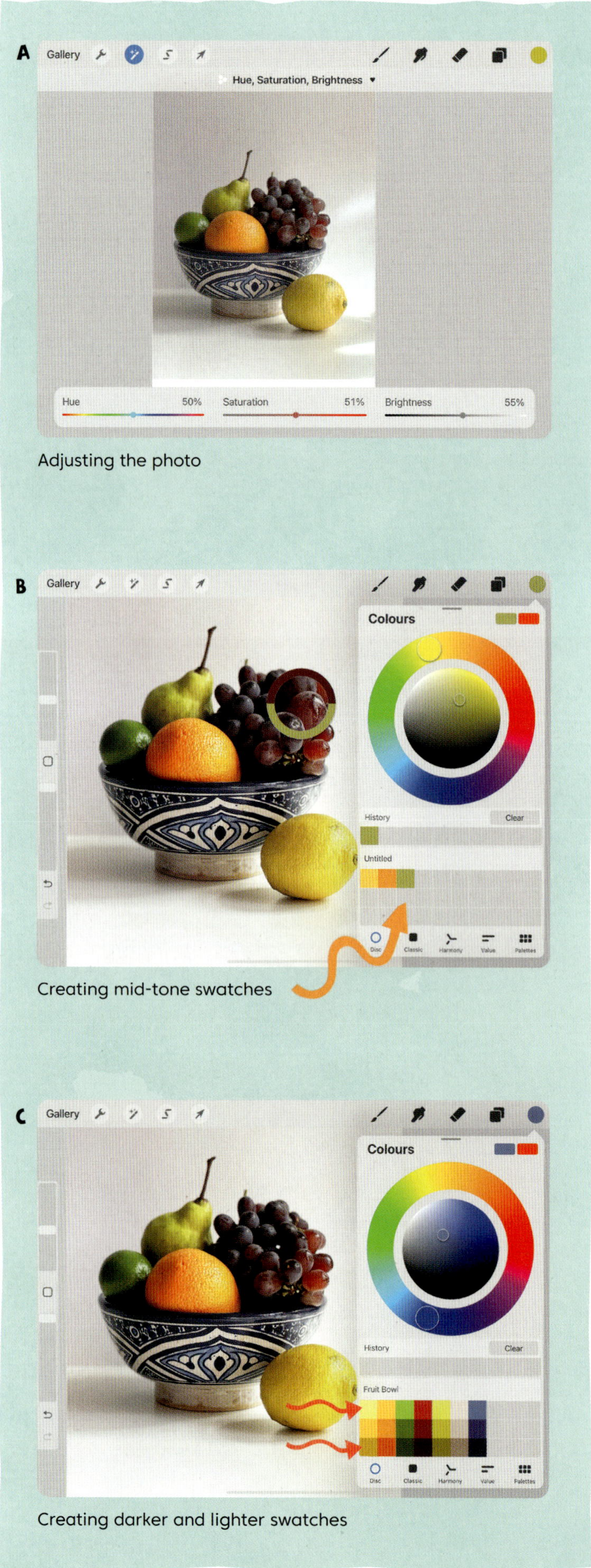

Adjusting the photo

Creating mid-tone swatches

Creating darker and lighter swatches

3. Establishing your intentions

Before we start sketching, let's take a moment to think about what we're going to create. You may have something in mind already, an idea of how you want it to look, or you may be completely open to how the end result turns out. Either way, it's good to focus in on your intentions and set the mood before you start.

STUDYING THE PHOTO

Look carefully at your reference photo and take a few moments to cast your eye over everything. Think about the shapes and how they interconnect. Try to simplify the composition in your mind. Trace the silhouette with your eye and compare the sizes within your composition. Really try to observe what is in front of you. Take a few deep breaths and relax your shoulders.

GOING DIGITAL

Now that you're drawing digitally, you have a lot of tools at your disposal to help you achieve your ideal composition. Select and move parts of the drawing. Resize, cut and copy. Work on your sketch until you're happy.

4. Starting to sketch

When you're ready, select the 6B Pencil or similar and a dark colour for sketching. Start to sketch the outline of all the shapes.

GO YOUR OWN WAY!

We're not looking for perfection here; we're looking for something that you find pleasing to your own individual eye. There is nothing wrong with wonky shapes and a bit of irregular scale. I tend to get things out of proportion when I'm drawing – I make things too big, I concentrate on parts of the drawing I love and leave out parts I don't like.

It's up to you! You may want to draw each individual grape or you might want to miss a few out and concentrate more on the details of the bowl. Start by drawing what you see, but if you feel like altering some shapes or distorting the perspective, go for it!

Here you can see my finished sketch. I stuck mostly to the reference photograph, but slightly changed the shape of the lemon and made the pear at the back a bit bigger. I probably missed out a few grapes. The point is not to labour over the sketch. Enjoy the flow but don't get bogged down in perfection and details!

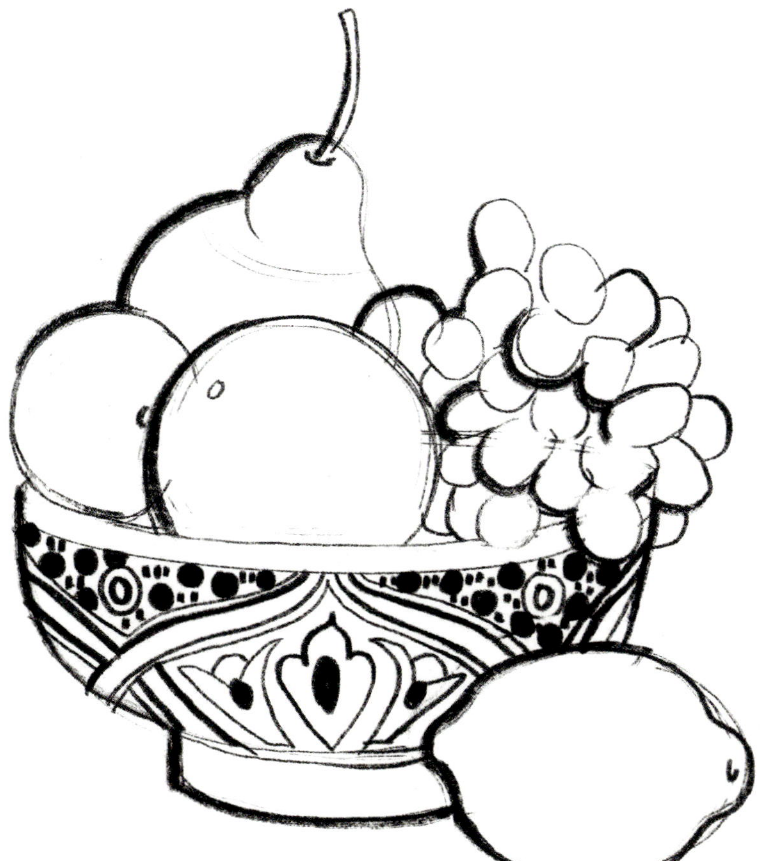

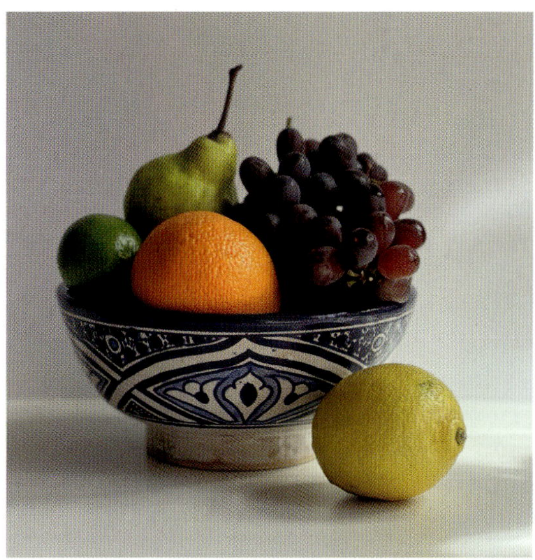

Note the differences between the reference and my sketch.

5. Adding the basic colours

Set the sketch layer to Multiply and lower the opacity to around 20% (**D**) so we can work with colour on a new layer underneath. We'll use the sketch as a guide for our painting. By keeping it on the top layer, we can toggle on and off while working on the layers below.

We'll now start to lay down the basic colours. Select the Acrylic Brush from the Painting section of the Brush Library. I'm going to start with the pear at the back. Use a mid-tone from your custom swatches and paint the sphere using light strokes. Build opacity where the fruit is in shadow but keep the colour soft where the light hits.

CREATE LAYERS

Use a different layer for each component. Keep hiding the sketch layer to check your progress. You should soon have something that looks like this (**E**).

Don't worry too much about the edges of the shapes for now – we'll touch up these later. Paint outside the lines rather than inside. Later, it will be easier to erase parts we don't need than to colour match and fill in gaps.

PENCIL GRIP

Try not to grip your pencil too tightly – a light touch will give pale results with a little brush texture. Pressing down hard will lay down more paint and create opacity. You'll soon learn how to build the colour in a way you like.

FIND THE LIGHT

I took the reference photo with natural sunlight hitting the top right-hand side of the composition. Think about the position of the light when you're painting.

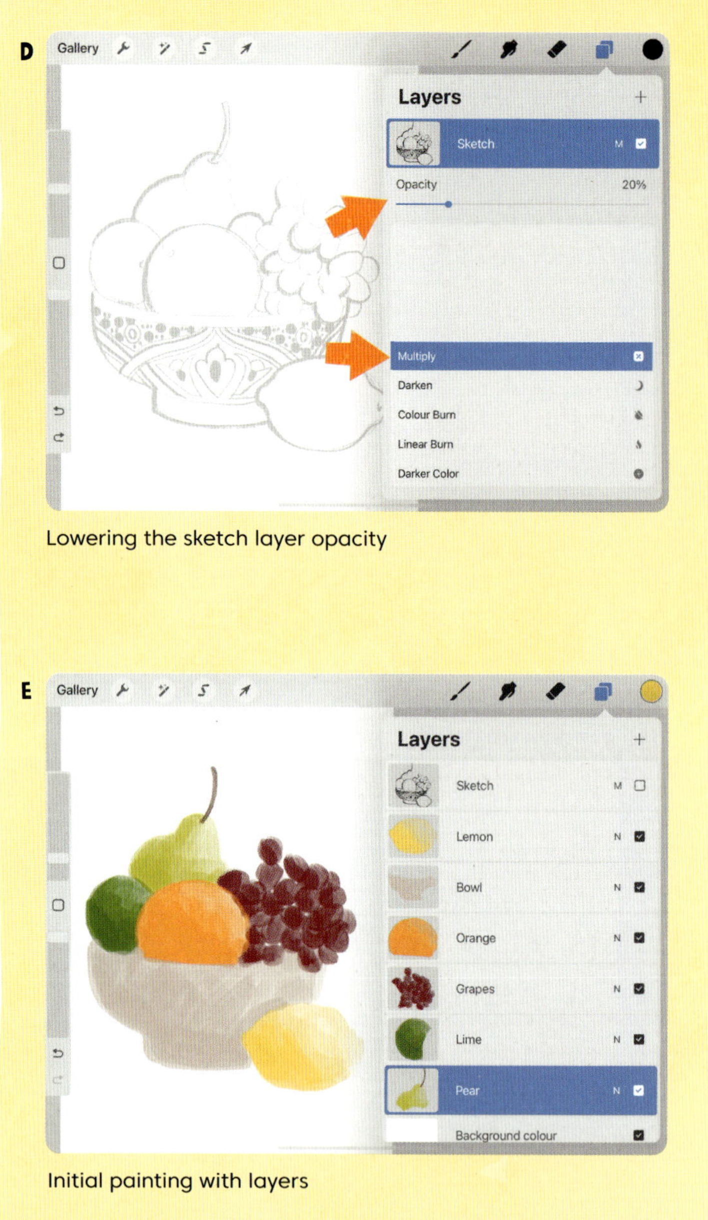

Lowering the sketch layer opacity

Initial painting with layers

6. Adding depth

Observe your reference photo and identify the areas that need to be darker. Quickly lay down some colour, taking care with the brush pressure sensitivity. Lay down some darker areas of colour on each fruit. Do it on the same layer if you're confident, or create new layers above to keep it separate and more editable.

I've also added a layer underneath everything else to add in a bit of shadow below the lemon and bowl (**F**). Set this layer to Multiply to act as a transparent shadow when we put some background in later.

BLEND MODES

Setting a layer to Multiply will usually darken the objects on that layer, and display some transparency depending on what is on the layer below. Experiment to see what happens. This blend mode is also great for shadows.

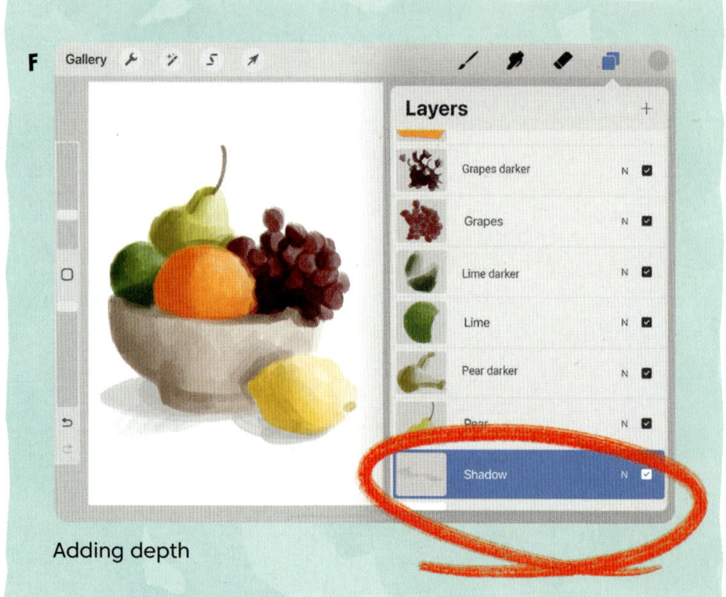

Adding depth

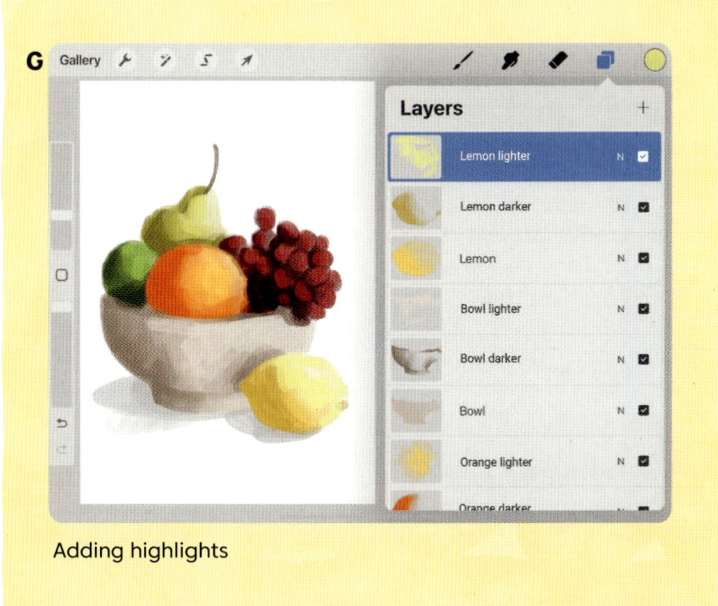

Adding highlights

7. Adding highlights

You should now start to see some form developing in the shapes. Repeat the process in the previous step, this time using the lighter colours in your palette. You can adjust the swatch colours at any time by using the disc, so you don't have to stick to your chosen colours. This initial palette is just using a starting point (**G**).

8. Merging the layers

For the next stage of this painting, I'm going to Merge some of the layers. But before doing this, it's a good idea to go back to the Brush Library and make a duplicate of your work. This ensures you retain all the individual layers in case you want to go back in and edit something further down the line (**H**).

WORKING ON THE DUPLICATE VERSION

Working now on the duplicate version, let's merge the individual fruit layers together so we can refine the shape and add more details. You can do this by pinching the layers together or by tapping each layer and selecting Merge Down. This way, we can refine the shape without editing colour, shade and highlights separately. However keep each piece of fruit separate so you have some edit-ability (**I**).

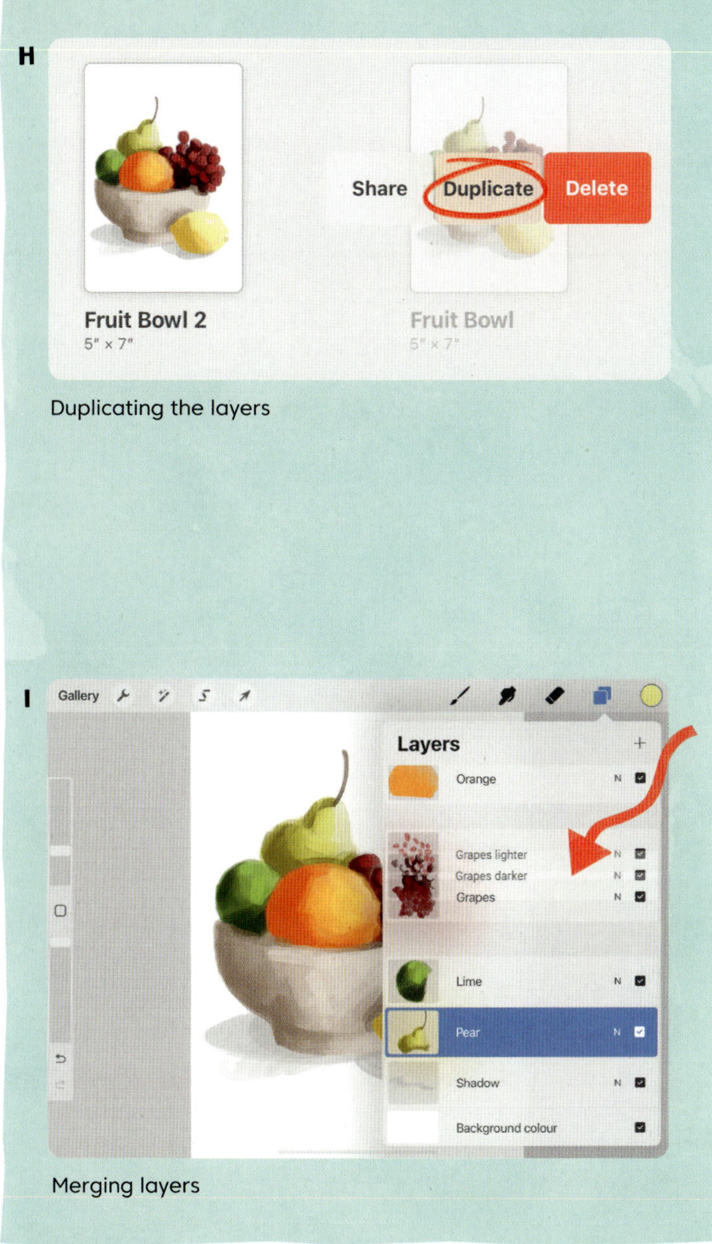

Duplicating the layers

Merging layers

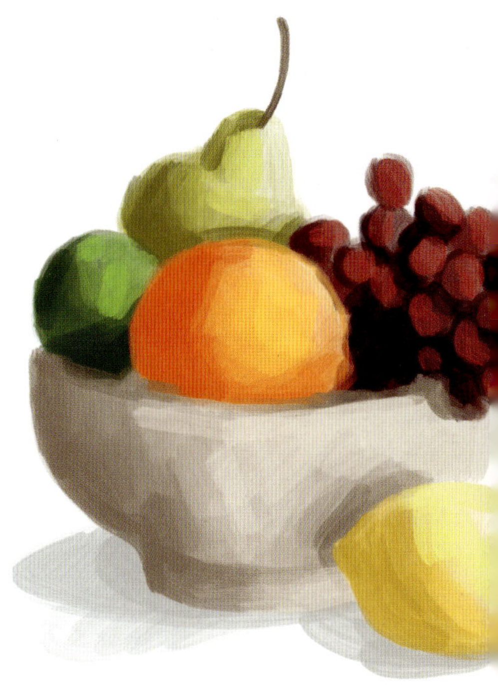

9. Refining the edges

I'm going to use the 6B Pencil as an eraser to tidy up the edges of the shapes. You may want to keep some of the painterly quality and that's fine, so try not to clean up any parts too much.

10. Painting the bowl

We're now ready to paint the design on the fruit bowl. If your still life has a plain bowl, you could leave it as is. Alternatively, sketch out a light pattern to add more interest to the piece. It's totally up to you.

SELECTING A BRUSH

The design on my bowl is hand painted, so I'll try to recreate that by using a watercolour-type brush from the Artistic section of the Brush Library. Locate the brush called Old Beach and duplicate it – we want to make a slight adjustment in the Brush Studio.

Tap on the duplicate brush and select Taper from the left-hand side menu. Scroll to the bottom of the list of options and tap on Classic Taper (**J**). Try the brush on the drawing pad – you'll see it looks more natural with a finely tapered start and finish to the stroke when you use pressure. Tap Done and return to the canvas.

USING A CLIPPING MASK

Create a new layer above the bowl. Tap on the layer to bring up the menu and select Clipping Mask (**K**). Select your brush and a colour, and paint the design. This will keep our decorative design within the shape of the bowl underneath. Draw out the design and add further layers for different colours if necessary (**L**).

CREATING A BACKGROUND

Create a new layer underneath everything else and fill it with colour to create a background. I'm using a pale pink that helps to make the fruit pop.

BACKGROUND OPTIONS

You can colour in the background by tapping on the Background layer and doing it from there. But I prefer to create an additional layer and keep the background white. You can create this layer anywhere and then hold and drag it to the bottom.

You may now notice some transparency on your painting where the pink is showing through. You have a couple of options here. You can either add more paint to those parts of the fruit, or you can create another layer on top of the background, underneath the fruit and the bowl. Add some white to bring back the lighter areas.

J

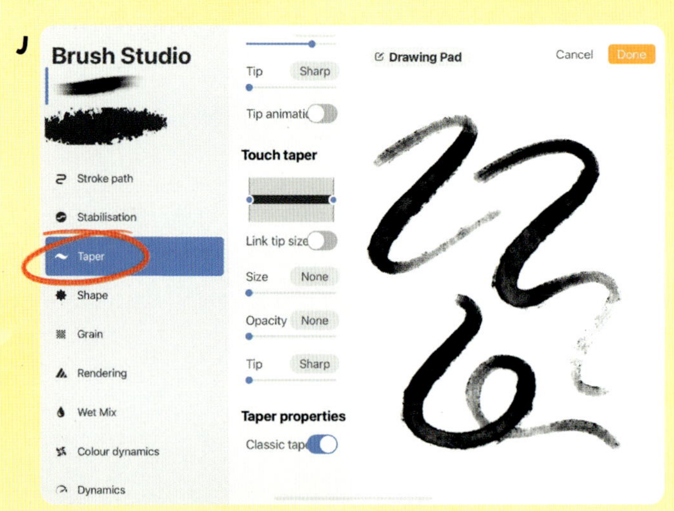

Adjusting the brush

K

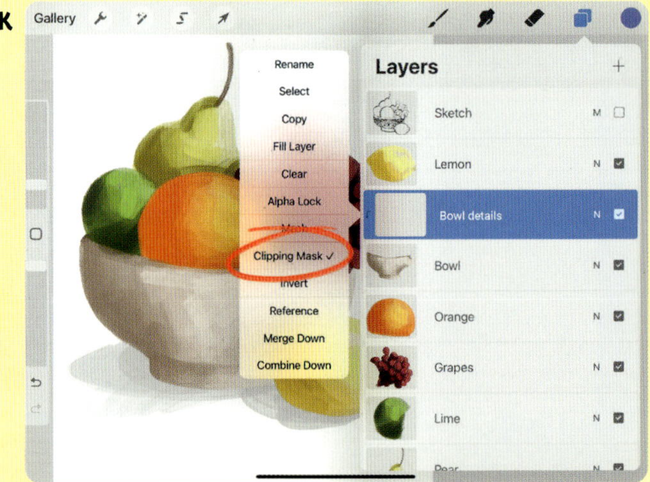

Creating a Clipping Mask layer

L

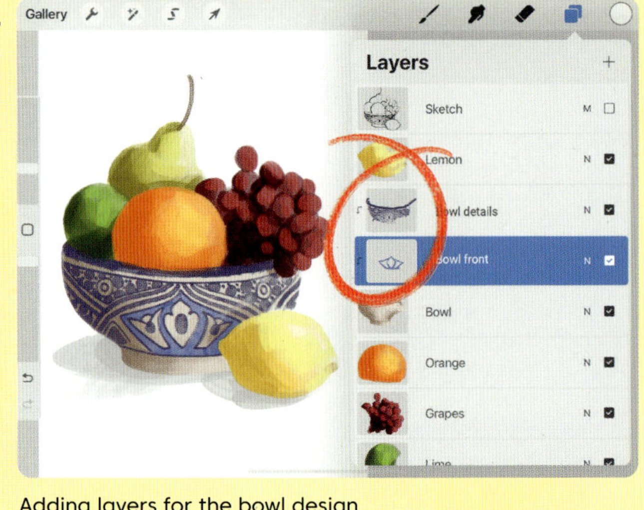

Adding layers for the bowl design

M

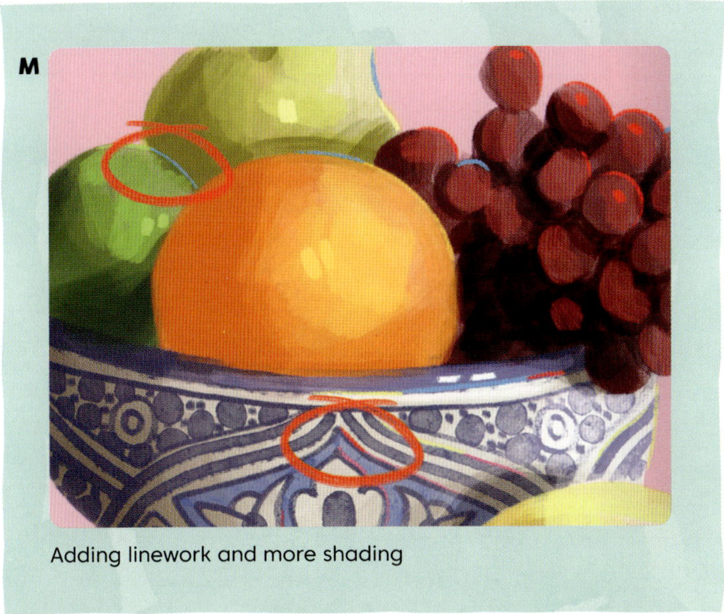

Adding linework and more shading

N

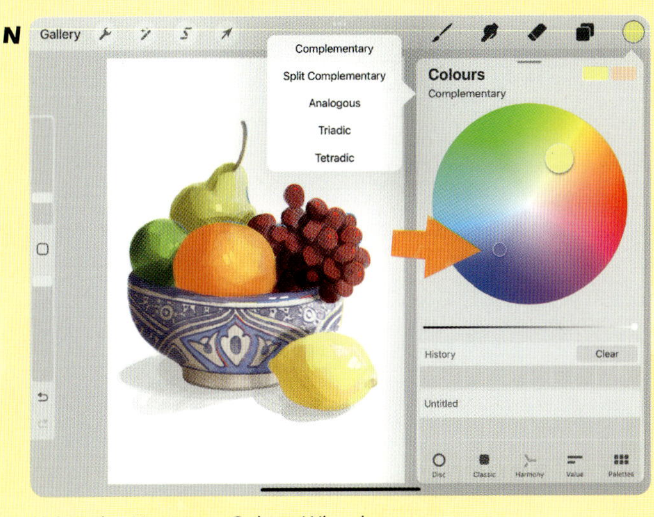

Using the Harmony Colour Wheel

O

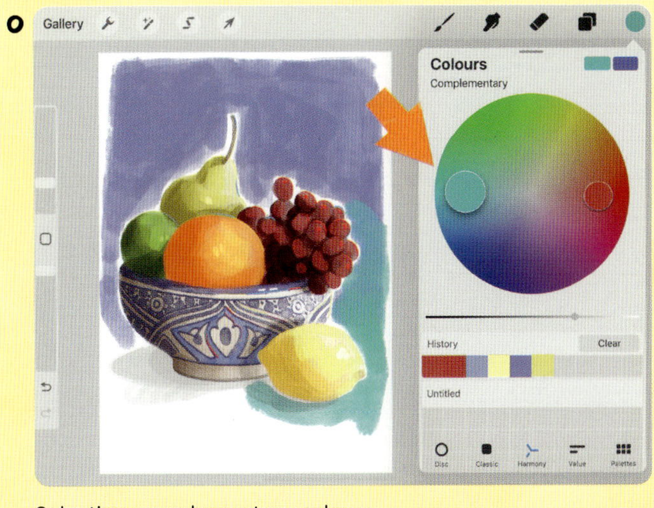

Selecting complementary colours

11. Finishing the painting

Take a minute to stand back – is anything missing? Do you need more contrast or shading? Perhaps you'd like to brighten some of the colours or refine the details.

ADDING FURTHER SHADING

I'm going to add an extra shade layer on top of the bowl. Again, I'll use a Clipping Mask to contain the brushstrokes and set the blend mode to Multiply (see Step 6). Adding another Clipping Mask layer set to Overlay will allow us to add highlights to the bowl.

ADDING LINEWORK

A fun way to make your work pop is with linework on a layer at the top, using brighter, contrasting colours to pick out small details. I've picked out some of the edges on the fruit and bowl with the 6B Pencil (**M**). Give it a go until you find something you're happy with.

12. Adding a background

Looking at the artwork now, I think it deserves a more painterly background. To help me choose the colour I'm going to use the Harmony Colour Wheel.

SELECTING A NEW BACKGROUND COLOUR

Hide the pink background layer and create a new layer above. Tap on the Colour options and select Harmony at the bottom. If you tap on Complementary at the top, you'll see all the other Harmony options listed – this is really for colour nerds so play around with it later!

For now, I'll select Complementary as I want to add a complementary background colour around the pear. Tap, hold and release the mid-section of the pear to bring up the pear's light green colour. The Harmony wheel now shows its complementary colour, so I'm selecting that to paint the background (**N**).

SELECTING A BRUSH

I'm painting in the background with the Gouache Brush from the Painting section of the Brush Library. This will give a painterly feel to the background but not enough texture to distract from the main piece. I'm leaving a little white space around the edge of the fruit and bowl.

I repeat this process above to identify the complementary colour of the grapes. In this case it is a turquoise, so I'm using that for the lower half of the painting (**O**).

REVISING THE SHADOW LAYER

Finally, I delete the shadow layer from underneath the objects and redo it on a new layer set to Multiply, with the turquoise. Just a couple of strokes with the Gouache Brush adds depth. I originally painted this layer on a white background with grey, but it is now a darker colour similar to the background so it looks more natural.

ASSEMBLE THE CARD

I exported the finished piece as a JPEG and printed it at home using matte photo paper.

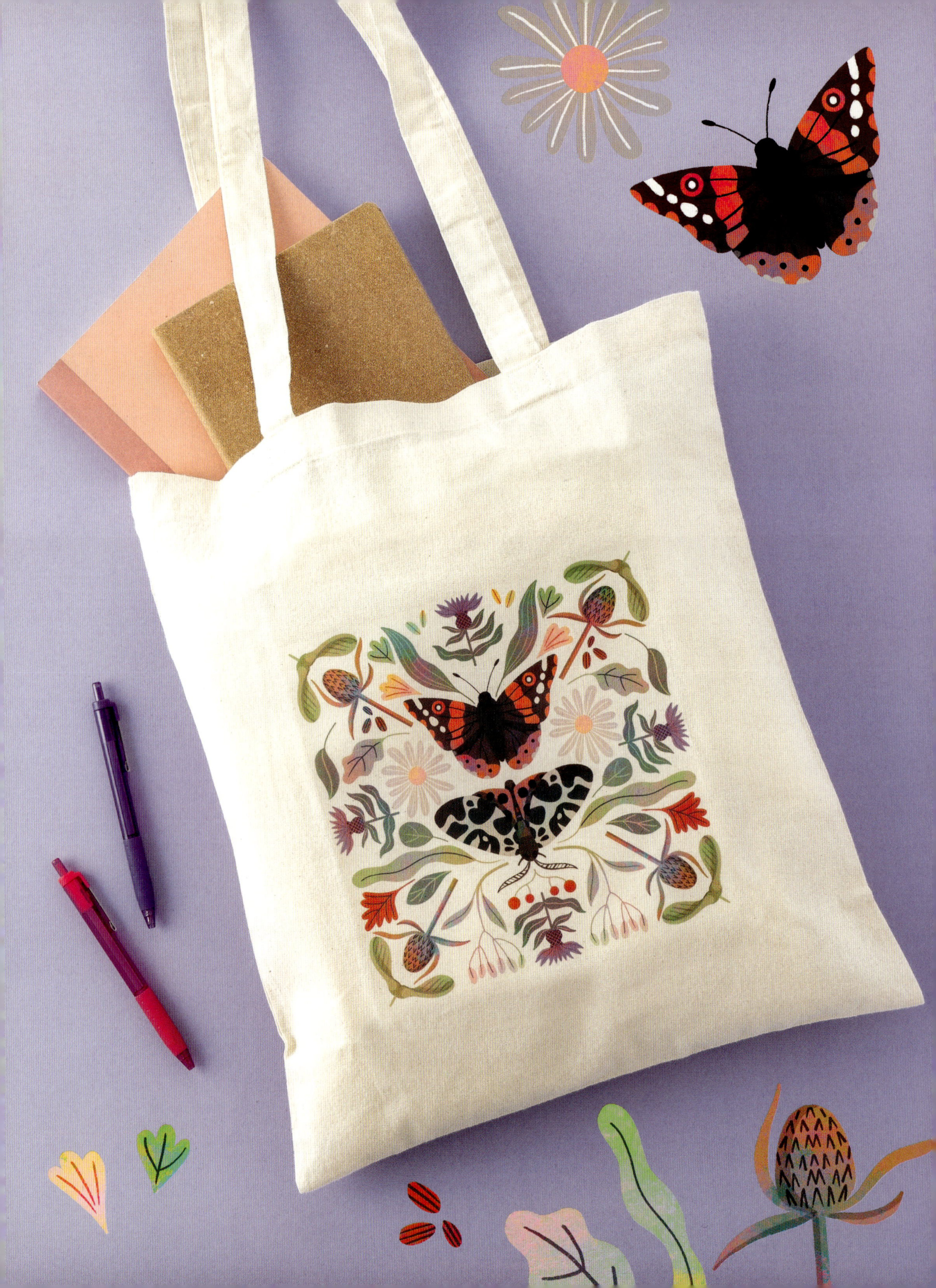

Natural Symmetry Tote Bag

Seeing your work brought to life on different accessories and products is a wonderful thing! By printing your design onto heat-transfer paper, it can be applied to many different surfaces. Blank cotton tote bags are inexpensive and make useful gifts. Even though it's a simple, flat surface, it still adds dimension and texture to your illustration.

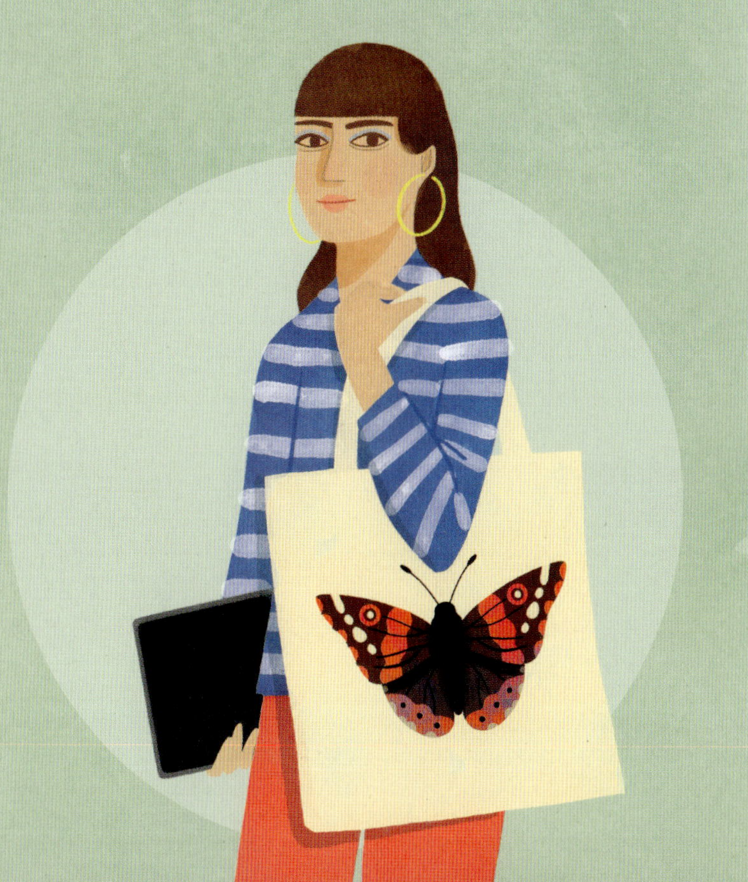

Built-in Symmetry Tools

Working digitally allows you to take advantage of some amazing tools that will help you enhance your creativity – instantly. The Assisted Drawing functions, including the Symmetry option in Procreate, are simple to use; once you get the hang of working with them, the possibilities are endless.

Sometimes I use the Symmetry tools to help me draw individual motifs that require a perfect mirrored shape. I then copy and paste them into my work, secretly pleased that no one will ever guess I used this brilliant tool! I find this kind of symmetrical drawing very relaxing – you can really work on it without thinking too much. Just let the shapes and lines flow from your brush.

To fully appreciate the power of Symmetry, we'll look at all the options and use them to help us make a stunning design that can be printed and applied to a tote bag.

1. Seeking inspiration

Symmetry is all around us – let's use nature as our starting point and really focus on shapes and lines. If possible, take a walk outside and look for inspiration. Collect leaves to draw from life, or take photos of plants and flowers. Butterflies and moths are also great subjects for this kind of project, and you may want to search for reference images online or in books and magazines.

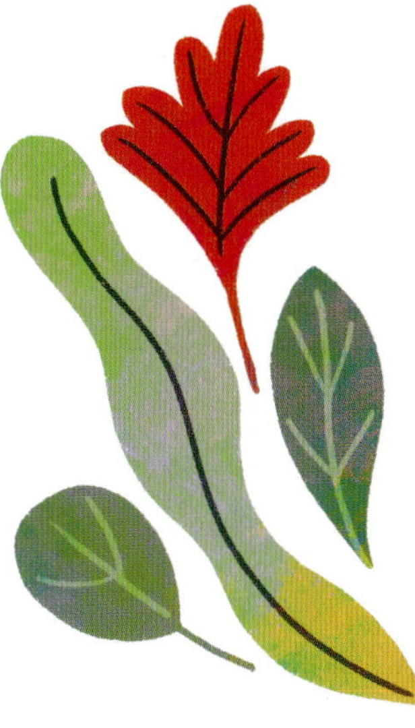

2. Setting up the canvas

For this project, I'm going to use a square canvas, 3000px by 3000px. Select or create this in the Gallery, then tap on the wrench icon to open Actions, then Canvas. Select Drawing Guide, then Edit Drawing Guide just below (**A**).

This will open the options and menus for all Drawing Guides. Tap on Symmetry (**B**), then Options to open the Guide Options.

3. Symmetry drawing – Guide Options

Let's have a play and get used to drawing with the different Symmetry Guide Options!

VERTICAL SYMMETRY

Select Vertical, and make sure Assisted Drawing is also selected (**C**). Click Done to return to the canvas.

Choose a smooth brush from the Inking section of the Brush Library. I'm using the Studio Pen sized at 10%. Another good brush for smooth outlines is the Monoline from the Calligraphy section. Try them both and see which you prefer.

Start drawing on one side of the vertical centre line and you'll magically see your drawing mirrored on the other! Draw simple leaf shapes and fill them with colour. Now you'll start to see the potential of this wonderful tool. Carry on and fill the page for practice.

ACCESSING ASSISTED DRAWING

If you tap on Layers, you'll see the word Assisted under the layer name. You can tap on the layer and turn Assisted Drawing on or off at any time. You may need to do this later on in this project.

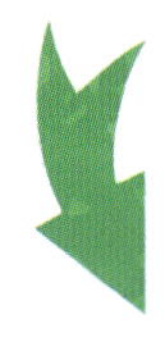

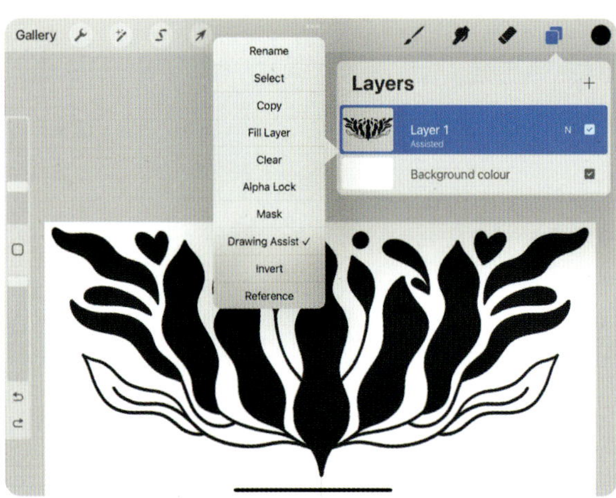

A

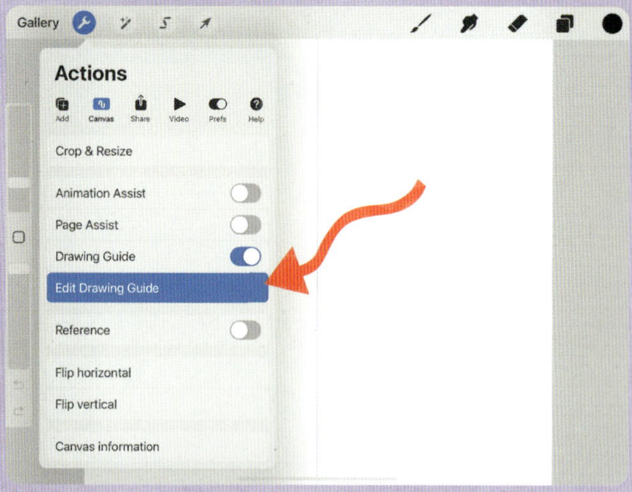

Select Edit Drawing Guide

B

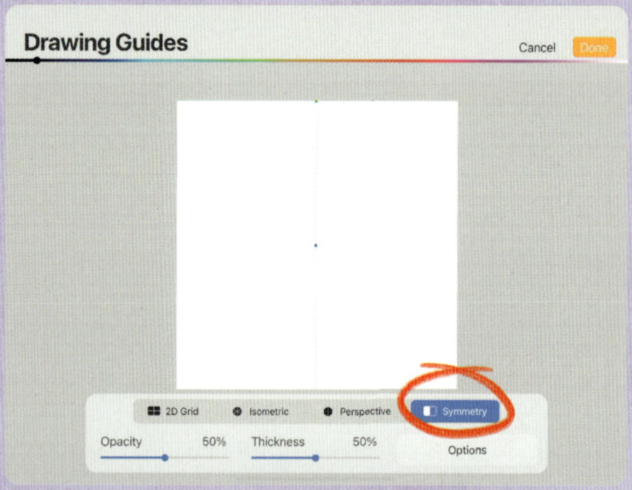

Select Symmetry

C

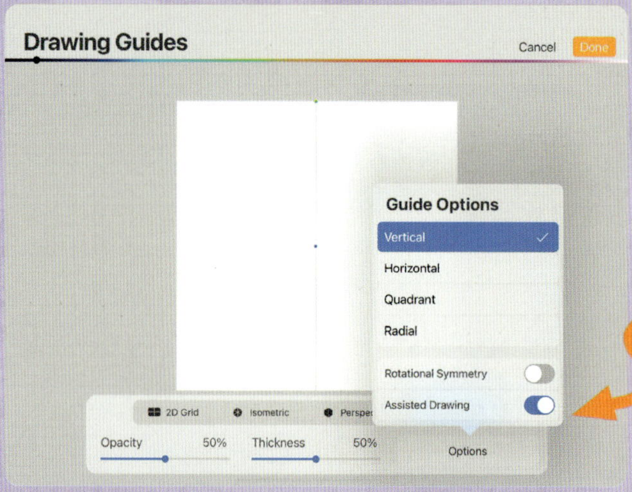

Select Assisted Drawing

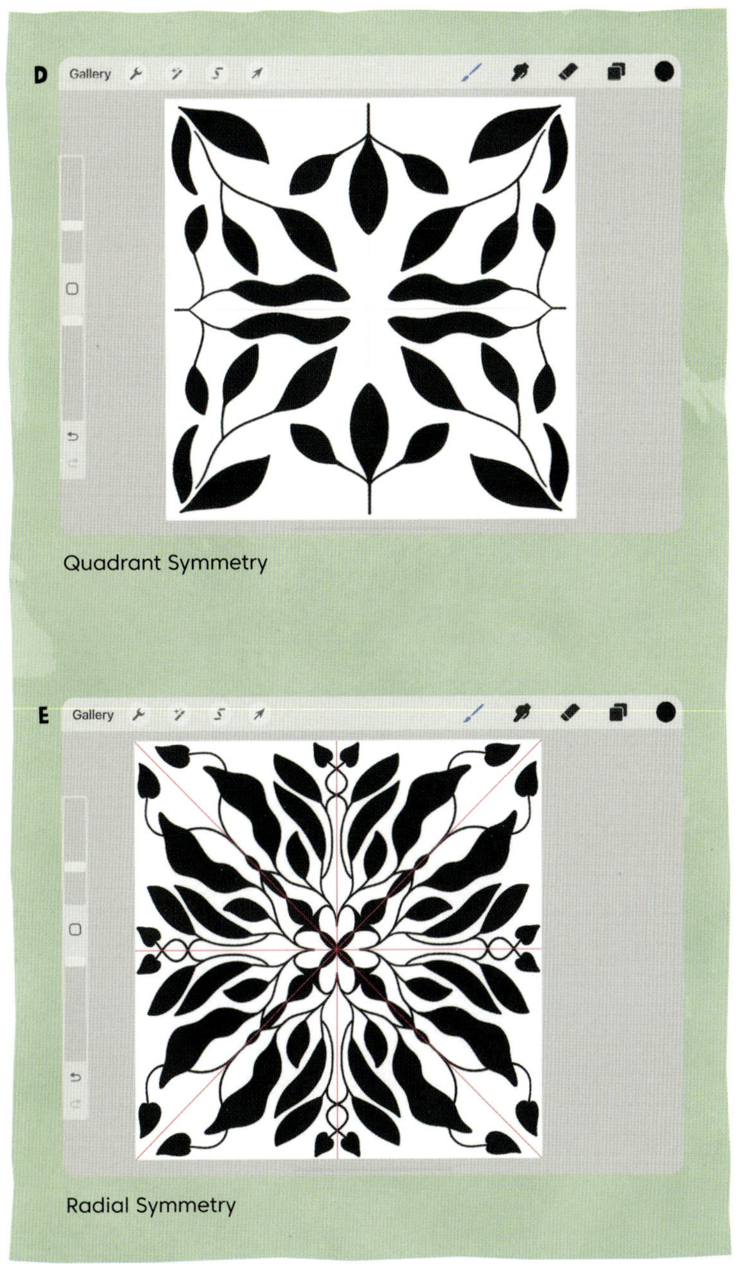
Quadrant Symmetry

Radial Symmetry

HORIZONTAL SYMMETRY

Go back out to the Gallery and create a new 3000px by 3000px canvas. We'll use this to look at the other Symmetry Guide Options. The next one in the menu is Horizontal, which does the same as Vertical but creates symmetry along the horizontal plane.

QUADRANT SYMMETRY

Next, select Quadrant. This will divide the canvas into four sections. Your design will be repeated four times along both the vertical and horizontal planes (**D**).

RADIAL SYMMETRY

Clear the previous canvas or open a new one. The next option is Radial, which divides the canvas into eight sections. When you start to draw here, you'll immediately see a design emerging – you only need a few lines and shapes to create a beautiful pattern (**E**).

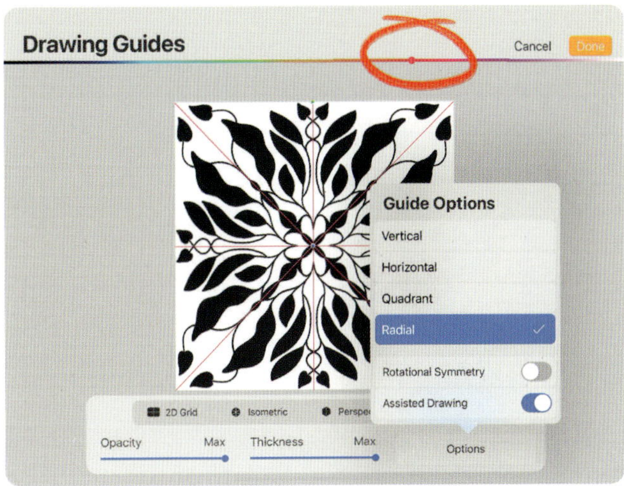

GUIDE COLOUR, OPACITY AND THICKNESS

At the top of the Drawing Guides menu, there is a coloured bar. Slide the dot on this bar to select a colour for your guides. At the bottom, you can also change the opacity and thickness. If you're struggling to see the guides as your design becomes busier, you can change the settings at any time.

4. Rotational Symmetry

Before we begin our tote bag design, let's look at another really cool feature. On a clear canvas, go back into Guide Options and select Radial, then also tap on Rotational Symmetry (**F**). This option will automatically reflect and rotate your drawing.

To understand this better, try drawing with this option on (**G**) and then off (**H**) again. Drawing similar shapes on both canvases will allow you to see more clearly how the rotation changes the design.

CREATING GUIDES

Drawing Guides can be moved around! Tap and drag the blue spot to move the guides around the canvas. The green spot rotates the guides. Tapping on the spot allows you to reset its position back to the default setting.

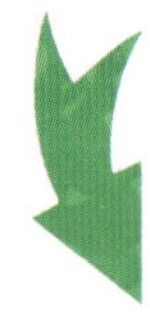

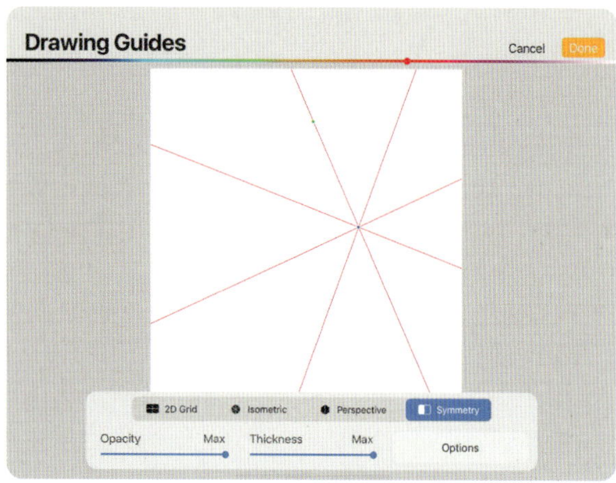

F

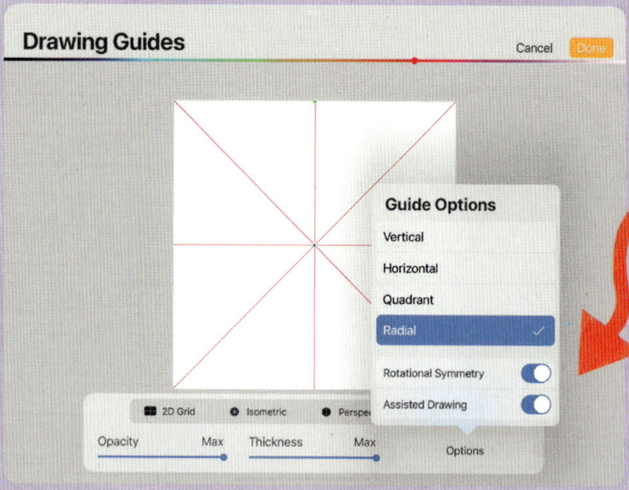

Select Radial Symmetry

G

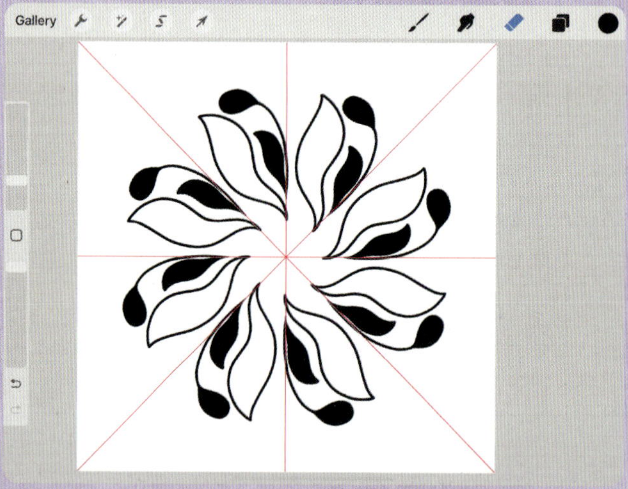

Rotational Symmetry on

H

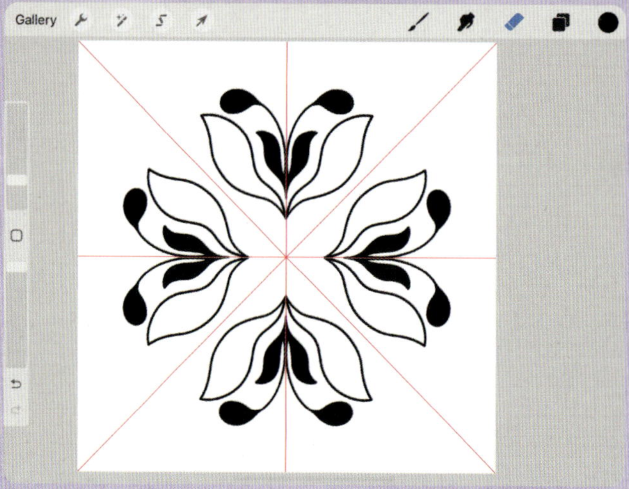

Rotational Symmetry off

I

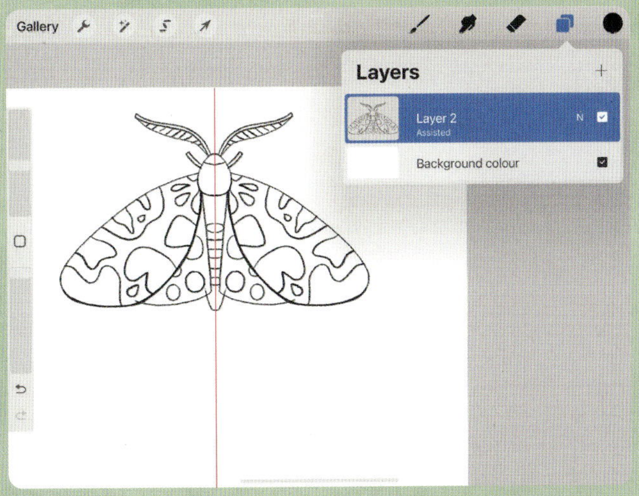

Establishing the sketch

J

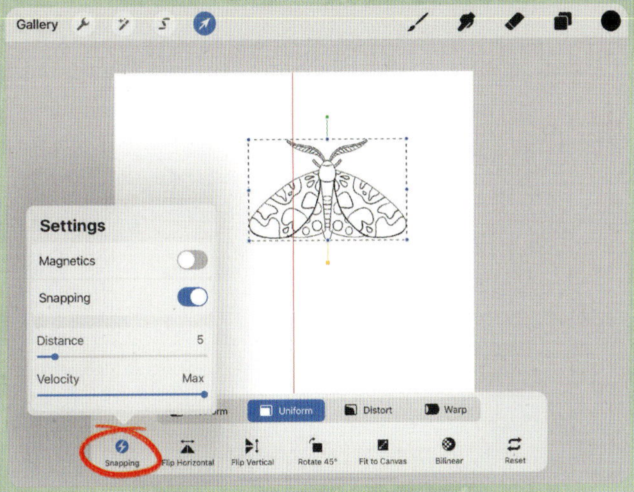

Selecting the Snapping option

K

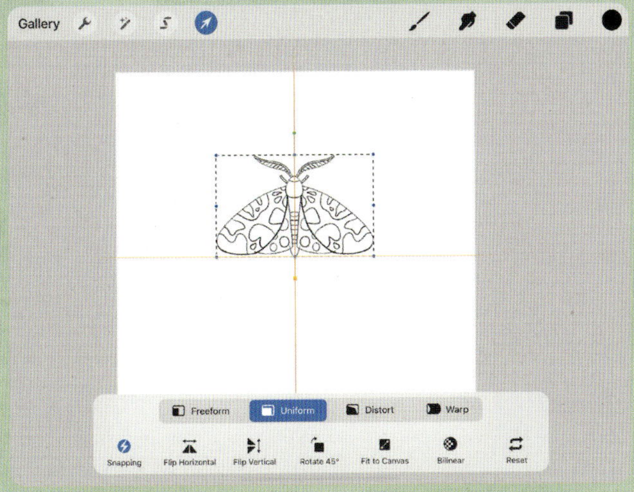

The design perfectly centred again

5. Starting the design

Now we have a good working knowledge of all the Symmetry tools and options, let's start to make a sketch for our tote bag design.

PREPARING TO SKETCH

I'm going to start by setting up my canvas for Vertical Symmetry (with Rotational Symmetry off). I have reference images in front of me to work from, and am starting with a colourful moth, sketching first with a 6B Pencil to get the shapes right (**I**).

SNAPPING TO THE GUIDES

I've sketched the moth quite large, so I'm going to scale it down a little, then move it further down the page. We need to keep the moth centred perfectly; however when scaling down, it moves across the page.

To get it back precisely on the Vertical Symmetry guide, we can turn on Snapping in the transform menu (**J**). This helps to place an object (in this case, the moth) by showing horizontal and vertical coloured guides, and assisting with the alignment automatically (**K**).

SNAPPING DISTANCE

On the Settings panel for Snapping, you'll see an option for Distance. The lower the number, the closer to the line you have to manually move an object before it automatically snaps into place.

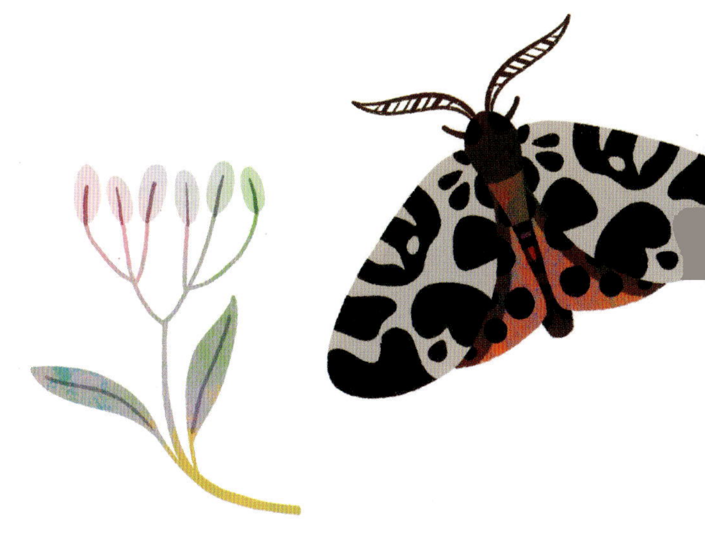

6. Adding to the design

Create a new layer for each additional motif. If you want to use Symmetry on a new layer, remember to turn on Drawing Assist from the Layers menu (**L**).

ADDING THE BUTTERFLY

I want to add another insect to my design, so I'm going to create a new layer. This time I draw a butterfly, again resizing and repositioning my sketch using Snapping. I also want to try turning this part of the design upside down, so I'm going to select Flip Vertical using the options in the Transform menu (**M**).

ILLUSTRATING THE CORNERS

Let's add corner elements, so first create a new layer and set the Symmetry Guide Options to Radial. Sketch your chosen shape – I'm using a sycamore seed pod from my reference material (**N**).

This is a good demonstration of how fast it is to build up your drawings using symmetry. I only had to draw half the seed pod next to one diagonal line, and I now have a complete shape in each of the four corners!

L

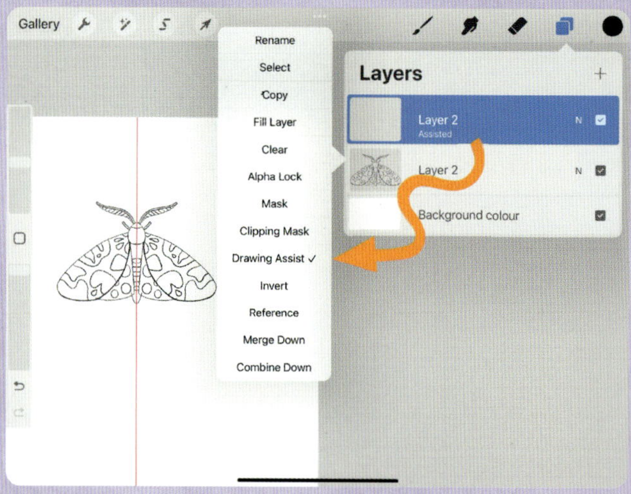

Creating a new layer with Drawing Assist

M

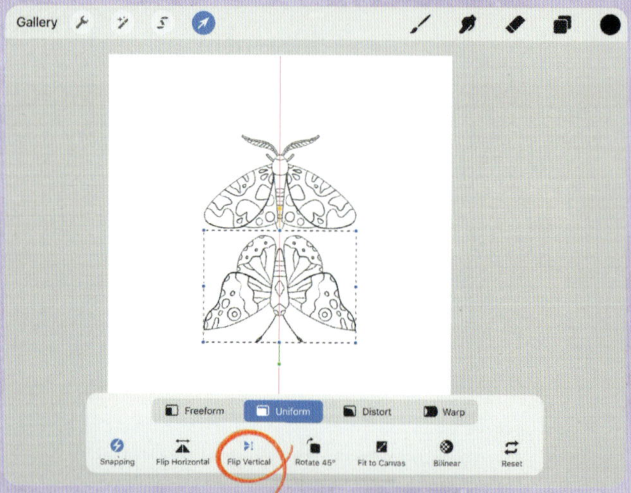

Flipping the butterfly vertically

N

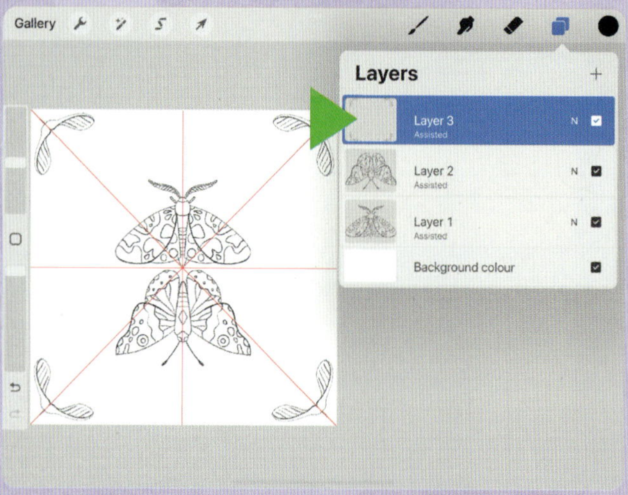

Adding corner motifs using Radial Symmetry

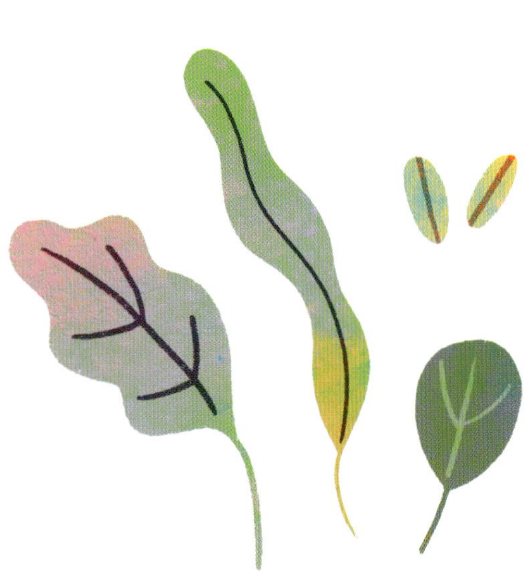

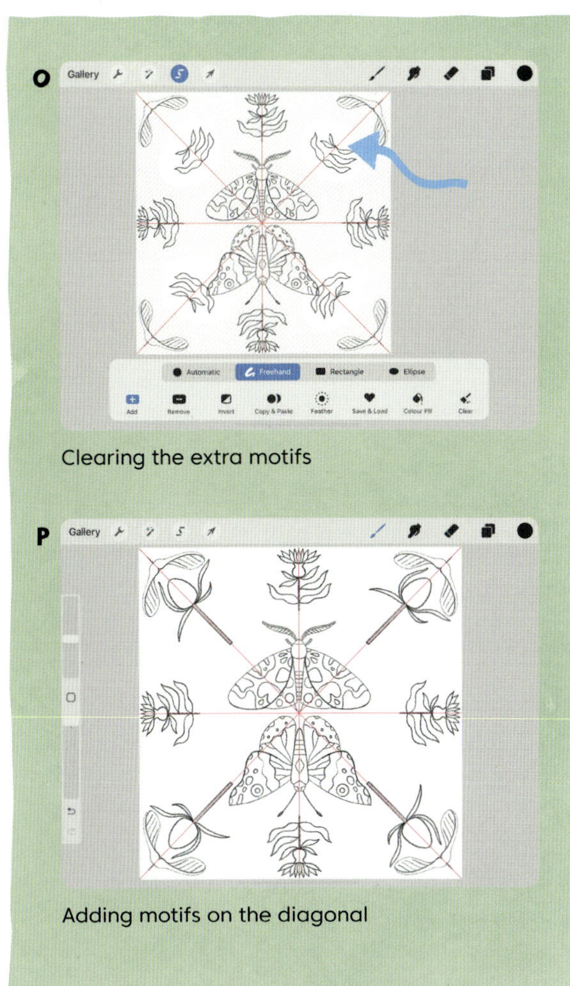

Clearing the extra motifs

Adding motifs on the diagonal

7. Mixing different Symmetry options

Let's create more elements for the design using what we've learned so far. Create another new layer.

ADDING NON-SYMMETRICAL LEAVES

Staying in Radial Symmetry, I'm adding a thistle shaped flower. However, I don't want mirrored symmetry for the leaves, so will enable Rotational Symmetry *after* I've drawn the head. This way the leaves will be repeated but I can have a non-symmetrical layout on the stem.

You'll be left with some extra shapes on the diagonal here but you can just select and clear these, disabling Rotational Symmetry first (**O**).

I'm going to repeat this technique to draw an elegant teasel shape on the diagonal, drawing the head and the stem with Radial Symmetry on, then enable Rotational Symmetry to draw the curved spikes at the base of the head.

Again, we just need to select and clear the extra spikes on the vertical and horizontal. You should now have something that looks like this (**P**).

VERTICAL SYMMETRY

For the rest of the design I'm going to work only in Vertical Symmetry, looking at the spaces I need to fill and choosing shapes and lines that will fit in without overlapping the other elements. By using Vertical Symmetry, I add more variety and an organic feel to the overall composition. Add as few or as many details as you like. We'll refine the design and decide what looks best at the colouring stage.

REFERENCE IMAGES

I'm constantly referring to my reference images. You don't need to copy exactly, but instead study the leaves and flowers, then draw them loosely to fit around your composition. This project will help you to stylize your drawings by creating simple shapes.

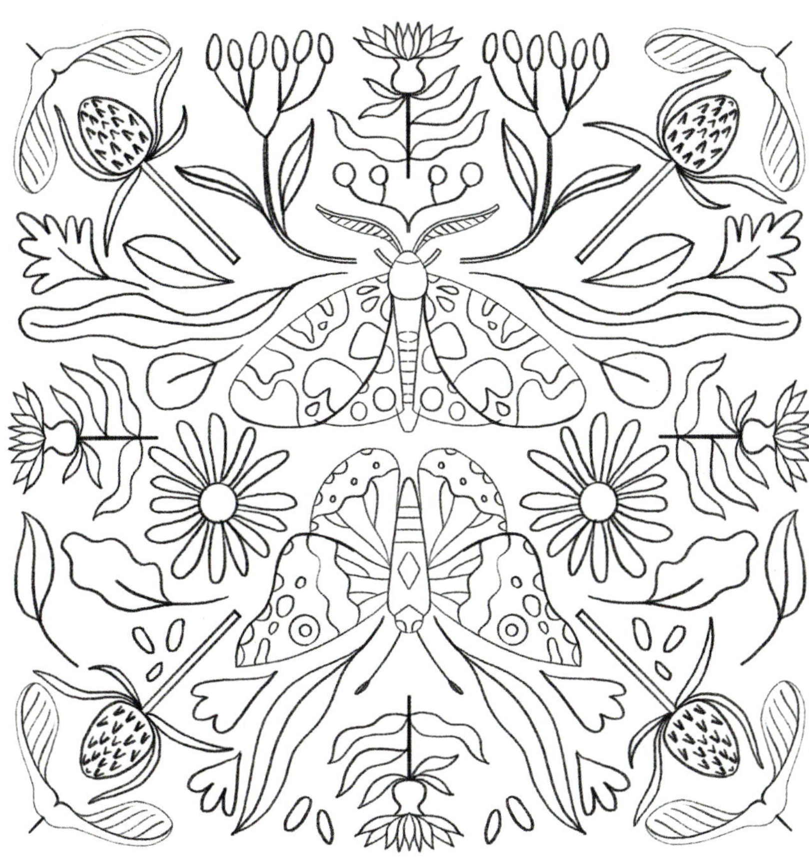

The final drawing

8. Colouring the moth

You can now pinch all the layers together. Set this new layer to Multiply and lower the opacity to around 10%. Create a new layer below and turn on Drawing Assist. We'll now start to colour our first motif – the moth.

CHANGING SYMMETRY

As we work through the illustration, the planes of symmetry will change, just as in the sketch. This may be a little challenging but I designed it that way to help you practise. Making mistakes will help you learn!

CHOOSING A BRUSH AND COLOUR PALETTE

First, select a brush – something with a little texture, but not too rough. Let's start with a brush called Dry Ink from the Inking section, its size set to around 10%. We're going to block in the colours, then add subtle texture on top. I'm going to select a few colours by eye based on my reference photos. A limited palette will suit this project, so we can play with the colours as we go along.

COLOURING THE MOTIF

Start tracing the lines of the sketch and filling in the shapes. You can Colour Drop for speed, but because this brush has some light speckles you need to make sure the shape is closed properly *before* dropping the colour.

DECIDING ON LAYERS

Try to think about which elements should go on each layer. I've started with the body, then the under wings, then the large wings on top (**Q**).

USING CLIPPING MASKS

Let's build up some of the details by adding in Clipping Mask layers above the wings. Don't forget to select Drawing Assist before you being (**R**).

I want to keep these motifs fairly simple and bold, but adding some shadow layers will bring them to life. I've created two separate layers, one above the body and one above the under wings. They are both Clipping Masks and set to Multiply. I'm using the Marker from the Inking section – with a couple of simple lines we have immediately added depth to the drawing (**S**). Turn off the sketch layer, lower the opacity of the drawing guide and zoom out to take a look. Once you're happy with the finished moth, group its layers.

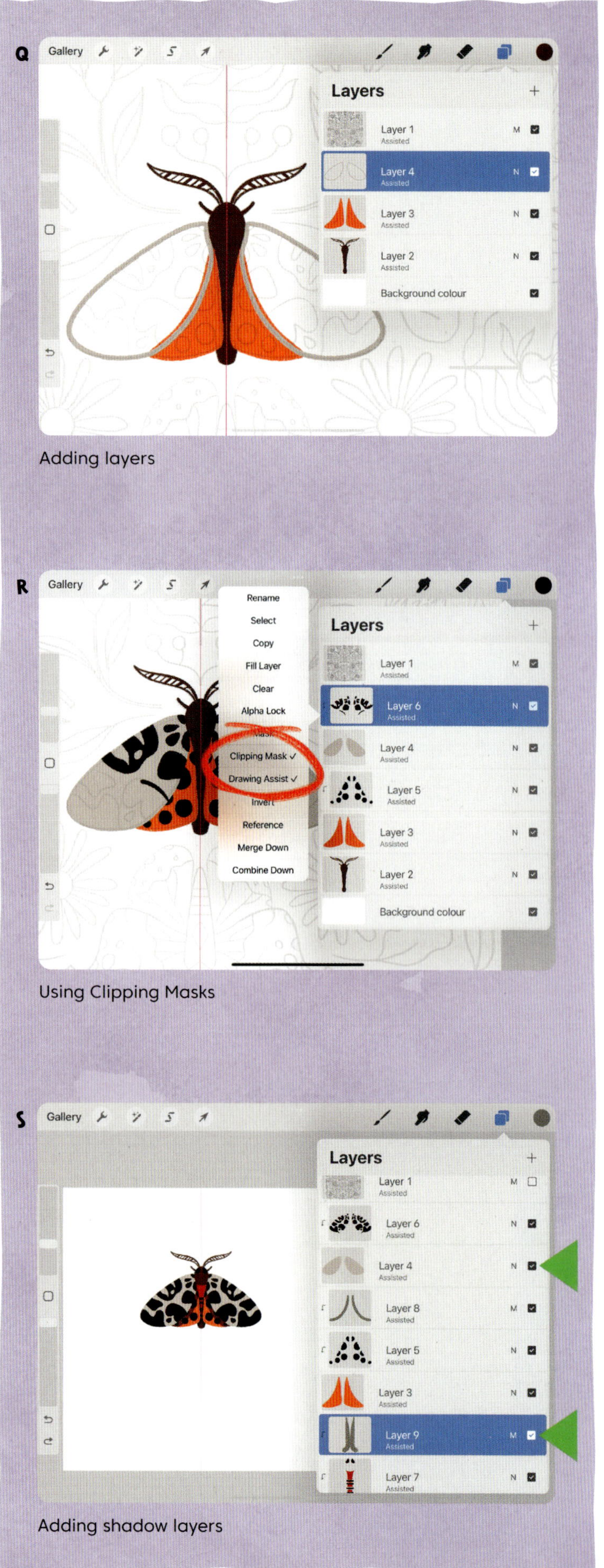

Adding layers

Using Clipping Masks

Adding shadow layers

T

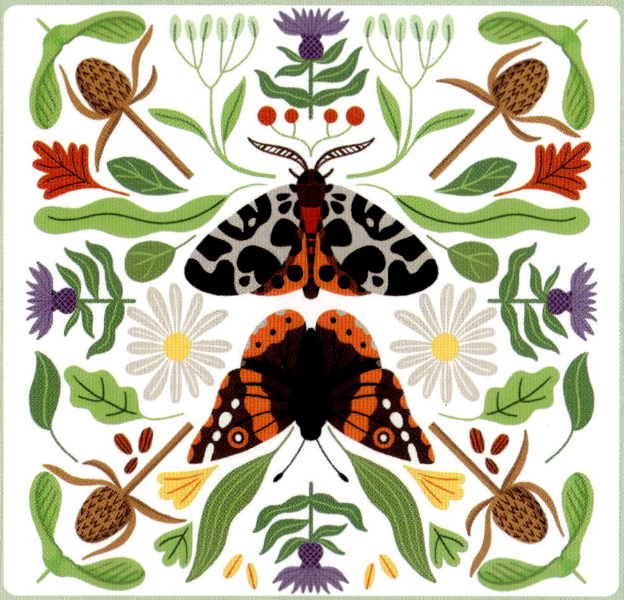

The final design – flat colour only

U

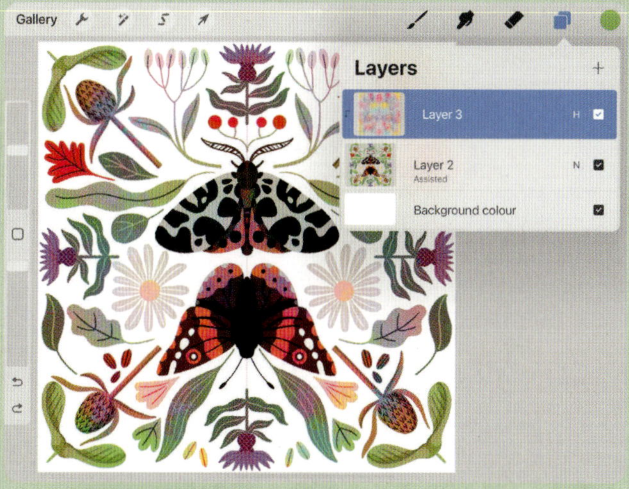

The textured Clipping Mask layer

V

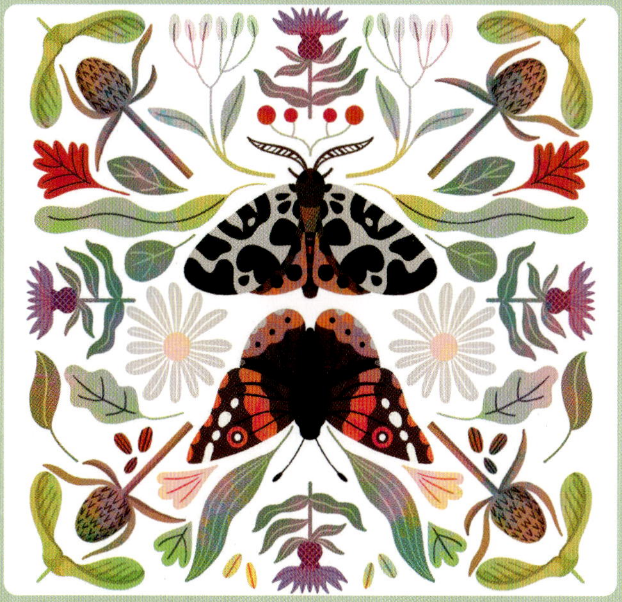

The final design – texture and extra hues added

9. Colouring the rest of the design

Move onto the butterfly, using the workflow you've learned in the previous step. Remember to switch your brush back to Dry Ink before you begin.

Continue with the other motifs, remembering to adjust the Symmetry options as you go. Add line and shadow detail on separate layers. Try to keep the different elements on their own layers so they're easy to edit later on. When you've coloured the whole image, it should look something like this (**T**).

When you're happy with the finished results, designs and colours, you can go to print. But, if you would like to add a bit of magic, read on!

10. Adding texture

Return to the Gallery and duplicate the canvas. We're going to use the copy to merge the layers, to add texture and break up the block colours.

PREPARING THE CANVAS

Delete the sketch layer and pinch everything else together. Create a Clipping Mask layer above and set it to Multiply. I'm leaving Drawing Assist *off* for this layer as I want the texture to be random across the design. I'm setting the blend mode to Hue, which preserves the tones and saturation on the coloured layer, but allows us to change the hue on the top. It's a little hard to explain but try it out – you'll see what starts to happen as you apply different colours.

APPLYING TEXTURE AND HUES

We can now play around with different brushes to add texture on this layer. I'm choosing Heavy Metal from the Industrial section of the Brush Library.

With complementary and contrasting colours, lightly pass the texture brush over parts of the work (**U**). For example, purple looks great on orange. Orange looks good on green (**V**). You can even throw in a colour that's not already in the palette.

HAVE FUN AND EXPERIMENT!

You can always clear or hide this final layer if you're not happy with it. The idea is to bring the design to life with a few subtle changes.

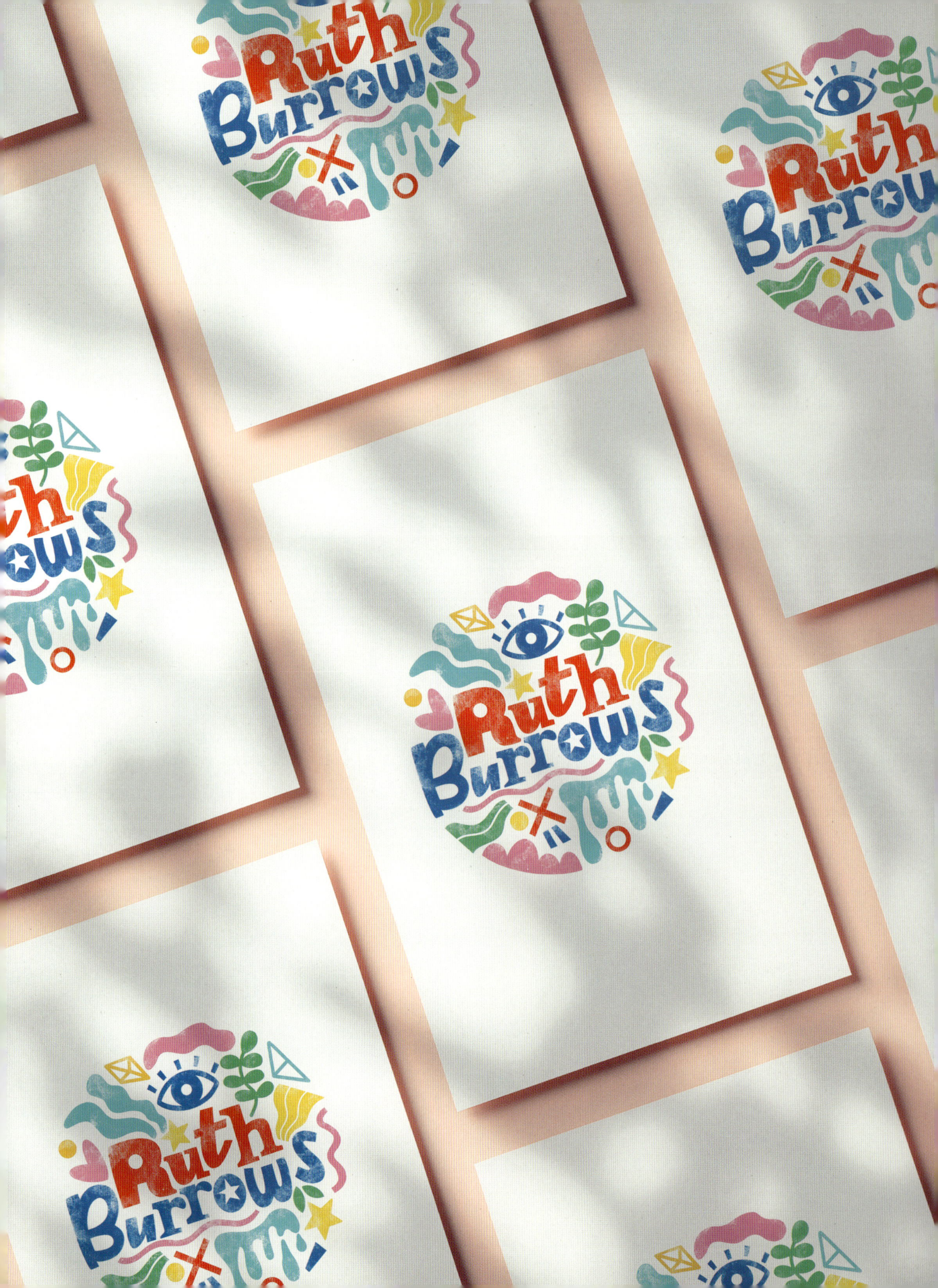
Ruth Burrows

Hand Lettered Logo Design

Use what you have learned so far to create a hand lettered quote. Many people shy away from hand lettering as they presume it requires a lot of practice. The trick is to forget that it's lettering! Letters are just shapes and lines – they can be blocks of colour or they can be textured and made up of brushstrokes or pencil marks. This project will reveal just how simple lettering can be.

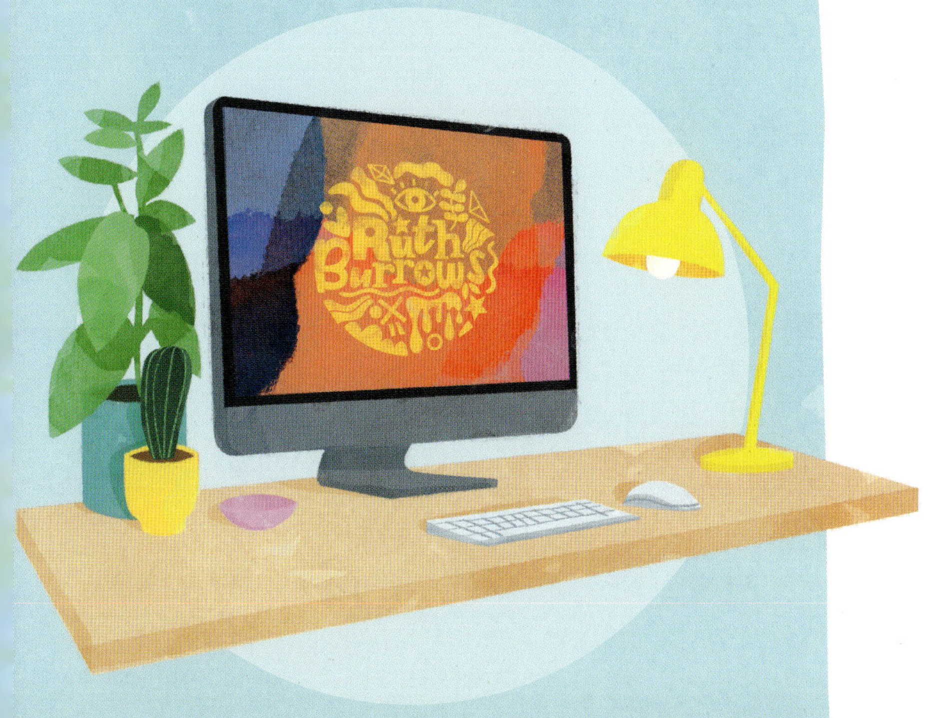

Lettering Made Easy

Hand lettering has become increasingly popular over the past few years. For companies or individuals that want a more personal, handcrafted look for their brand, script-based fonts are the answer. Here, we're going to look at ways to create hand lettering in Procreate.

Hand lettering your name will help you to understand and develop your style. Choose lettering elements that you like and combine them with colours you love. You'll not only create lettering personal to you, but also a style that others will recognize as belonging to you. As long as the type is legible and readable, it can be made up of anything you like! Hand lettering creates a freedom around what you want to say and how you say it.

This makes the project ideal as a starting point for developing your brand as an illustrator. You'll create an artwork that features your name, so it will be ideal to use as a logo or website header. You could have it printed onto labels for your products or make a rubber stamp to use on handmade business cards. The possibilities are endless.

1. Preparing your canvas and mindset!

Let's dive straight into this simple project by opening a new square canvas. 3000px by 3000px at 300 dpi will be a good size, giving scope for scaling the design up or down in size if you decide to print later on.

We'll start by looking at some font shapes and styles, but we don't get want to get tied down by convention. There are no rules here – we'll just add some text and type our name to start with, then look at how some of these letters can be put together. Focus on the process! If you're a font purist or a calligrapher, please look away now...

2. Adding text

Open your new canvas, tap on the wrench icon, tap Add and select Add Text (**A**).

A text box will appear on your canvas and the keyboard will pop up. Type your name in this box and then tap the two letter "Aa" symbol on the top right-hand side of the keyboard (**B**). This will bring up the Font and Style options.

SELECTING A FONT

I'm choosing just a couple of different fonts to look at. Don't worry if these fonts aren't included on your iPad – we can work with what's installed on there for now. I'm not going into any detail about font styles – we're simply looking at the shapes and using them for reference. The first one I have chosen is a serif font called Georgia (**C**).

SERIF OR SANS SERIF?
Serif fonts have extra strokes at the end of their letterforms. Sans serif are clean with no extra details.

Serif

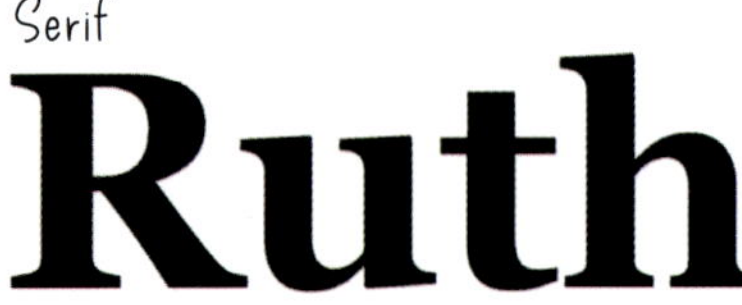

Sans serif

Ruth

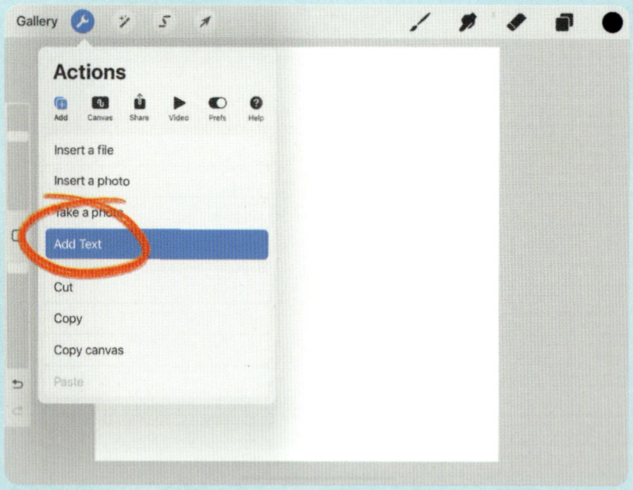

Accessing the keyboard

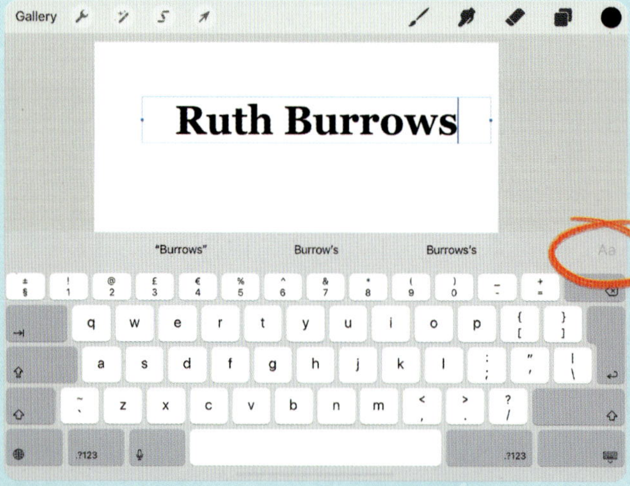

Preparing to choose a font

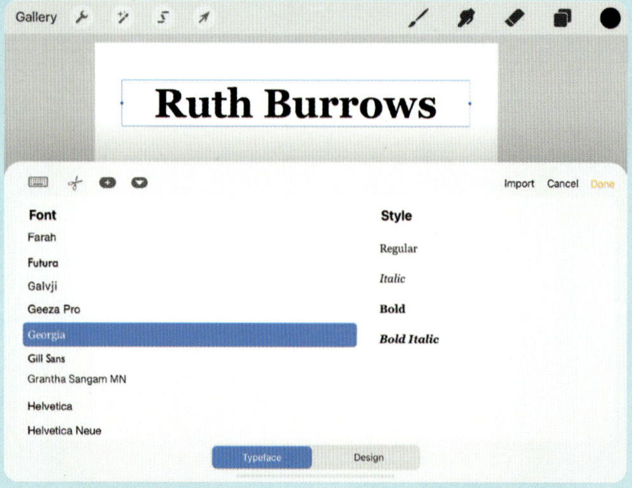

Font and Style options

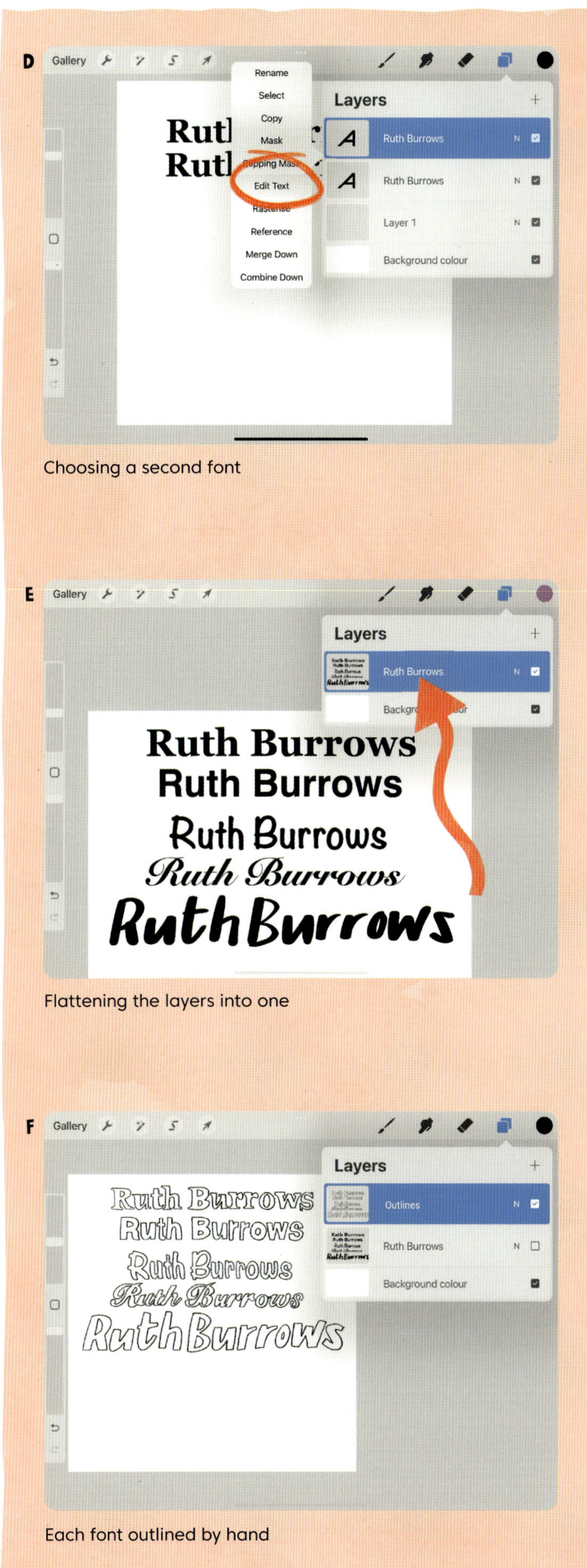

Choosing a second font

Flattening the layers into one

Each font outlined by hand

3. Changing fonts and writing by hand

Duplicate the text layer, and move your name down a line as I have. Tap on the duplicate and select Edit Text (**D**). Follow the previous step again to choose a different font style. Repeat this process until you have your name written in four different fonts, each on their own layer.

WRITING YOUR NAME BY HAND

In addition, choose the Brush Pen from the Calligraphy section of the Brush Library, and write your name in your own handwriting (you can use the default Layer 1). It can be joined up, lower case or upper case. It doesn't matter. Just write your name as you like to see it written!

PREPARING THE TEMPLATE

When you have your five layers, group them together and flatten into one (**E**). We're just using this for reference, so the type no longer needs to be editable.

Lower the opacity of this new layer to around 10% and add a new layer above. We're going to trace these examples to give us some outline shapes to work with.

TRACING THE LETTERS

Let's use the 6B Pencil – we want to create a sketched outline rather than actually writing our name.

The tracing does not need to be exact. In fact, wonky lines will only add character so enjoy the process. Embrace the mistakes! Forget about the words and concentrate on the shapes and lines.

When you're done, hide the template layer and have a look at what you've created (**F**).

It should definitely have a handcrafted look about it, and I'm sure there will be parts that you don't like. But there will also be parts you love, so the next step is to chop up this layer and choose your favourite shapes and styles to make up your very own unique, hand lettered name artwork!

4. Choosing and rearranging the letters

Scale down your traced lettering to make room on the canvas to create the new name. Don't make the lettering too small, as we're still working with this layer.

1. Look carefully at your lettering and choose your favourite shape for the first letter of your name.
2. Use the Freehand Selection tool to trace round the letter, then hit Copy & Paste to save it on a new layer.
3. Drag the letter down to the clear space on the bottom half of the canvas and scale up if necessary.

Repeat this process for the other letters. Choose shapes that fit well together. You can chop and change as much as you want, but keep each letter on a separate layer – they'll be easier to move and edit later (**G**).

Keep copying, pasting and rearranging until you have a quirky but well balanced piece to work with. I also add in some decorative motifs for fun. You may choose to put your surname on a different line. We're creating something now that looks more like a logo, so the layout can be any shape you like.

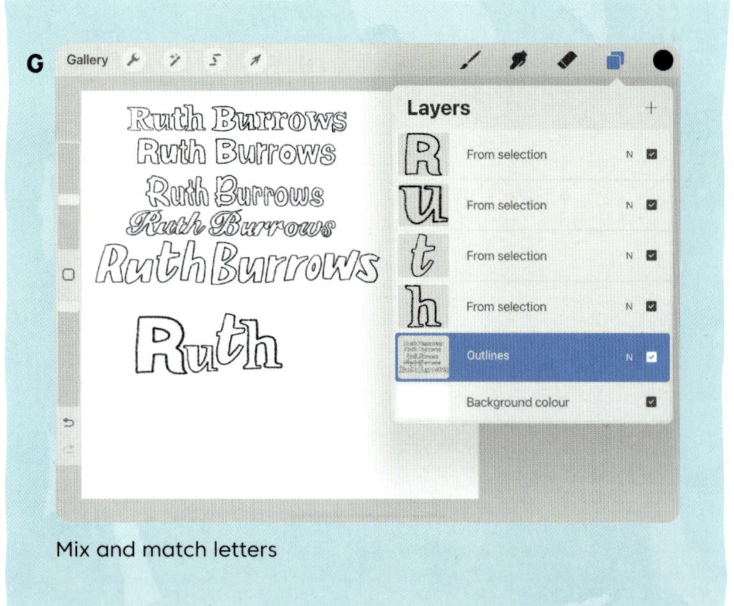

Mix and match letters

5. Refining the letters

When happy with your layout, go back to the Gallery and duplicate the canvas. Keep a record of everything we've done so far – we want to delete and merge some layers now, so let's do that on the duplicate.

Delete the traced layer and pinch all the others together so we have one layer to use as a reference. You may need to scale it up a bit and centre it on the canvas. Lower the opacity (**H**) so we can use it as a guide for drawing and colouring our final letters.

OUTLINING AND BLOCKING

I haven't quite decided which colours or textures I would like to include in the final lettering, so I'm going to create a clean outline of each element and fill it with a block of black for now. Black will contrast well with the white background.

REFINING

Now it's time to start refining the shapes. I'm using the Monoline brush from the Calligraphy section of the Brush Library (**I**).

ERASING WITH CURRENT BRUSH

If you have any wobbly lines or imperfections, tap and hold on the eraser, and a message will pop up that says "Erase with current brush". That means it will erase with the same brush you have selected for drawing. In this case, the Monoline.

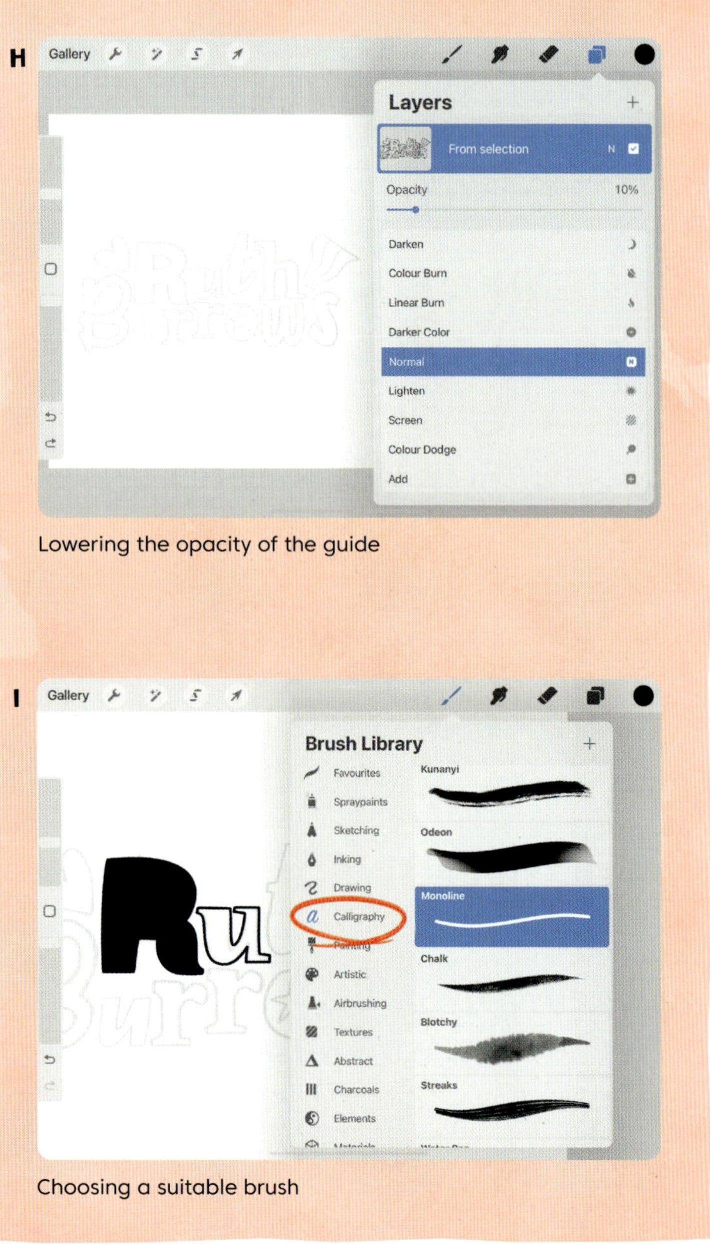

Lowering the opacity of the guide

Choosing a suitable brush

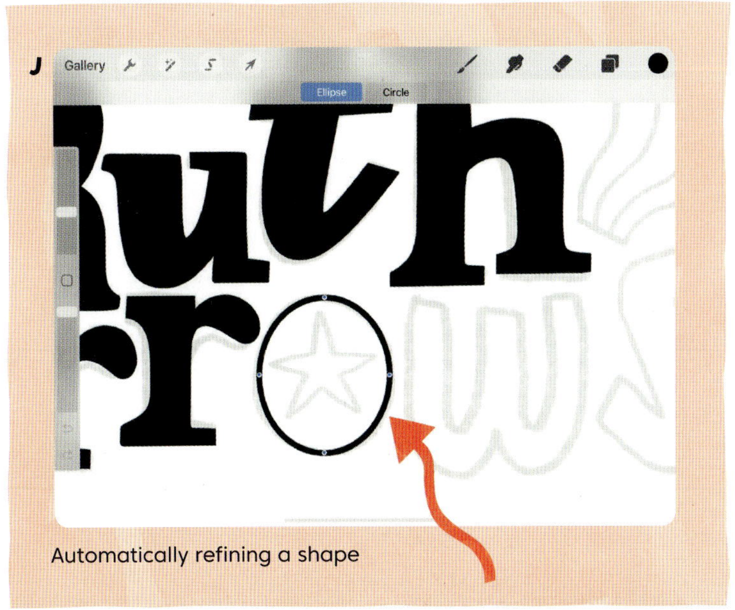

Automatically refining a shape

CONTINUE REFINING

Carry on outlining and blocking until your hand lettered logo is complete. Don't forget that you can draw a line, then hold the pencil down to straighten or edit the shape – useful if you want to tidy things up (**J**).

However, you may want to keep all the imperfections for a real handcrafted style – that's fine too! I usually end up somewhere in between, with clean shapes and textured fills.

When you have finished outlining and filling, you should have something like this:

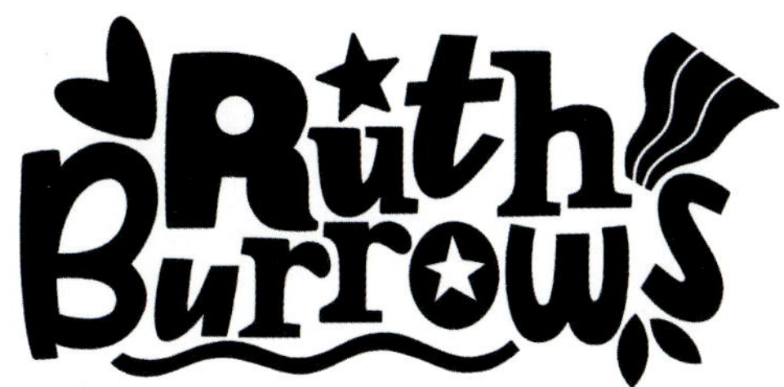

The design works pretty well in black and white, and could easily be used as a logo for business cards or social media, so save this as an editable file. I've exported mine as a PSD file (Photoshop) and AirDropped it to my laptop.

6. Planning for colour and composition

I'd like to try some colour and texture, and maybe fill out the space with more motifs to make a circular picture suitable for use on a social media profile.

SPLITTING UP THE MOTIFS

So let's duplicate the canvas once again. Delete the sketch layer on the duplicate, and instead of merging the other layers together, you might want to split them up again to make colouring easier. You can use the Freehand Selection tool to do this, then swipe down with three fingers and tap Cut & Paste. I've split up my motifs onto layers as shown (**K**).

ADDING A CIRCULAR GUIDE

As a guide for the space I have to fill, I'm adding a circle filled with a light colour on a layer underneath everything else (**L**). Do this by tapping on the Selections tool and selecting Ellipse. Drag down from the top left-hand corner to create a circle on your canvas. Whilst your pencil is still on the screen, tap and hold with one finger to constrain the ellipse into a perfect circle. You can then drop colour into the selection on the new layer.

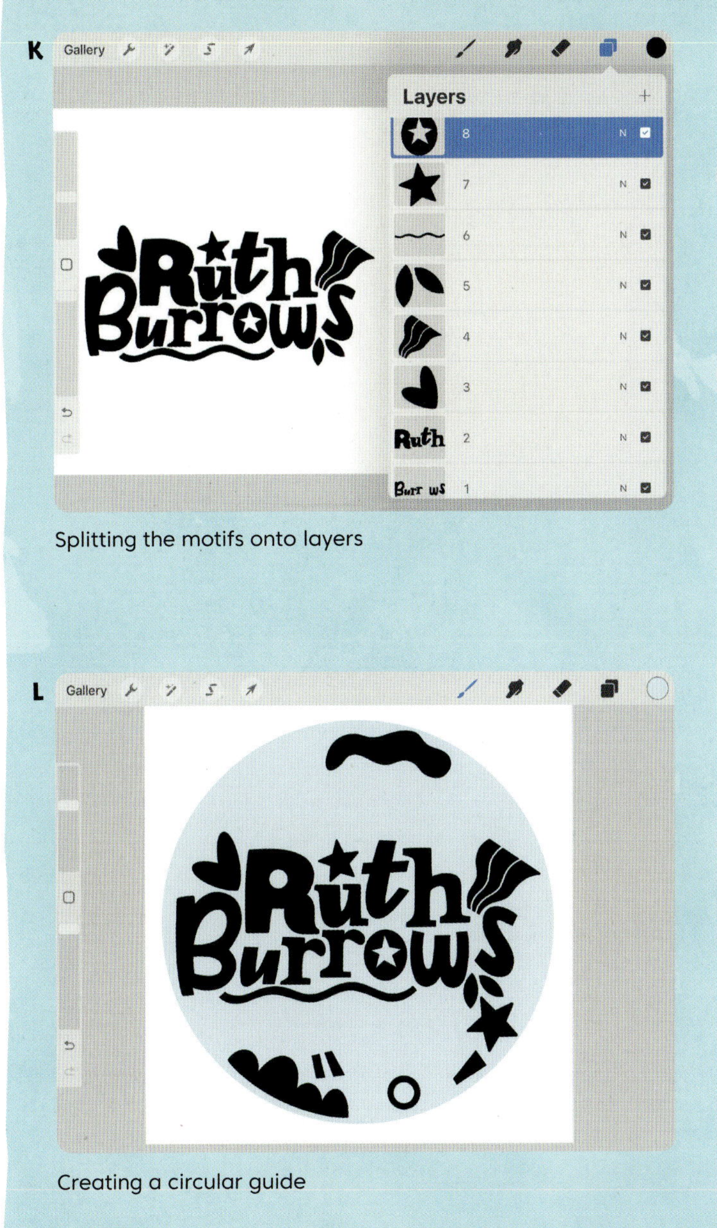

Splitting the motifs onto layers

Creating a circular guide

FILLING THE FRAME

Resize and position your lettering to fill as much of the circle as possible. I'm now going to freehand some shapes and motifs to fill the area. You can of course sketch them in first if you feel the need, but sometimes it's nice just to work freely and see what pops up!

I ended up with a lot of motifs and doodles on my piece. I'm really happy with the way it turned out, so I'm going to go ahead and add some colour.

The final logo in black and white.

7. Adding colour and texture

I want a vintage stamp effect, which is very easy to achieve with a brush called Rusted Decay (from the Industrial section of the Brush Library). Each motif in my design is on a separate layer, so colouring will be a little time consuming but super easy.

1. First, I'll hide my circle layer. It was just a guide, and you can bring it back as a background colour later on if you want so don't delete it.
2. Select a shape by holding two fingers on its layer. Once selected, hide that layer and create a new layer above.
3. Brush lightly within the selection, using the Rusted Decay brush.
4. Work through the design, selecting layers and colouring as you go (**M**).

I'm using a palette of my favourite bright colours, and by varying the pressure on the pencil can create the desired vintage stamped effect with just a few strokes.

MANAGING YOUR LAYERS

Keep an eye on your layer count by tapping on the wrench icon, selecting Canvas, Canvas Information and then tapping on Layers. If it looks like you're running out of layers, duplicate the canvas and merge some existing layers on the duplicate. Try to keep your original black shapes in case you want to edit or re-colour.

Finding ways to work with the layer limit in Procreate is challenging, but you'll soon find your own workflow and devise ways to deal with it (**N**).

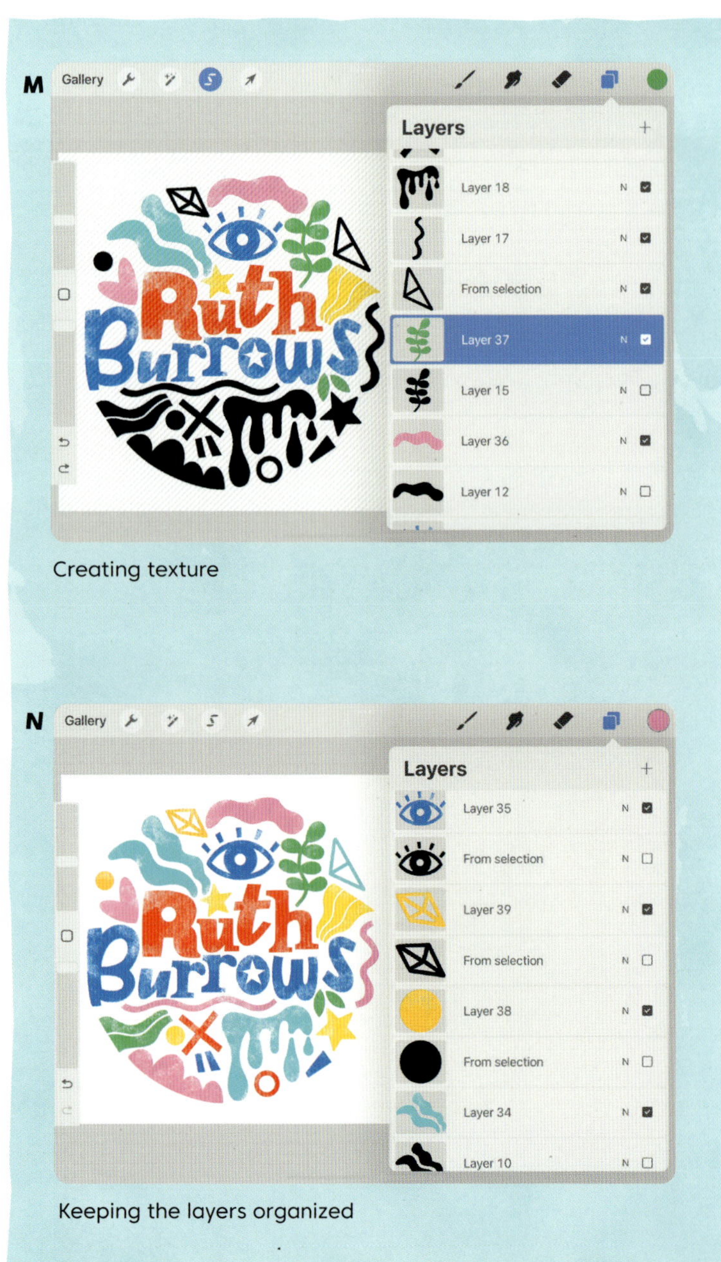

Creating texture

Keeping the layers organized

The final logo in full colour.

STAY ON BRAND!
Remember, you have saved all the motifs separately so you can use them as part of your branding. Think about using them for stickers, as a repeat pattern on wrapping paper or as a background for your website.

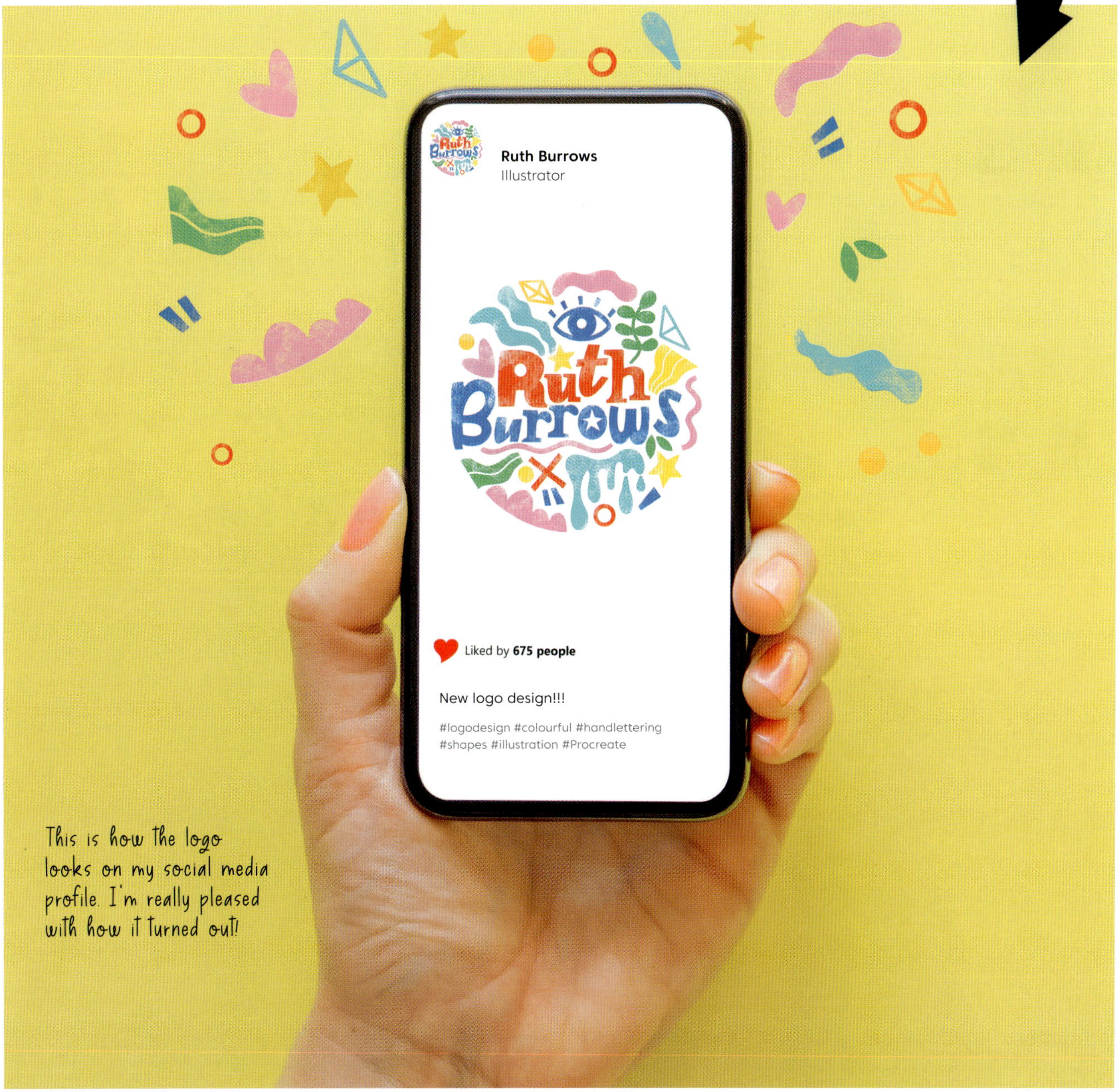

Ruth Burrows
Illustrator

Liked by **675 people**

New logo design!!!

#logodesign #colourful #handlettering
#shapes #illustration #Procreate

This is how the logo looks on my social media profile. I'm really pleased with how it turned out!

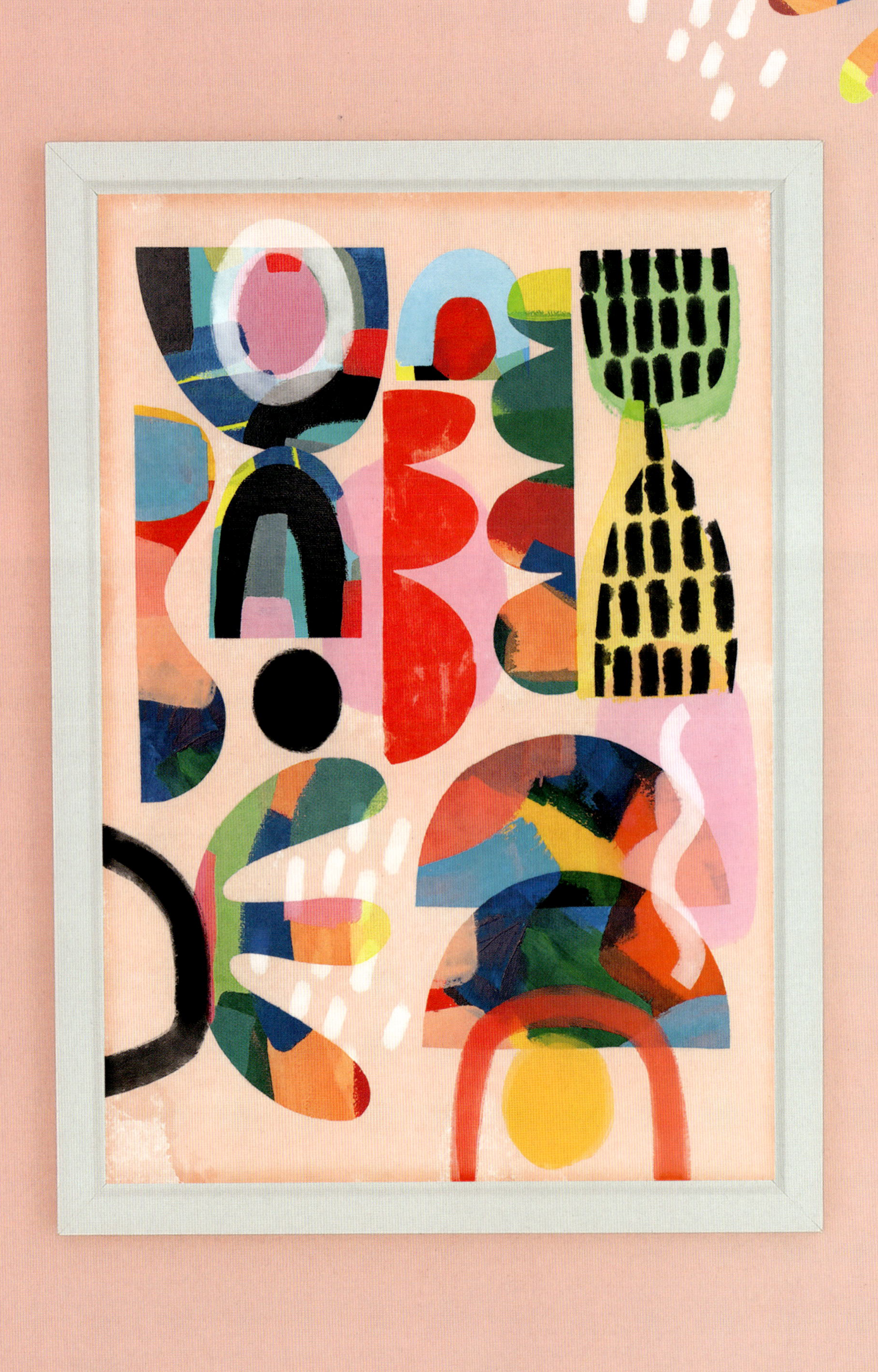

Abstract Collage Wall Art

Making a digital collage is a fun and relaxing thing to do, and it also has the potential to make great wall art. You can incorporate colours that match or complement your interiors, then scale up the finished design to print, frame and display. This kind of art can be uploaded to online stores that print on demand – you'll create your own unique gallery wall in no time!

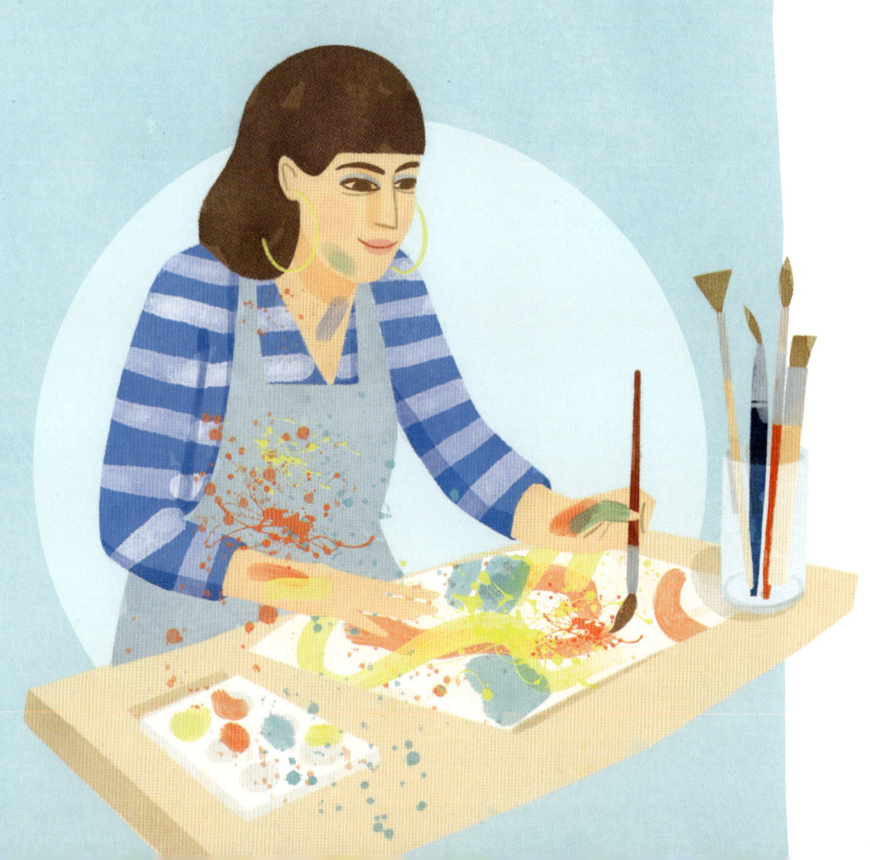

Art for Art's Sake

As an Illustrator drawing pictures every day, many people ask me what I do in my spare time, to which I answer, "I make more art"! I'm always itching to try new things, I have several unfinished canvases (both digital and traditional) and half filled sketchbooks. Creativity is an endless journey and all the stops on the way are a new idea or project.

I also love to mix traditional media with my digital art. It's a great way to utilize those unfinished pieces or spark creativity for a completely new project. Sometimes it's nice to just play around with abstract shapes. Add some mark making to the mix and just see where it takes you – no plan required!

1. Getting arty

To start this project, let's take a break from the screen and get more hands on. Set up a workspace where you can lay out some of your favourite art supplies. If you have time, spend the whole morning playing with paint and ink. Work outside if the weather is nice or put on some music. Work without thinking – it doesn't matter what you create. We're going to cut up your traditionally made creation and use it to make a bold digital statement piece!

2. Inserting artwork and cutting out shapes

For this project, let's create a canvas at 300 dpi, 4000px wide by 5000px high. This size will give us quite a few layers. Also, if we want to scale up the design later, it will allow us to do so without losing resolution.

IMPORTING TRADITIONAL ART INTO PROCREATE

The easiest way to import your art is to photograph it with your iPad or phone. Once your art is in the photo gallery of your device, it will be easy to insert onto the canvas.

I'm selecting two images, each with bold, colourful strokes that will work well together (**A**). After adding them to the canvas, I use the Rectangle Selection tool to select the main parts of the artwork I need by tapping on Copy & Paste. This way, you can discard the edges of the paper or shadows from the original photo (**B**). You can discard the unedited photo layers.

EDITING THE IMAGES

If you would like to brighten the photos, you can edit them in the Adjustments menu using the Hue, Saturation and Brightness sliders. Curves is also a good option for adjusting colour and contrast, so spend a few minutes playing with these settings. If you would like to apply the changes, undo them or reset the image, just tap anywhere on the screen to bring up the options. You can also cancel from here and exit Adjustments entirely.

SELECTING PARTS OF THE IMAGE

Once I have my chosen images on the canvas, I begin choosing sections of them using Freehand Selection, then tap Copy & Paste to copy them to a new layer (**C**). Because I may want to copy other parts of the original image later, I preserve it on its own layer.

Keep the Freehand shapes simple – the complexity is in the brushstrokes and colours. I typically use half-circles and organic leaf shapes. Think Matisse paper cuts! I'm also refining the shapes as I go along using the 6B Pencil as an eraser. This is not strictly necessary but softens up the edges.

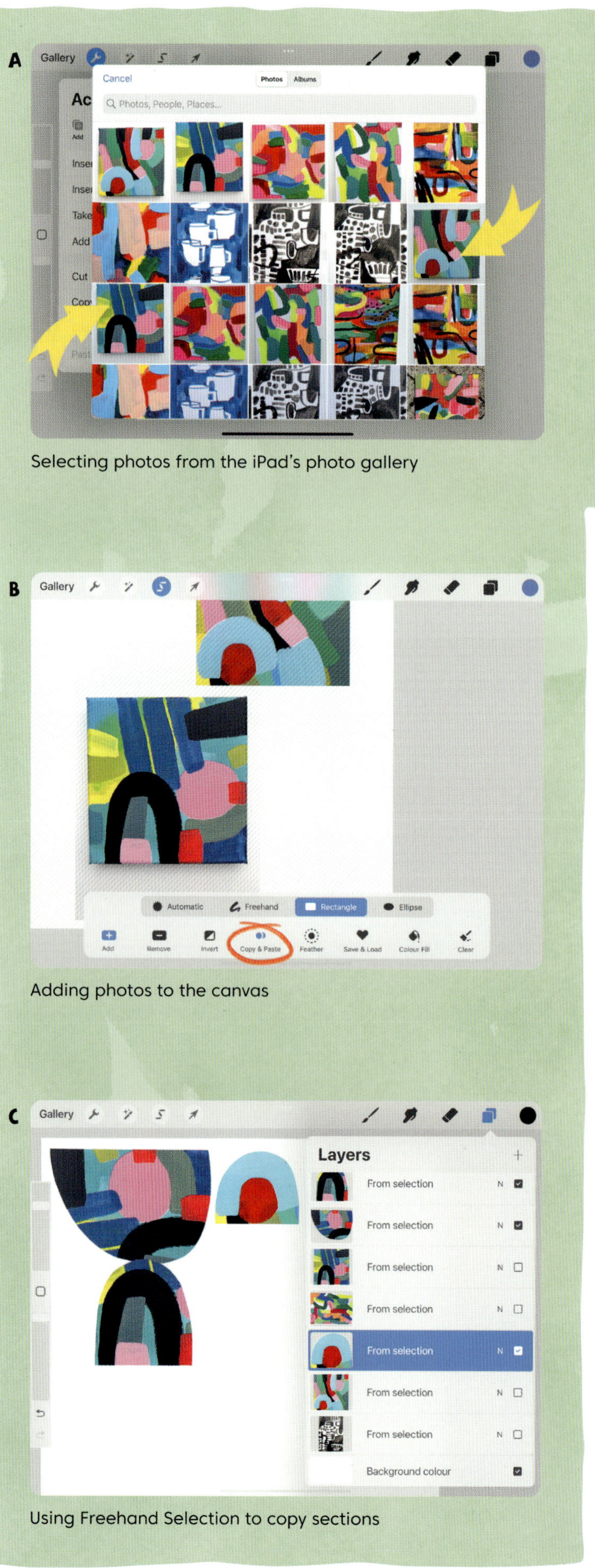

Selecting photos from the iPad's photo gallery

Adding photos to the canvas

Using Freehand Selection to copy sections

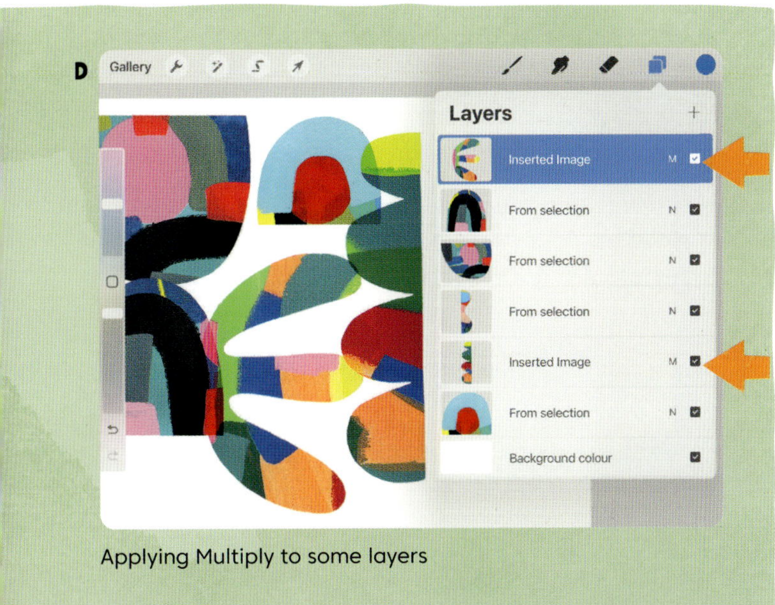

Applying Multiply to some layers

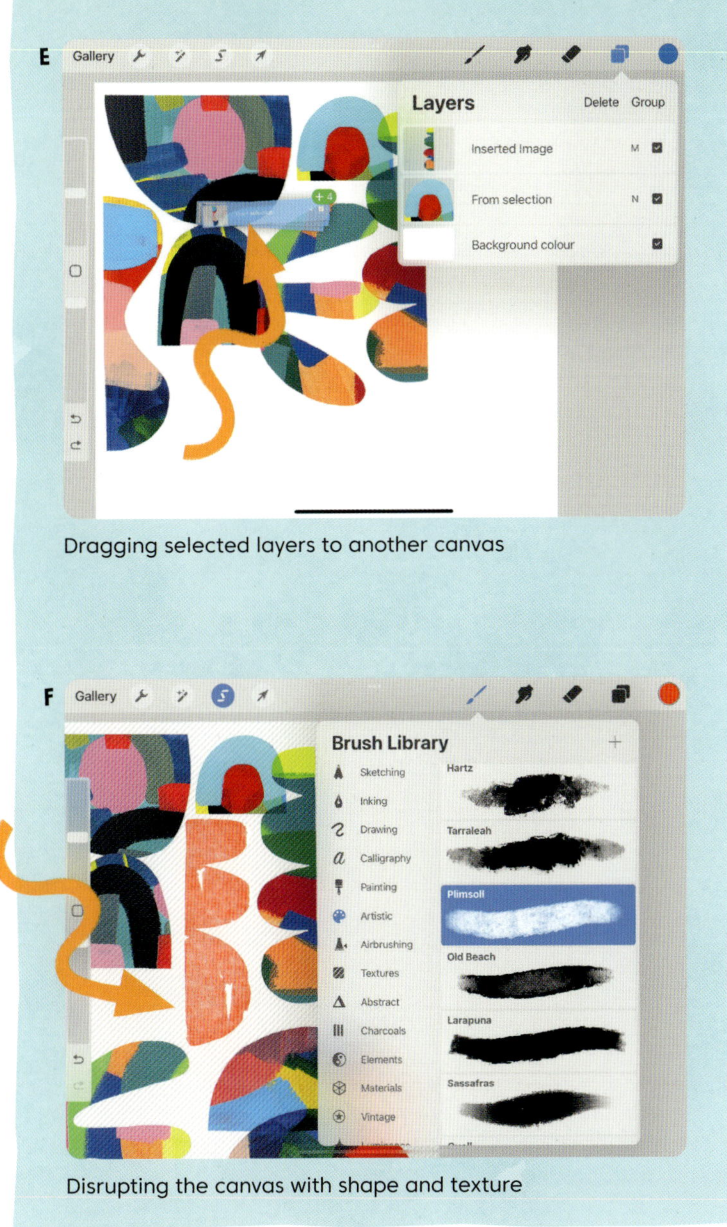

Dragging selected layers to another canvas

Disrupting the canvas with shape and texture

ORGANIZING THE LAYERS

I'm enjoying the negative space, but want to overlap some shapes. The order of the layers will also make a difference, so to re-order them, simply hold and drag each one up or down in the Layers panel (**D**).

I have about eight shapes on my canvas now. I've moved them around, leaving some space for digital input. I've also changed the blend mode to Multiply on a couple of the layers to allow colours and shapes on the layers below to blend and contrast with the shapes above.

3. Adding a digital shape with texture

For the next stage, let's create shapes using digital tools. Go to the Gallery and duplicate your canvas. Open the duplicate and delete the layers we're not using. If we need any other original artwork, we can go back and drag it from the first version. Keep the cut-out shapes you want to use and discard everything else.

DRAGGING BETWEEN CANVASES

You can drag shapes from one canvas to another by swiping right on the layers you would like to drag across. When they are all highlighted in blue (**E**), use one finger to drag them away from the layers palette. At the same time, with your other hand, tap Gallery in the top left. You will go back out to the Gallery – keep your finger down on the selected items, then tap the canvas where you would like to drop the shapes. This requires a bit of dexterity, but with practice, you'll soon get the hang of it!

ADDING THE FIRST DIGITAL SHAPE

Look at the way the shapes are filling the space. It's good to have a combination of overlapping shapes, pieces that stand alone and negative space – the shape of the gaps in between. We want to create a block of colour that looks as if it was painted traditionally!

Create a new layer and use the Freehand Selection tool to draw a shape. We'll fill this with a textured brush – Plimsoll from the Artistic section of the Brush Library (**F**). This has a lovely canvas-type texture built in, which matches nicely with my traditional artwork. You can increase the size to about 40% and keep full opacity. I like to redraw similar shapes, but feel free to experiment!

When I pass the brush over the selected shape the first time, I leave some gaps – I fill these in the second time, and may pass over a third time to add more texture. Try to recreate a natural looking fill. Once again, I'll take off the hard edges with my eraser.

ADDING COLOUR

You can pick the colour from one of your cut-out shapes so that it blends in nicely, or choose a completely contrasting colour. Remember, this is playtime! Explore and enjoy the process.

4. Digital mark making

For the second shape, I keep the same Plimsoll brush but this time fill the selection with short marks. As soon as I have created this shape, I decide it will look good set to Multiply with a bright colour underneath.

ADDING COLOUR TO THE SHAPE

I pick a green directly from one of the cut-outs and make a new layer. I pick a nice watery brush called Old Beach from the Artistic section – I'm going in freehand for this as I want it to look like a quick watercolour wash (**G**).

5. Creating the background

At this point, I start thinking about the background colour. I usually have about two-thirds of the work done before I consider this, when there will be enough colour on the page at this point to make a decision. In addition, having a background will make it easier to commit to the final pieces.

CHOOSING THE COLOUR

I want to create the background with a textured brush, but will choose the colour first. I like the light peach colour in the original painting, so have selected it with the eyedropper tool. I'm adding a new layer underneath everything else and filling it with this colour.

I pick colours intuitively. As mentioned previously, I'm a bit of a rule breaker when it comes to colour, and spend time trying out different backgrounds until it just seems to look right. Try different colours until you're happy with it. You'll know when you've hit on the right one!

With that new background layer selected, I'm using the Hue, Saturation and Brightness sliders (in the Adjustments menu) to refine the colour. It's worth trying different hues before making the final decision. When you're happy, either tap the screen and select Apply, or tap again on the Adjustments icon to save the changes (**H**).

ADDING TEXTURE

Delete the test background layer and recreate using a textured brush. The Quoll brush, in the Artistic folder, is great for this. Set the size to 50%, keep the opacity at 100% to create the effect of a large paint roller (**I**). Pass it roughly over the canvas two or three times to create the effect you want.

G

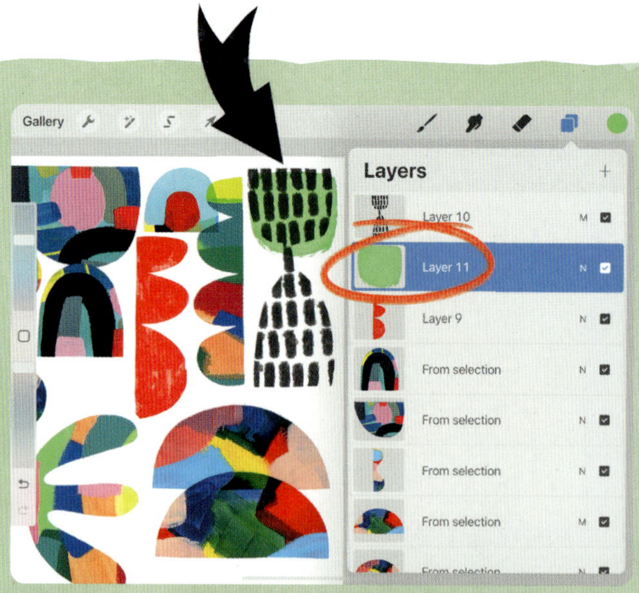

Adding additional colour and marks

H

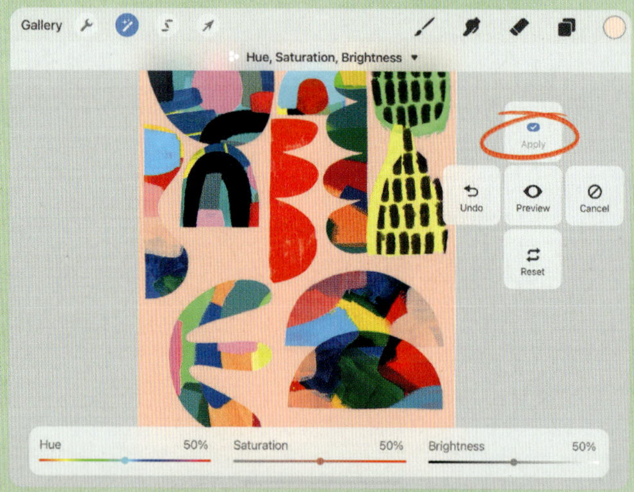

Choosing the background colour

I

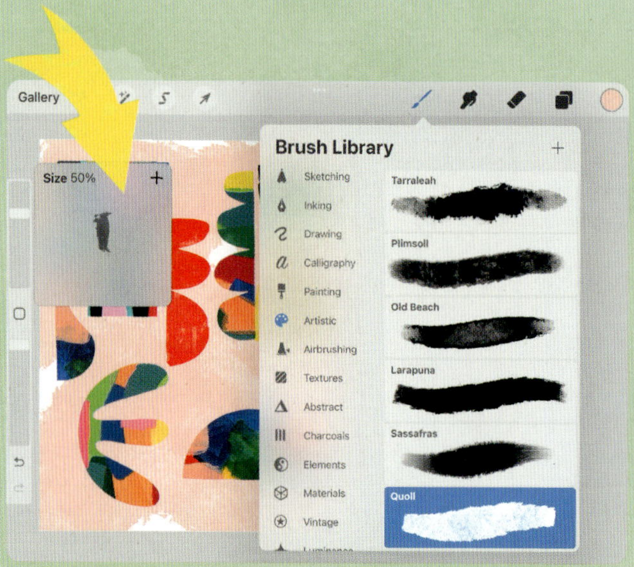

Adding texture to the background

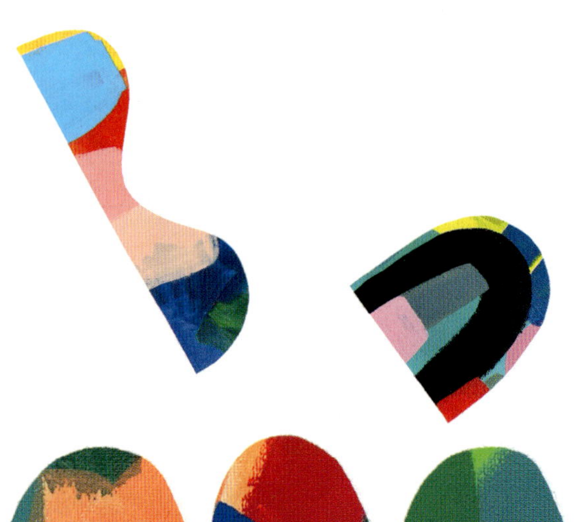

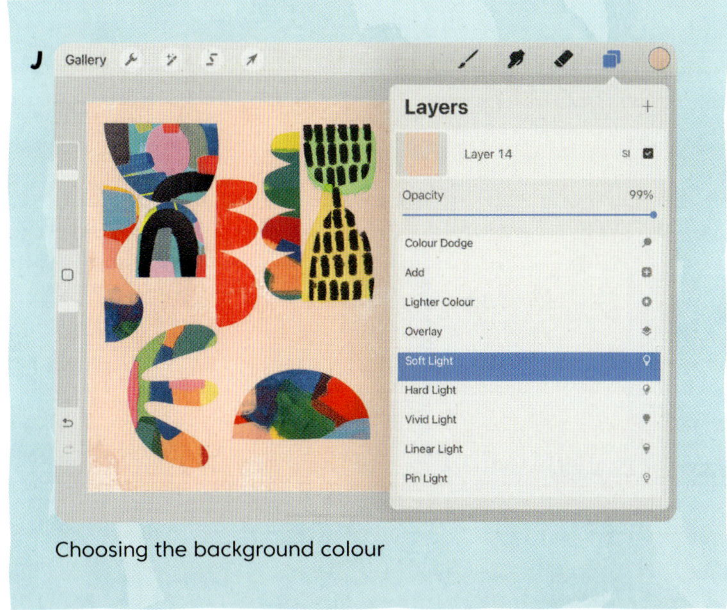

Choosing the background colour

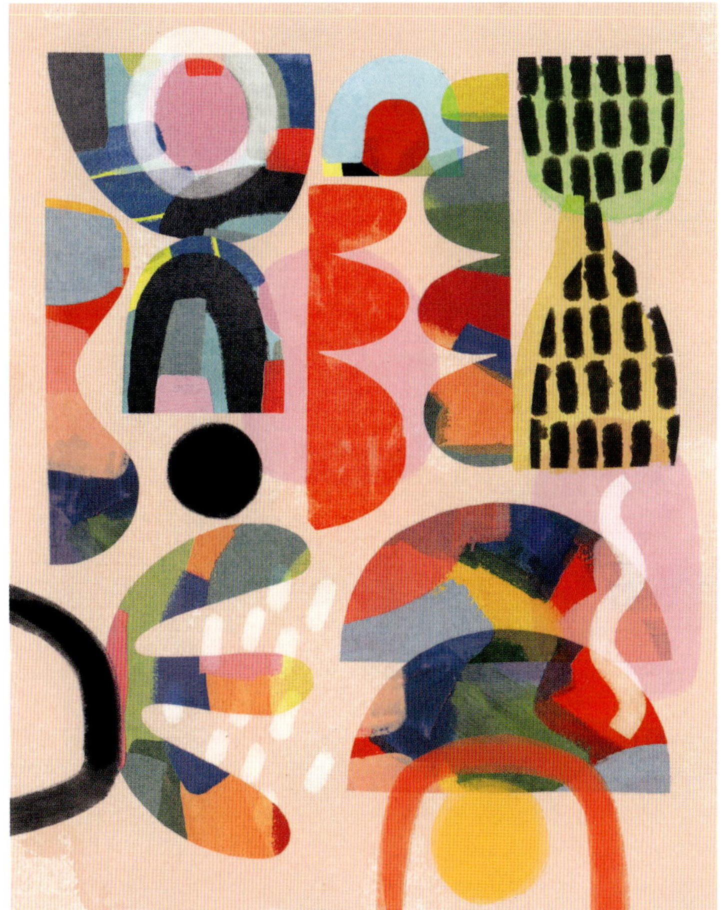

The final artwork, blending traditional and digital art.

MAKING A BLENDING LAYER

I make another textured layer with the same colour, which I'll use to knock back the colours in the design. To do this, I drag it above all the other layers and set the blend mode to Soft Light (**J**). This is a subtle effect, but it blends the traditional and digital together. If you want to include this layer, you can also play with the opacity to see how if affects the overall look.

DISCOVER MORE

Use this project to take a deep dive into Layer blend modes. The secret to natural looking work has much to do with how layers interact and blend with each other.

6. Disrupting the canvas

To finish my artwork, I'm adding marks, lines and shapes with the Gouache Brush from the Painting section of the Brush Library. This brush is a nice natural looking brush that will give you a painterly stroke. You could also try other brushes to find one that matches your traditional artwork. I just want to add some elements to "disrupt" the shapes I already have on the canvas. I'm disturbing anything that looks too uniform or repetitive by introducing new shapes, marks or lines. I'm also working on new layers, dragging them up or down to see how they work together.

This is a therapeutic process – just relax and have fun with it. Walk away and come back to it later or start another piece to pair up with this one. This is *you* time!

SO YOU'VE FINISHED – NOW WHAT?

Knowing whether a piece of work like this is finished or not can be difficult. You may have a gut feeling, or you can take the opinion of friends or family. Either way, I'm sure at some point you would like to see it framed and hanging on the wall in a stylish interior! It may also look good as a throw cushion or a set of coasters that other people would love to have in their home.

Read on for advice about how to get your design printed and made into a product for sale.

7. From iPad to product

You may have started to think about monetizing your art. If others regularly admire your work, how can you take this a step further to display and sell it? If you're new to this idea, a great way to start is to upload some designs to a Print on Demand (POD) website such as Society6 or Redbubble to see your artwork transformed into accessories and homestyle. See Monetizing Your Art for advice and ideas.

TESTING, TESTING!

Adding your work to online product mock-ups is a great way to test it. It's like taking a step back to see your artwork in the context it may eventually be displayed. You might see parts of the composition you're not happy with or colours that need tweaking.

You can then go back into Procreate and make any adjustments you like.

EXPORTING AND UPLOADING YOUR ART

To allow you to preview your work as part of a product, create an account at one of the popular POD websites. Follow the next few steps to get started.

1. Tap on the wrench icon to open Actions, tap Share, and choose JPEG. I'm going to Save to Files and choose Documents on my iCloud Drive (**K**).
2. Rename your file so it's easy to find when you want to upload to the site (**L**).
3. Once saved, open your browser and sign into your account on the POD site. Navigate to the area where you add your work and upload the JPEG from your files.

There may be a few more steps, depending on the site you choose, but eventually you should see a page much like the one here (**M**).

You can now scroll through to see your work mocked up onto many different products. Tap Edit and you'll see options for resizing, repositioning and so on. If you're ready, you can follow their instructions to list the item in your shop. Otherwise, just save as a draft!

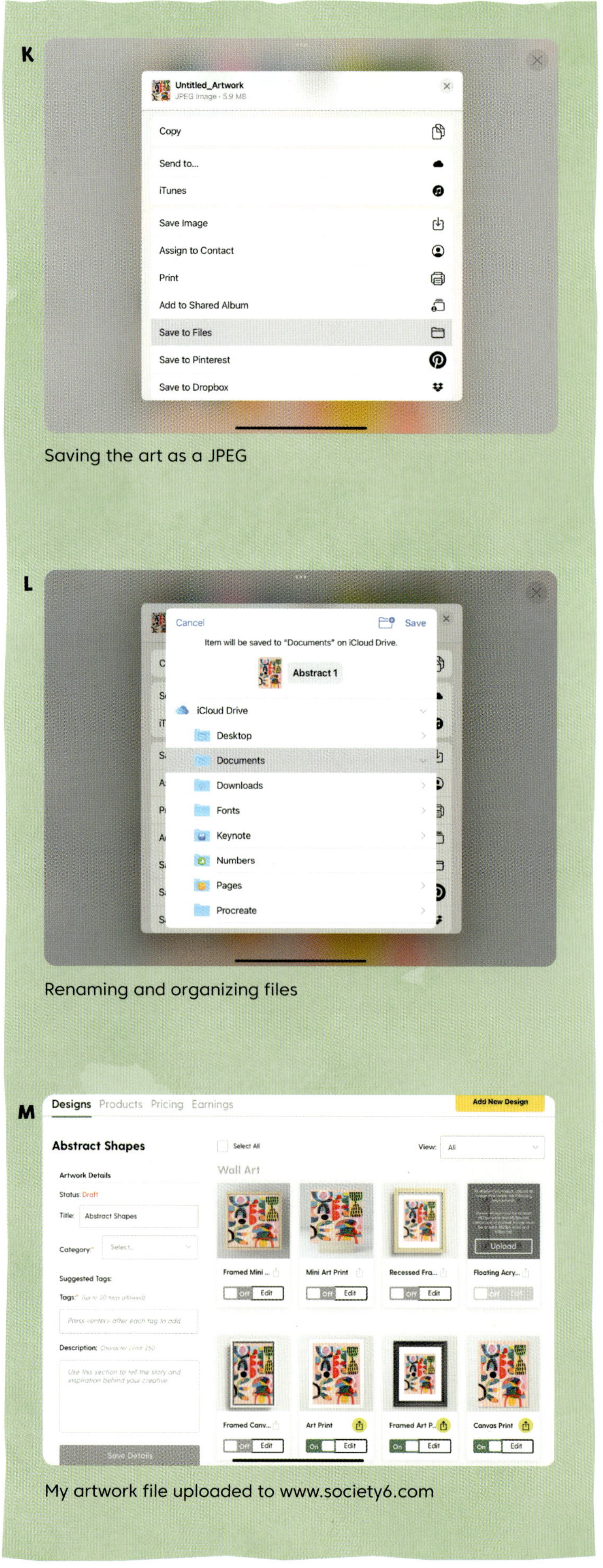

Saving the art as a JPEG

Renaming and organizing files

My artwork file uploaded to www.society6.com

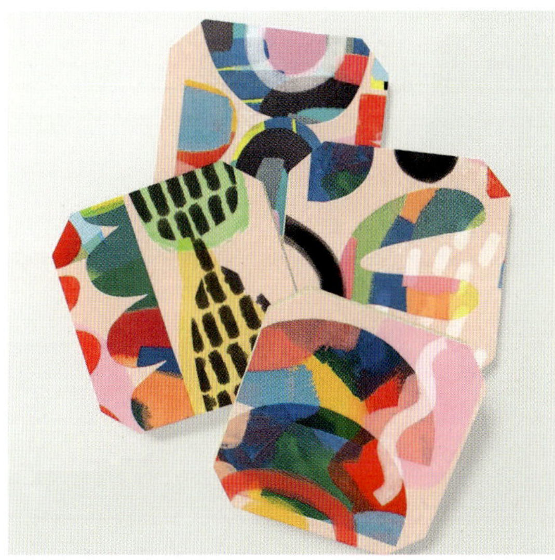
Preview created using www.society6.com

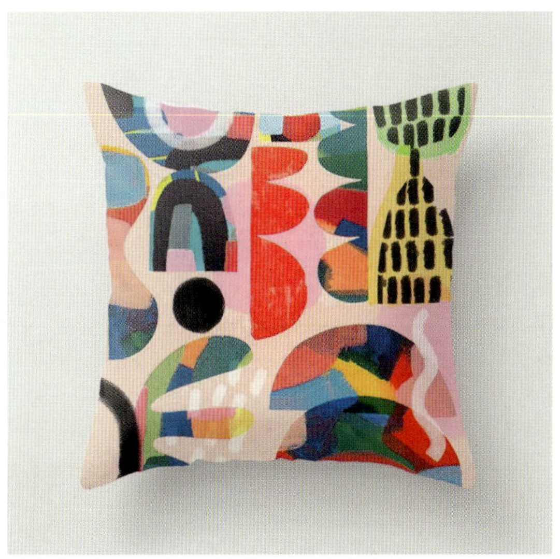
Preview created using www.society6.com

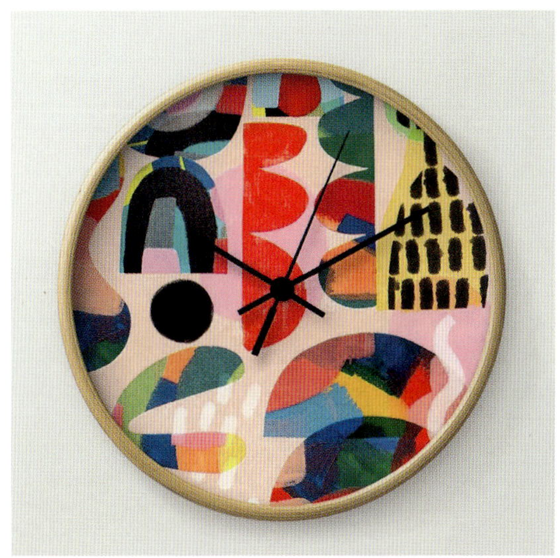
Preview created using www.society6.com

PRINTING & SELLING ON DEMAND

- POD sites are a fantastic, free resource for viewing your work on a range of products. Do a bit of research and sign up for an account.
- Sites such as those mentioned are big, and sell the work of thousands of artists. Being a successful seller on these sites takes a lot of time and work. It's a good idea to build up a collection of artworks before publishing for the public to see. If I go to someone's online shop or POD shop front, I would be disappointed and less likely to buy if they only had one or two designs.
- Add links to your shop front from your social media platforms and own website to drive your followers there. I found www.wix.com helpful very helpful when setting up my own website.
- Here, I've shown my artwork uploaded to POD site www.society6.com, and previewed it as a set of drinks coasters, a cushion, and even a clock face.

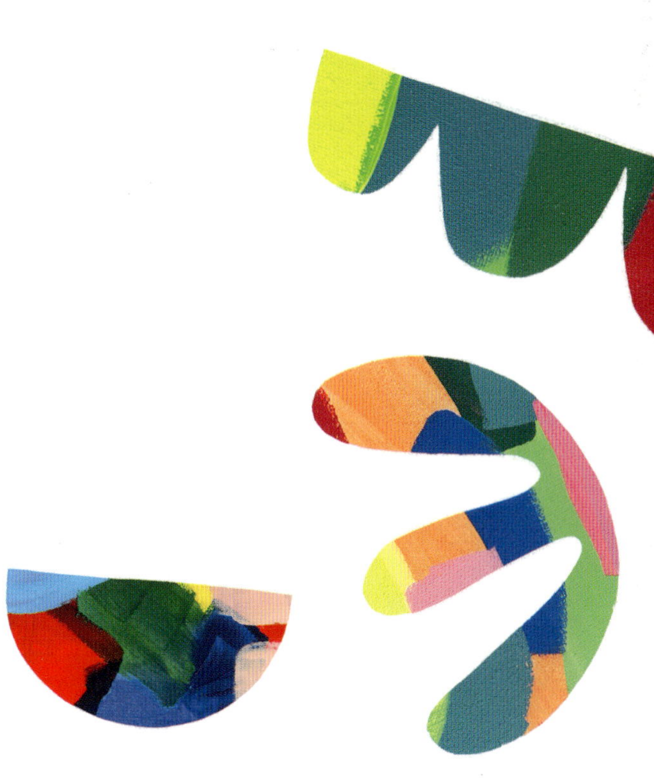

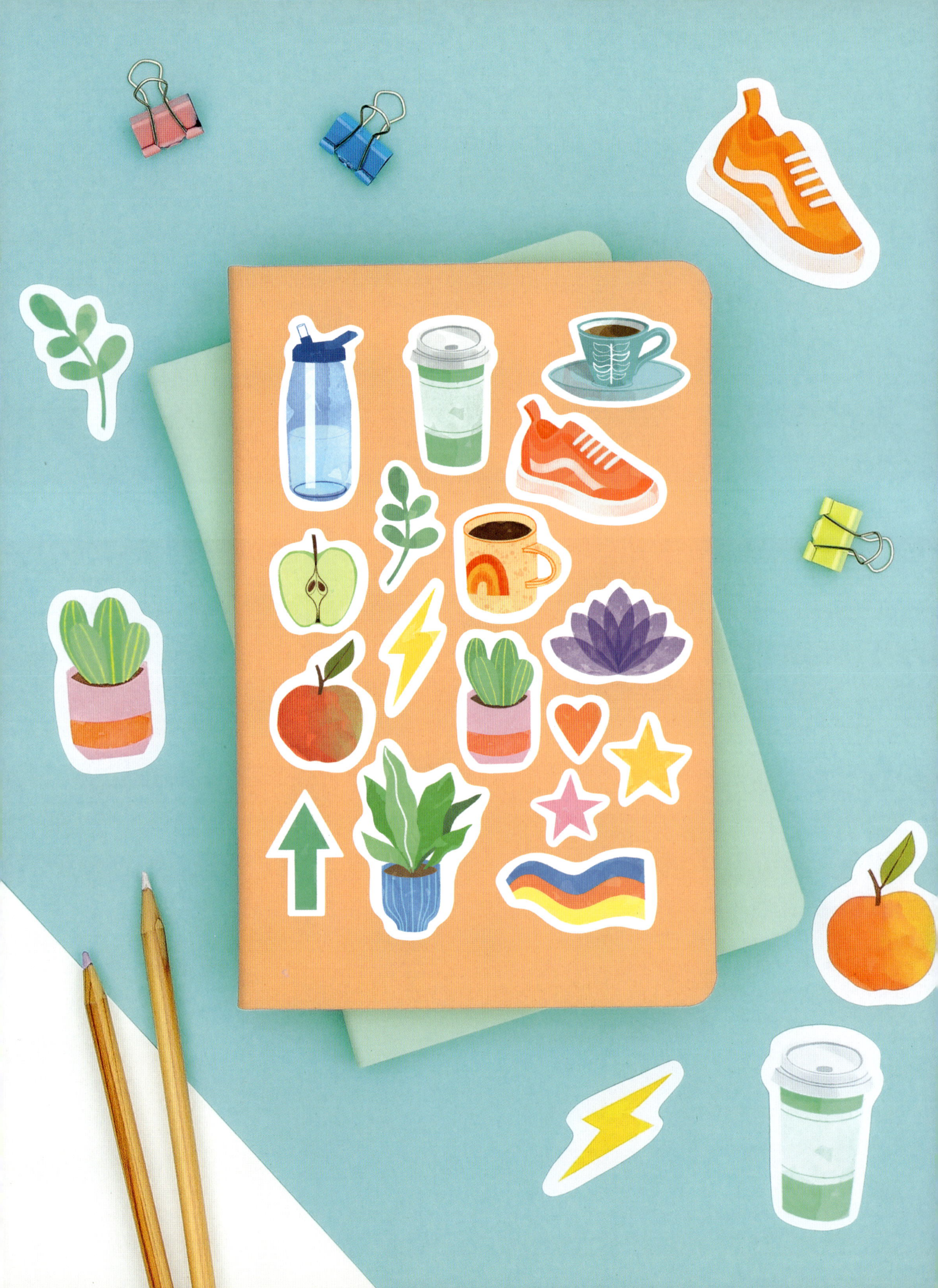

Print & Cut Stickers

Stickers are not just for kids, so it's no wonder that making DIY stickers has become really popular. They offer little bursts of colour to decorate your laptop, add a positive affirmation on your travel cup, or adorn your phone case with cute characters. Lots of us are using these little sticky instant-artworks to brighten up our day. In this project, I'll guide you through the process of illustrating your own set of stickers. This is also an ideal opportunity to experiment with what you've learnt so far.

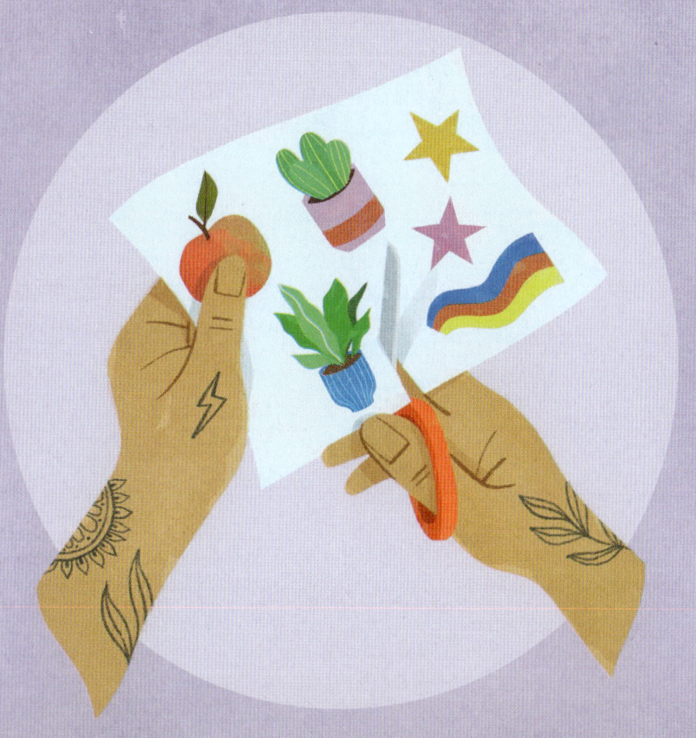

Finding Your Style

When I first started thinking seriously about a career in illustration, I became obsessed with style! I spent a lot of time looking at the work of artists I admired and wondering how they did it. How did they come up with the magic formula of technique, expertise and talent that resulted in such attractive, clever and marketable work? The simple answer? Keep working! Keep experimenting, put in the hours and don't give up. You'll get there.

As you work through the projects in this book, you may start to discover styles that you enjoy. Maybe you love flat, graphic shapes, or you're developing a more painterly style. Are you keen to test some retro-style brushes, or experiment with importing more textures? Whatever it is, I encourage you to embrace your own way of working and try any of these and more on your sticker designs. This simple project is ideal for working on your style as you follow along with the simple steps.

Each little motif is a tiny work of art, but takes only a few minutes to create. You can try different techniques for each sticker. Play with brushes, colour and layers. I'll show you my approach for creating the artwork but then you're on your own! I'll also give you tips on using reference material for inspiration and preparing the file for printing.

1. Brainstorming your ideas

When I approach this kind of fun project, the first thing I do is have a little brainstorm in my notebook. Think about themes you might want to include, and the style you want to use to create your stickers. You can search online for inspiration, but limit that to no more than ten minutes – you don't want to become overly influenced by the work of others

Here are a few of the ideas I jotted down before starting this project:

- Drinks – water, tea, coffee
- Food – fruit, healthy snacks
- Exercise – walking, gym session, wild swimming
- Self care – meditation, beauty treatments
- Nature – plants, flowers
- Positivity – stars, rainbows, arrows, fun shapes

2. Using reference material

Let's set up a new canvas – I'm choosing standard A4 size (2480px wide by 3508px high). We'll create the stickers at this size but probably rearrange and size them down a little before we print.

FINDING YOUR REFERENCE

Let's bring in a reference photo to help us with our sketching. In this example, I'll start with the subject of coffee. A quick online image search brings up lots of options for a coffee cup. Select a simple shape – don't labour over it. This is just to get you started!

MULTITASKING

Let's use the iPad's multitasking feature to help your workflow. Tap and hold on your chosen image, a few options will pop up including copying the image and pasting it onto your canvas, and adding the image to Photos to insert from within the Procreate app.

However for me, the iPad's Split View and Slide Over funtions are the best for viewing reference material. You can keep the larger working space for Procreate, and flick through the images in a separate, smaller window to the side. To bring up these options, tap on the three dots at the top centre of your screen (**A**) to reveal three options: Full Screen, Split View and Slide Over.

Tap on Split View to minimize and move the app to the side, allowing you to choose another. Choose Procreate so that the two apps are displayed side by side, and use Slide Over to create more sketching space. You can now use both windows simultaneously to sketch and browse (**B**).

Tap on Slide Over and follow the same steps. You'll now have the smaller browser window floating *over* Procreate (**C**). For me, this is the better option for viewing reference material as you can keep the larger working space for Procreate and have the images in a separate window at the side to flick through.

Play around with the multitasking options to find something that suits your working style.

MIX, MATCH AND INVENT

Use the reference photos to help you get the shape right, rather than creating a copy. Take elements from different sources and combine them in your own original artwork. Avoid using brand names or logos, which carry the complication of copyright. Anyway, it's much more fun to invent your own!

A

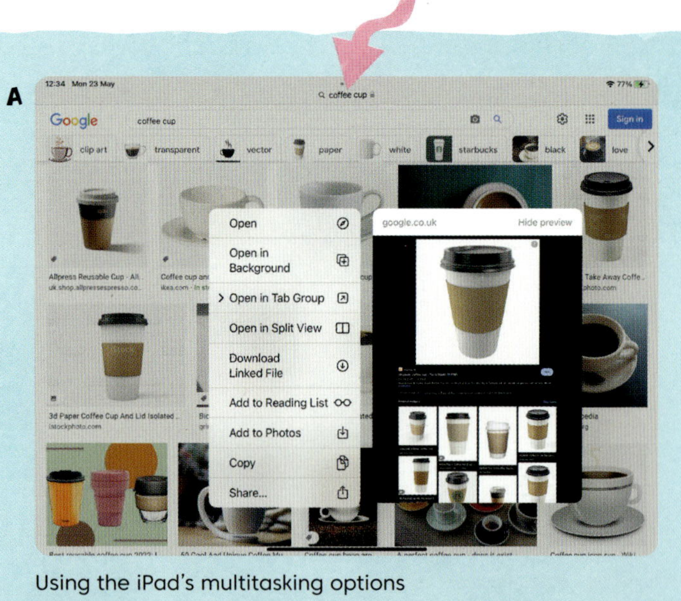

Using the iPad's multitasking options

B

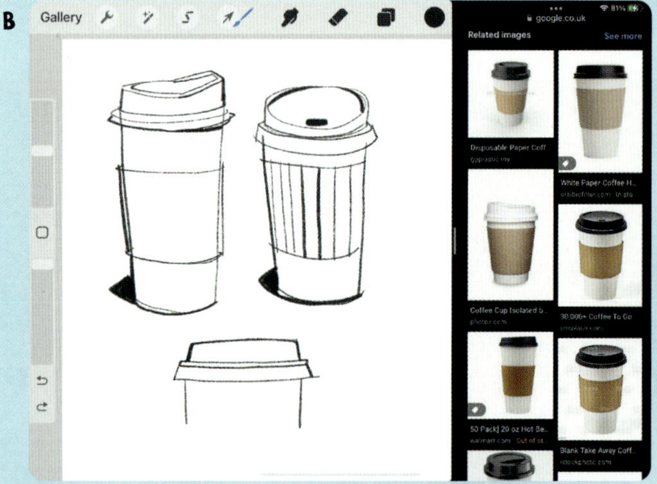

Using Split View

C

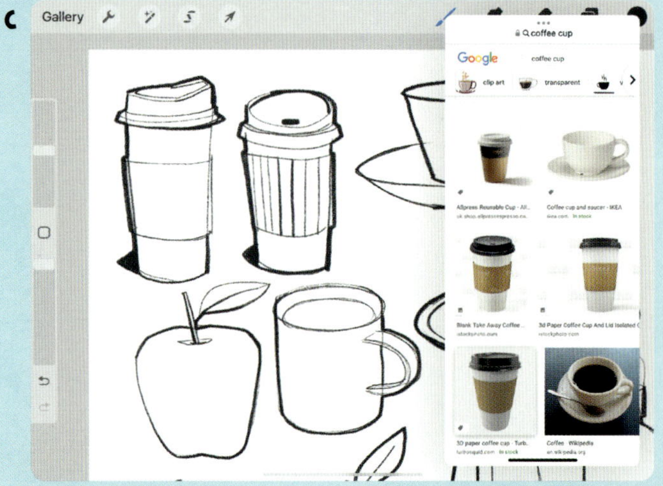

Using Slide Over

3. Sketching and doodling

Now we have reference material to hand, let's start sketching. I select my trusty 6B Pencil from the Brush Library. Try to sketch quickly and loosely at first – don't worry about perspective or perfecting shapes and layout. Just get down all your ideas as quick sketches. Fill the page with one or two options for each icon. Move them around and resize them proportionally until they are all a similar size and the sketch sheet is filled.

At this point I'll go back out to the Gallery, duplicate the sketch sheet as a backup (**D**), and rename it to avoid confusion

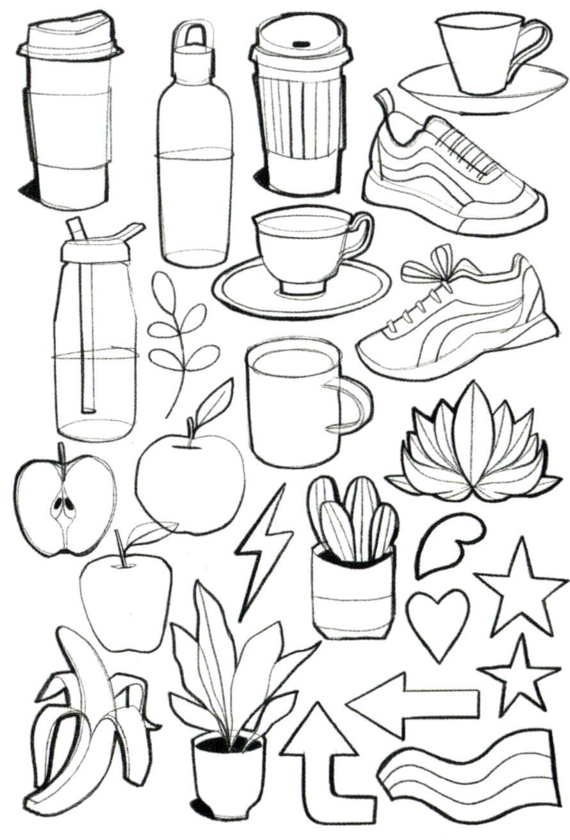

Collect the sketches together on the page.

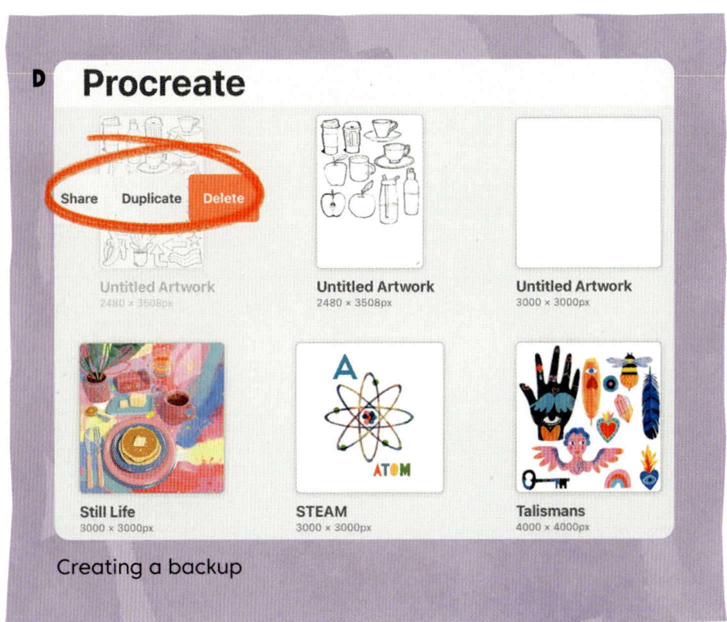

Creating a backup

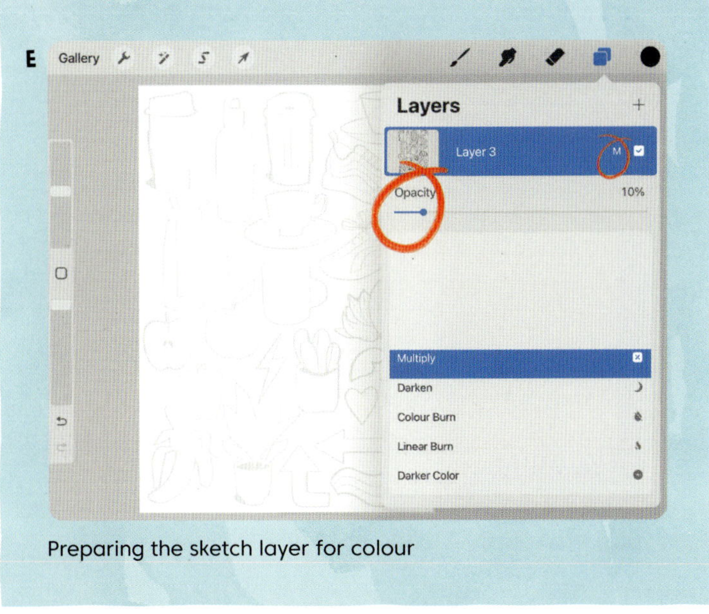

Preparing the sketch layer for colour

4. Preparing to colour

Let's now lower the opacity of the sketch layer, tapping on the N of the selected layer and using the slider to lower the opacity to around 10%. Set the blend mode to Multiply so we can keep it on top of the artwork and work below it without blocking any details (**E**).

WASTE NOT WANT NOT

If there's anything you don't like, cut and paste the offending motif onto a new layer and hide the layer rather than delete it. You may go back to it for another project!

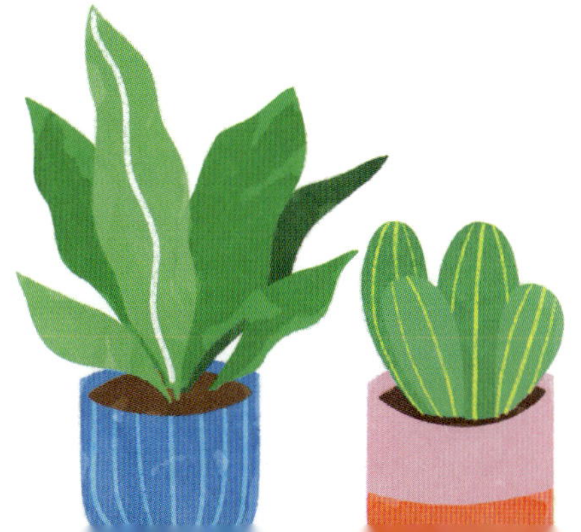

5. Adding colour

Let's start with a simple technique I turn to often, using the Selections tools, a watercolour brush, and the 6B Pencil and Eraser. This technique will give a nice natural finish but keep the colours bright. The watercolour brush I'm using is part of a set I bought online from www.maxpacks.com.

LAYING DOWN COLOUR

Zoom in on one of the potted plant icons and create a layer underneath the sketch. Use the Freehand Selection tool to draw around the shape of the pot. Once selected, take a watercolour brush, choose a colour and paint within the selection. Then tap on the Selections button to deselect the shape (**F**).

MAKING ADJUSTMENTS

Another technique I love to use is to duplicate that shape and play around with the Hue, Saturation and Brightness options in the Adjustments panel (**G**). Once you're happy with the effect, merge the two layers. If you want an even more natural looking finish, use the 6B Pencil as an eraser to refine the edges of the shape (**H**).

Use the same technique to build up the image, using new layers for the soil and the plant itself (**I**).

6. Adding details

Next, we'll use a Clipping Mask layer to build up some design details.

USING A CLIPPING MASK

Create a new layer above the pot, tap on the layer and select Clipping Mask from the menu (**J**). On this layer, trace the stripe on the pot with the Freehand Selection tool (**K**), select your brush and a contrasting colour. The colour is not only contained within the selected area, but also within the shape of the pot (**L**). I also used this method to darken the areas of the cactus at the back to create depth.

ADDING SIMPLE LINES

When printed, the stickers will be quite small, so the only extra detail I add is a few lines with the 6B Pencil to add detail to the plant (**M**). It's best to hide the sketch layer at this point and zoom out to see how it looks. You can always go back in to add more detail or take it away later.

Group your coloured layers together and give the group a suitable name. Keep the sketch layer separate and always on top.

F

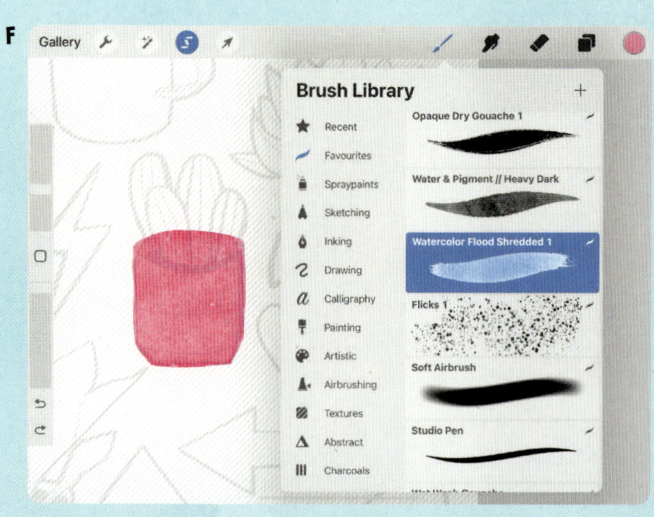

Painting using Freehand Selection as a guide

G

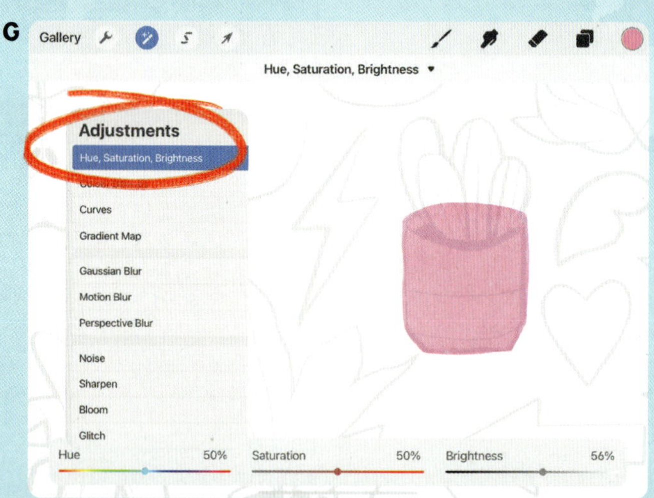

Adjusting colour using Hue, Saturation, Brightness

H

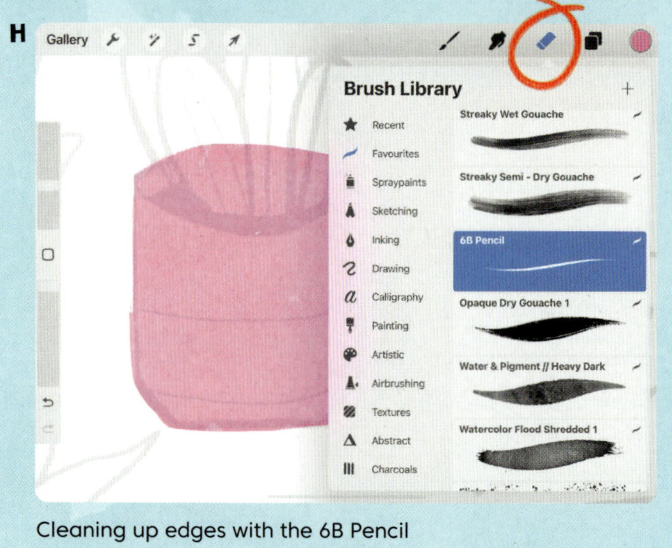

Cleaning up edges with the 6B Pencil

I

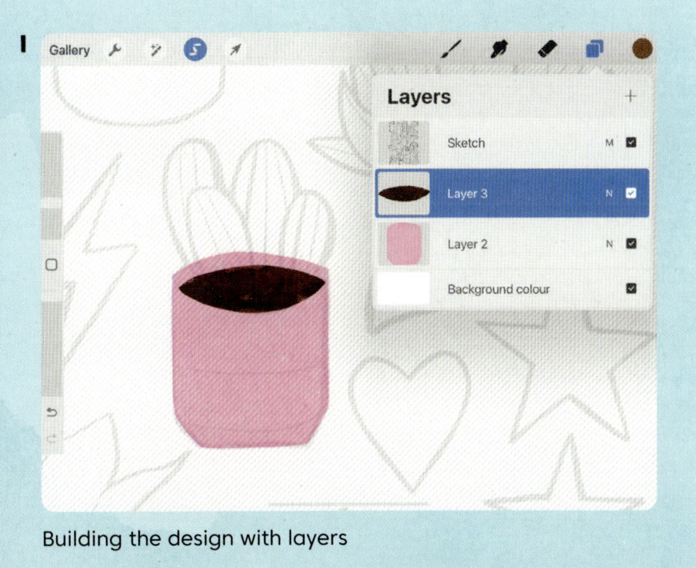

Building the design with layers

LAYERS OF RESOURCES!

I love the option of keeping all the layers so I can edit endlessly. I constantly reuse and recycle my artwork and having editable layers means you'll save time by not having to redraw. You can go back to your layered files over and over to alter and adapt to suit your needs.

J

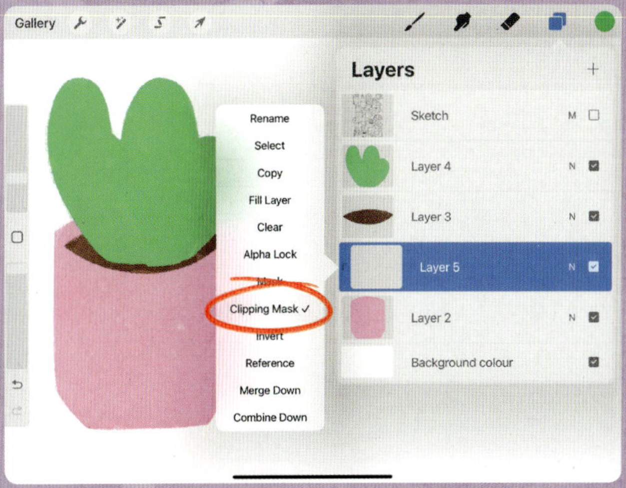

Creating a Clipping Mask layer

L

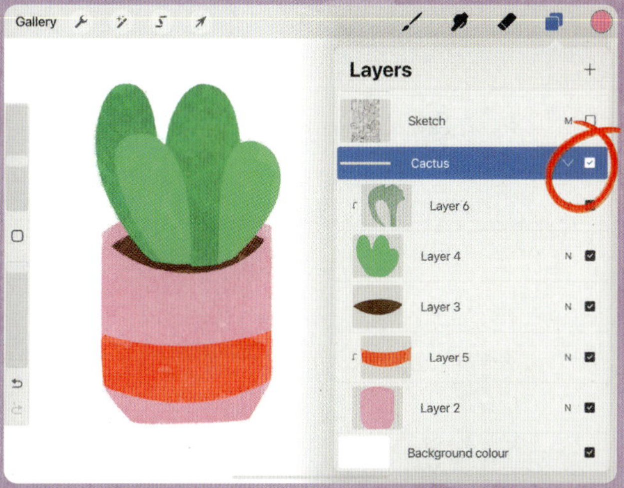

Creating depth with Clipping Masks

K

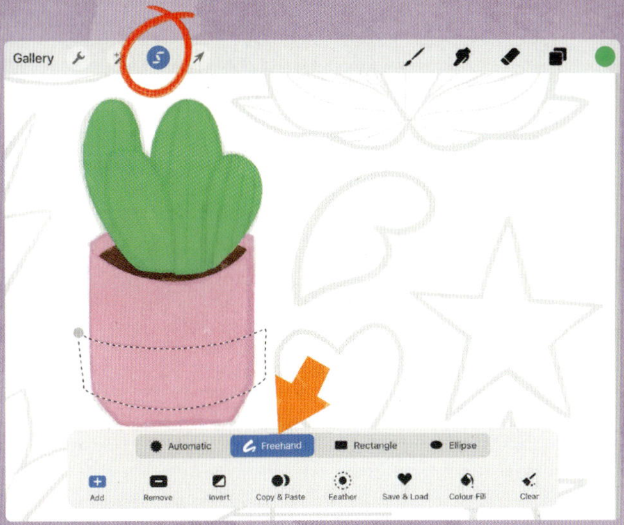

Drawing the outline of the colour band

M

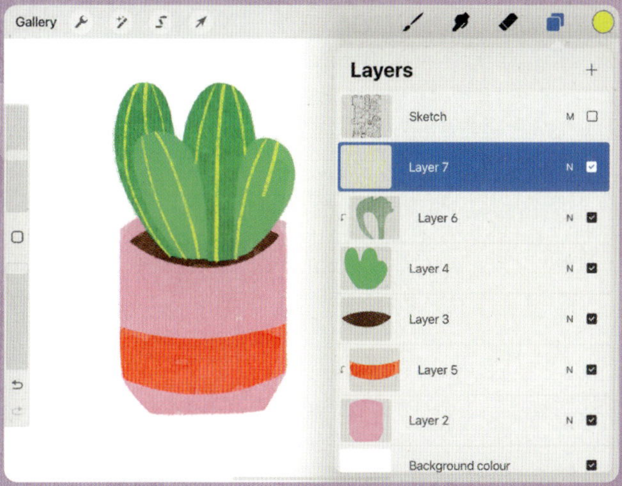

Adding minimal detail with the 6B Pencil

7. Working with layers

Now you're on your own! Continue to use these steps, or even devise your own workflow. Work through the page, grouping the layers to keep each sticker isolated (**N**).

LAYER LIMITS!

Now you're creating freely and having fun, so why does it end abruptly halfway through? You can't create any more layers... You may actually have run out of layers!

Depending on your iPad model, your layer count may be limited (**O**). Simply put, this is a technical issue due to the iPad's memory. But don't worry – newer iPads with higher specifications can support more layers, and there are workarounds for older models.

If you followed the steps so far, you have probably used about seven or eight layers grouped together to create a single icon. Twenty-five icons on your page means your layer count could reach up to two hundred.

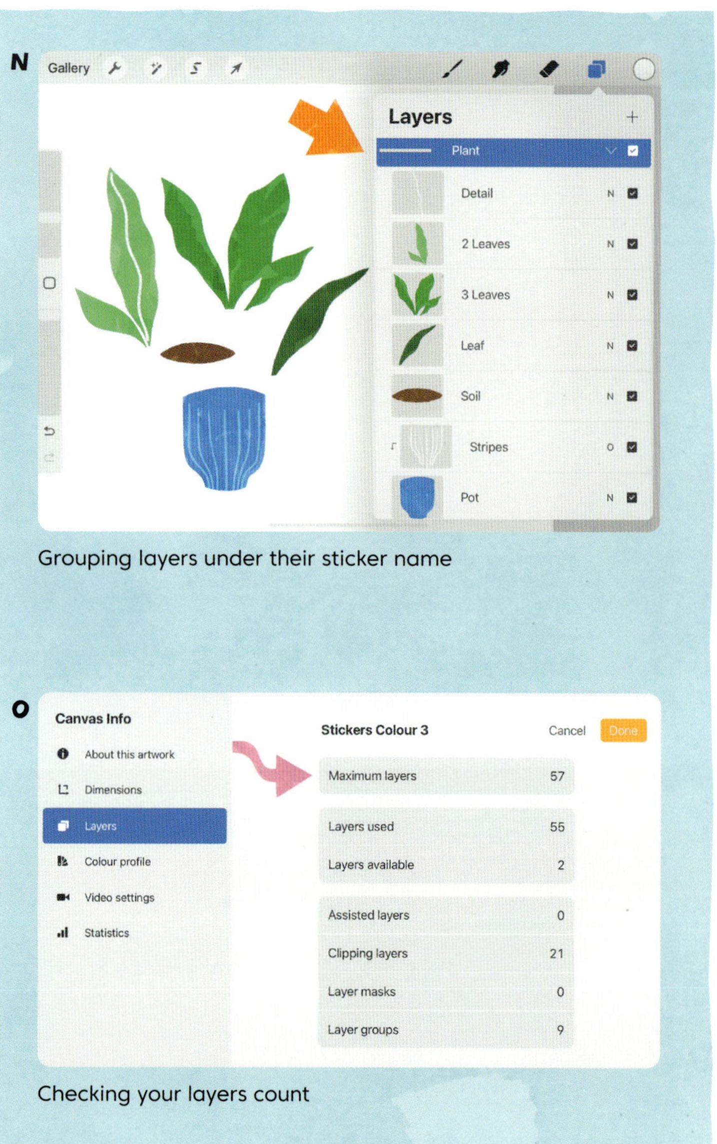

Grouping layers under their sticker name

Checking your layers count

MAXIMIZING YOUR LAYERS ALLOWANCE

When you're close to your limit, go back to the Gallery, duplicate your work, and rename and open the duplicate. Merge any groups you're not working on (these are still layered in the original artwork saved in the Gallery) to free up space for new layers. When you're close to the maximum again, repeat these steps. I sometimes have multiple canvases for one artwork, but I can keep all the layers. Tap, hold and drag artworks together in the Gallery to organize them into Stacks.

Once you've finished colouring your mini artworks, you should have a page that looks something like mine.

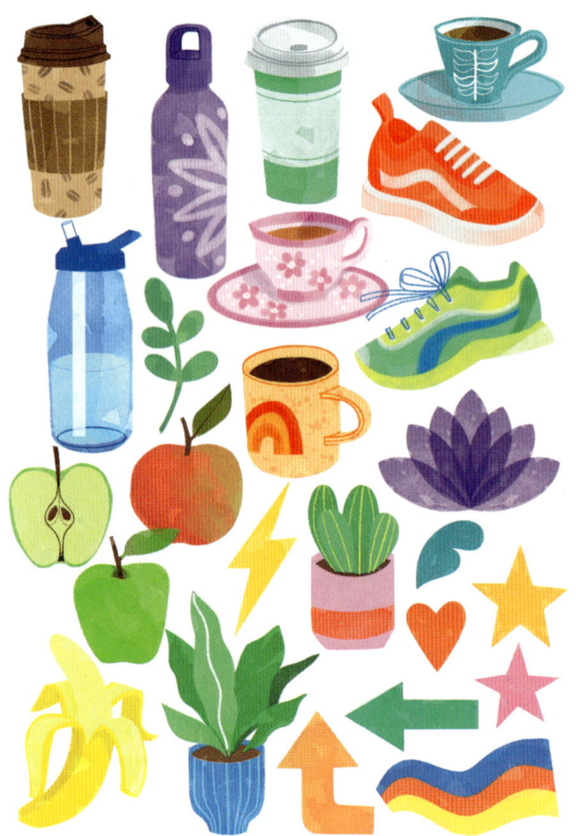

Your page of completed artwork!

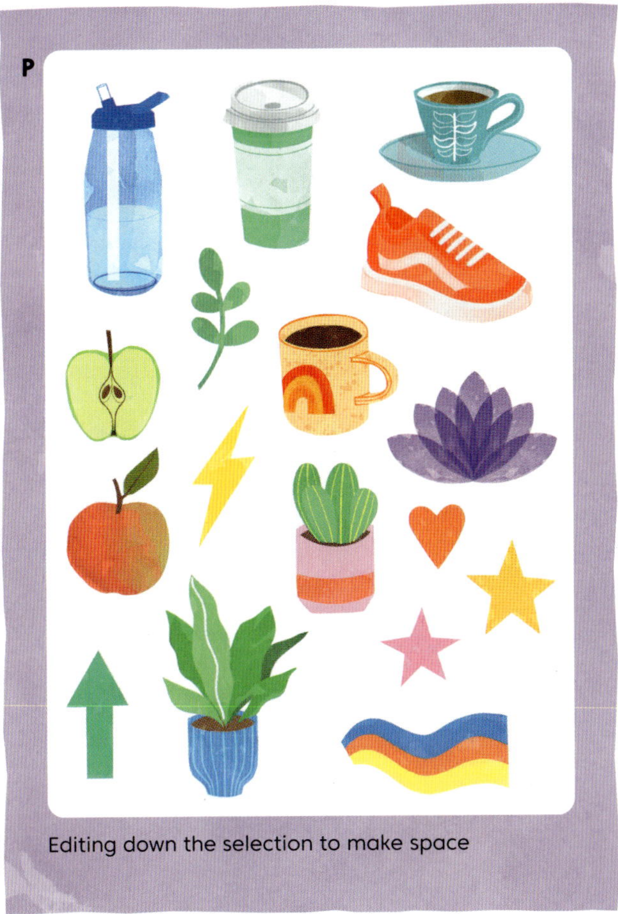

Editing down the selection to make space

8. Spacing the stickers

We now need to create a bit of space around each icon and ensure nothing is overlapping. Make sure you're working on a duplicate canvas so you can now flatten all the groups with each icon on a separate layer. I'm going to hide or delete a few icons from this canvas to free up space (they are stored in previous versions so you won't lose them forever!). Arrange the icons to be evenly spaced. Don't be tempted to resize them to help them fit – for technical reasons I won't go into now, you'll lose quality, so keep resizing to a minimum. With your page looking similar to mine (**P**), we can prepare the images for printing and cutting.

9. Outlining the stickers

We'll create a white background and border for each sticker, so change the canvas background colour to medium grey to show the white. Do this by tapping on the background colour layer – the Colour Disc will open.

SELECTING THE PEN AND COLOUR

Create a new layer underneath your first icon and select something like the Technical Pen from the Inking section of the Brush Library, or Monoline from the Calligraphy set – a smooth and fully opaque brush will produce a clean, sharp edge. Select white from the Colour palette.

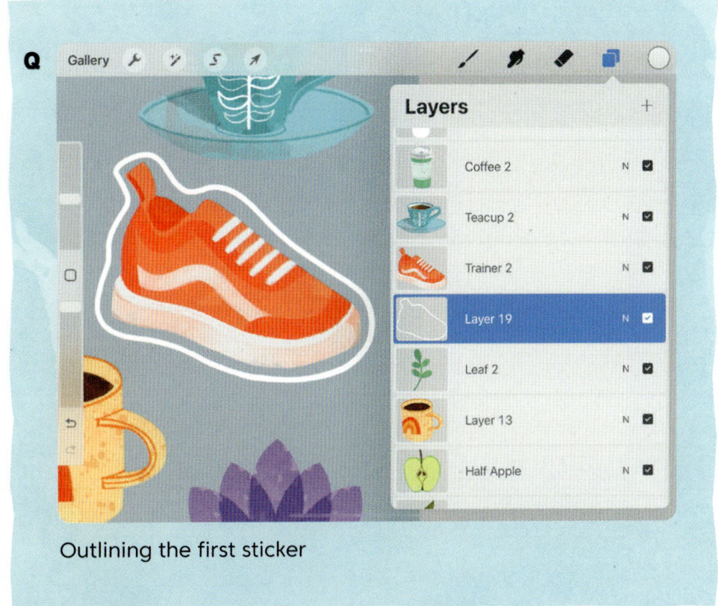

Outlining the first sticker

SELECTING PURE WHITE

Double tap on the inner disc near the white area and pure white will be selected instead of light grey, which you might otherwise select if you're doing it freehand.

Outline the icon, leaving space around the edge (**Q**). Keep the line smooth and simplify the shape to make it easier to cut around. Refine wobbly areas, using the same drawing pen as an eraser to correct any parts of the line that become too wide. Make sure you close the line so you can drag and drop white into the centre to fill and create the background.

Congratulations – your first sticker is ready! Create borders for each icon. Keep them on separate layers and group them when done to move the border and icon layers together.

10. Printing the stickers

Your sticker sheet is now ready to print. You can print straight from your iPad if you have it set up. Alternatively, export it and send to your computer.

If you're using a cutting machine, export the sheet as a PNG file and upload to the design program that comes with your machine.

Don't worry if you don't have this equipment, just print on a sheet of sticker paper and cut around the smooth outlines you have created with a pair of small sharp scissors!

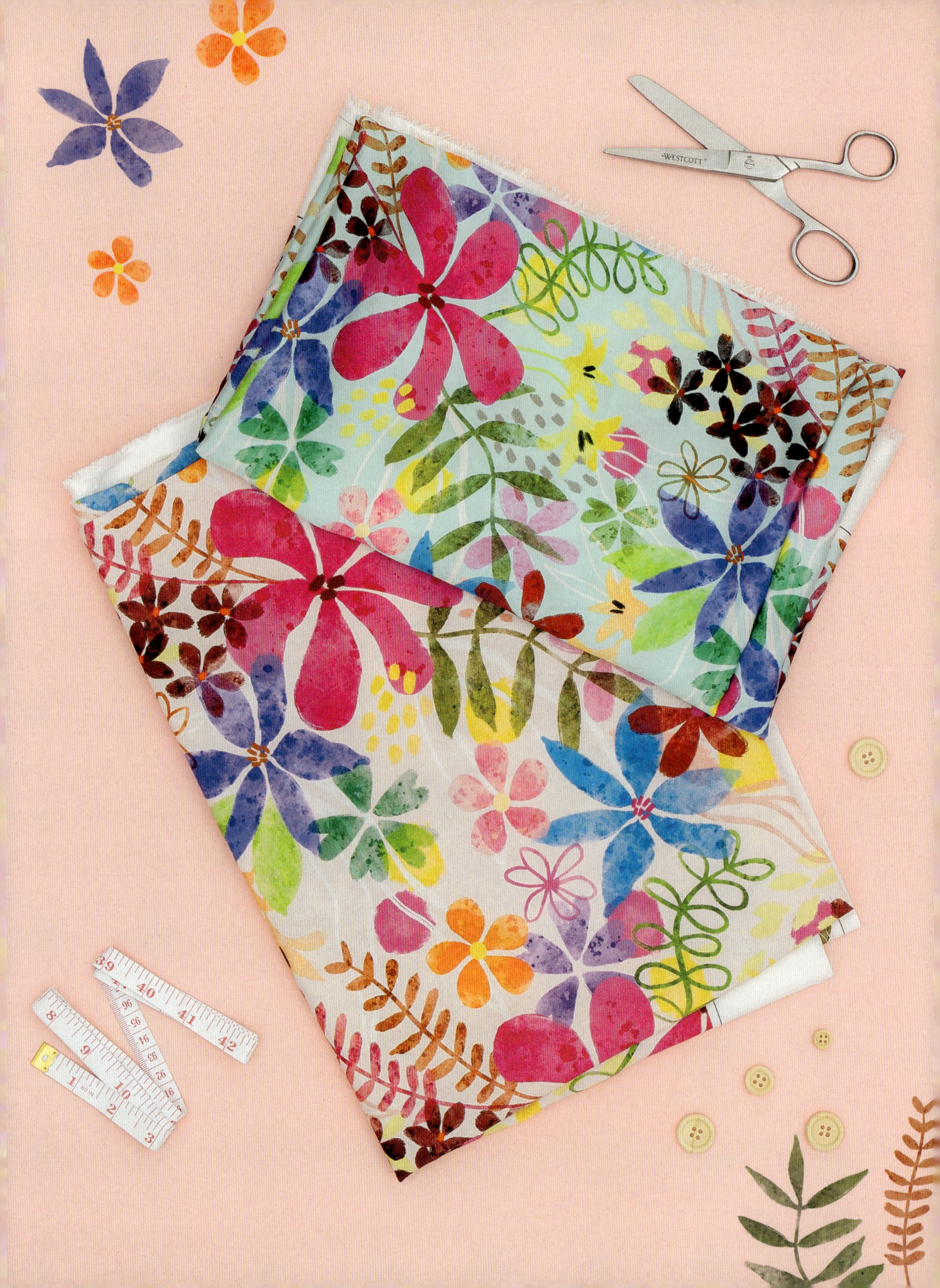
WESTCOTT

Repeat Pattern Fabric Design

Being able to create a repeating surface pattern is a great skill to have as an illustrator. It's a versatile technique that can be used in so many different ways. Once you master the details of how to build a seamless repeat pattern, you'll enjoy putting together collections using new designs. Patterns can also be created from work already in your portfolio.

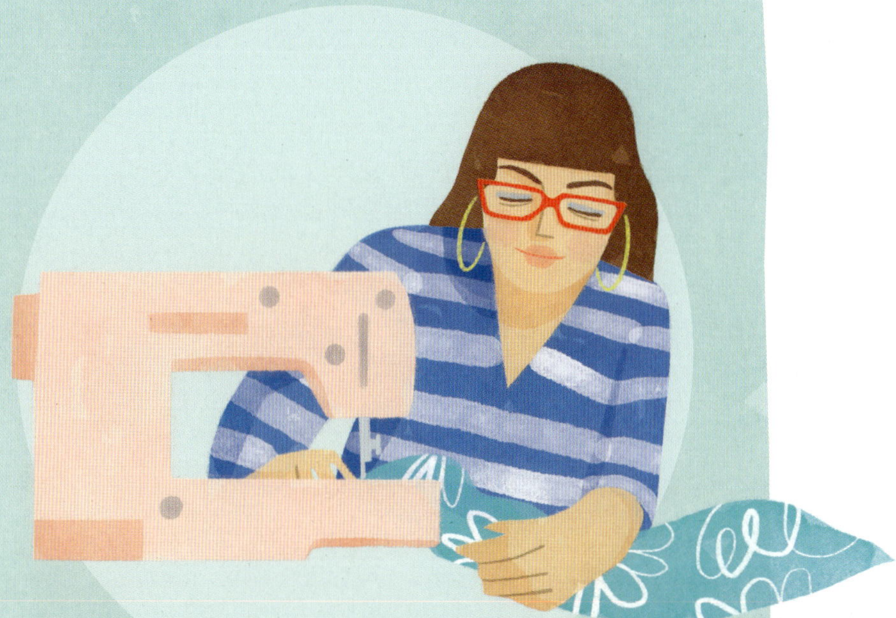

Pattern-making

There are a lot of different ways to create a repeating pattern. Some techniques can seem complicated and long-winded, but in this project, I'll show you a basic and simple way to make your own patterns using only the Procreate app.

The base of the pattern will be a block or tile that, when stacked together, will create the seamless repeat. The success of the pattern lies in building up a well balanced tile, and so here we'll experiment with simple techniques and tricks to make that happen!

I'll also show you how to replicate a painterly looking watercolour style using brushes already included in the app.

1. Finding inspiration

Sparking ideas for designing patterns is not difficult! Look around your house at the soft furnishings or wallpaper. Your wardrobe will no doubt be full of patterned clothes – you may have big and bold florals or tiny ditsy prints. Stripes, polka dots and checks also come under the umbrella of pattern. Have a browse through a department store, either online or in town. Look closely at the motifs in a pattern and try to see how they repeat. Do they appear in a straight line or is the pattern stepped or "dropped" to make it appear more random? Let's jump into how our pattern tile will be put together to better understand how a repeat pattern works.

2. Understanding a repeat tile

Before we begin, I would like to explain with a few simple diagrams, how a repeat tile is made. Understanding this before we create any artwork will enable us to work through this project with ease.

CREATING THE BASIC DESIGN

I've drawn a simple design in the middle of a square canvas, making sure no parts are touching or hanging off the edges (**A**).

I can repeat this tile as it is (**B**), but the demarcation between the blocks is very visible.

CREATING A BLENDED REPEAT

I want to fill in the spaces and blend the pattern together to achieve a seamless repeat. Here is the process I'll use:

1. The design is first cut exactly into quarters (**C**).
2. Each quarter is flipped both horizontally and vertically. The central corner of each quarter is now on the outer corner (**D**).
3. When the quarters are rejoined, there is a prominent gap between each one (**E**).
4. The gaps are filled with further freehand shapes (**F**).
5. I'll now be able to stack this design vertically and horizontally, the pattern repeating seamlessly (**G**).

This resulting pattern is known as a full drop repeat. The are are many other ways to make a repeating pattern, and if you enjoy this project I encourage you to research some other methods. You'll learn what works for you and soon devise your own way of working.

For now, use this simple technique on this project.

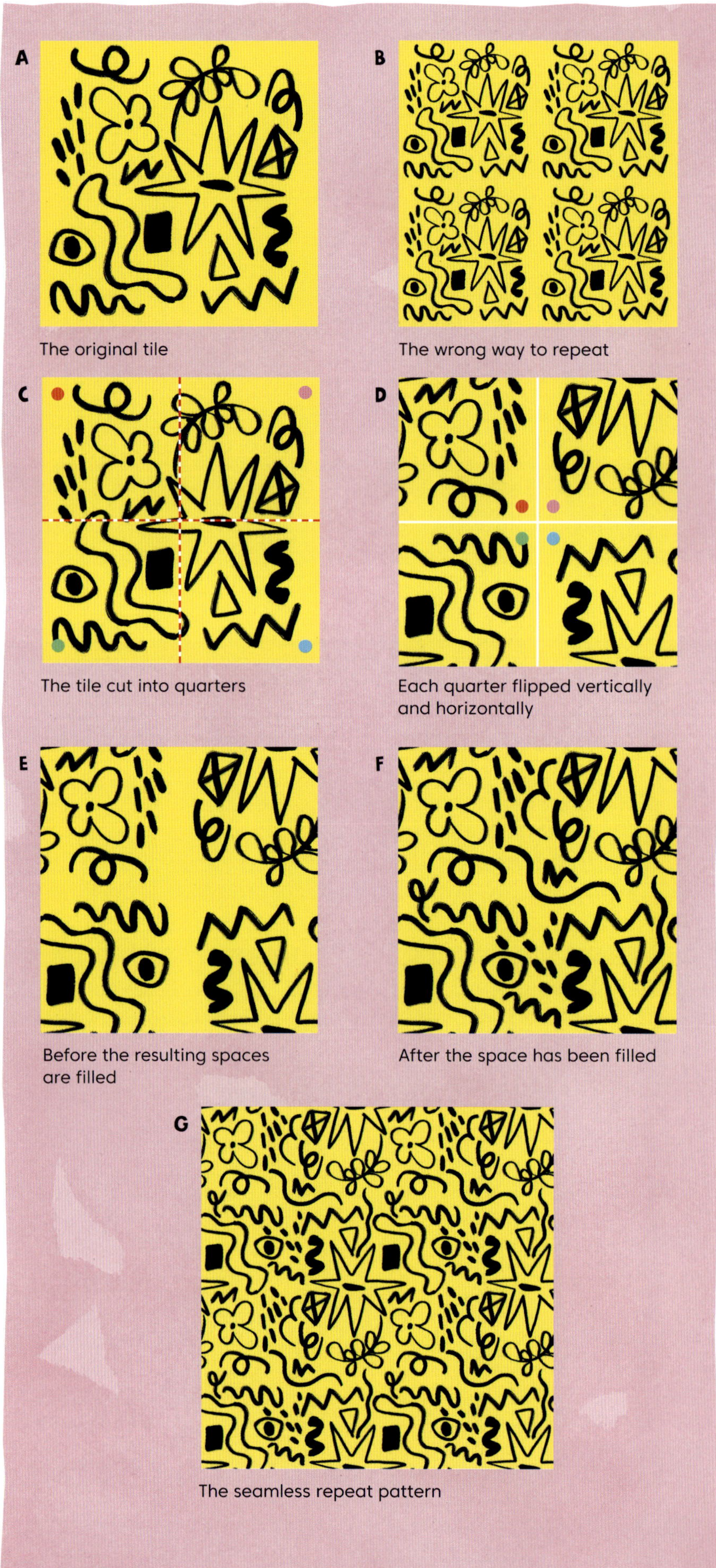

A: The original tile

B: The wrong way to repeat

C: The tile cut into quarters

D: Each quarter flipped vertically and horizontally

E: Before the resulting spaces are filled

F: After the space has been filled

G: The seamless repeat pattern

H

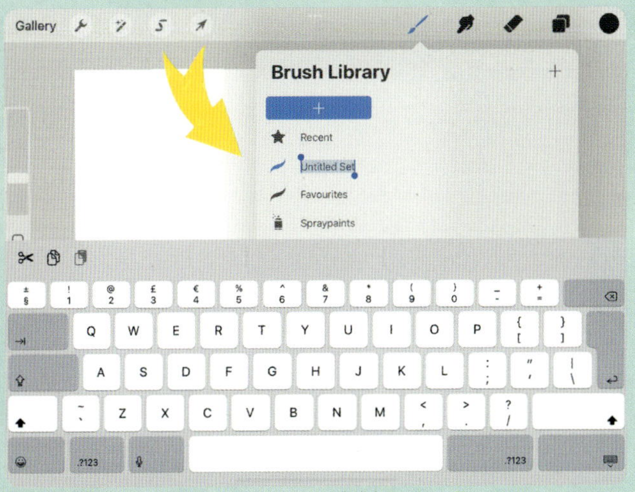

Creating a Brush Library project folder

I

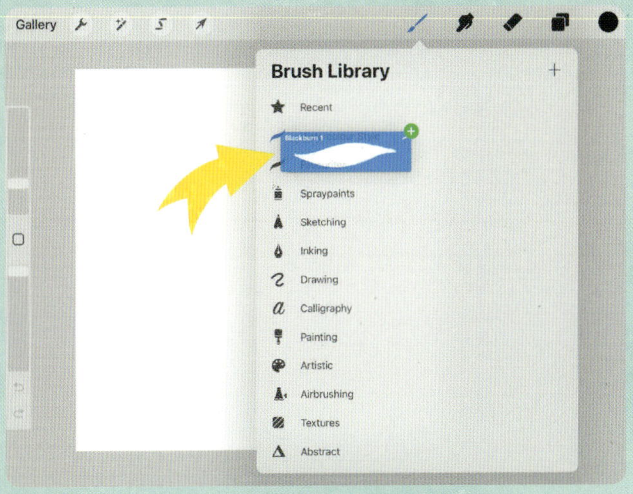

Selecting a brush to copy into the project folder

K

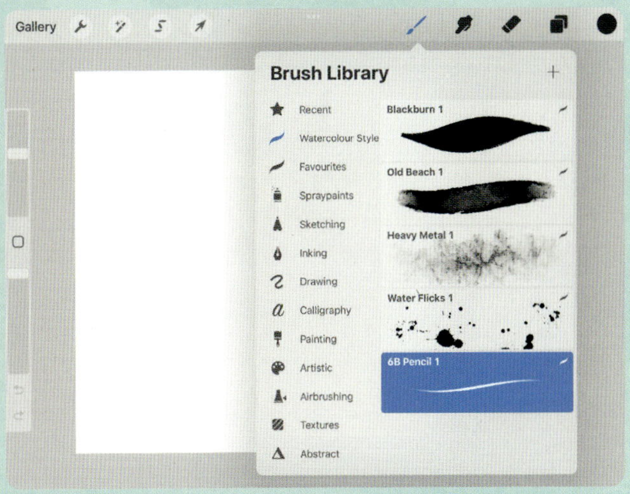

The complete brush collection for this project

3. Watercolour brushes

Before we begin the repeat pattern process, we'll draw and paint our motifs in a watercolour style. Set up a square canvas – 3000px by 3000px will be a good size to start with.

IMPORTING AND ORGANIZING BRUSHES

You can purchase and import watercolour brushes to use for this project. Simply download the purchased brush to your files. Then open Procreate's Brush Library and tap + in the top right-hand corner. From there, you can navigate the folders on your iPad to find the brush file. Tap on the file to import it directly to your library.

Alternatively, I'll show you a really simple technique to create a watercolour style with a few brushes that are already included in the app.

Let's first create a new folder to hold the brushes so we can easily find and select them.

1. Pull down on the Brush Library list and you'll see a blue button with a + sign.
2. Tap on that to create a new brush set and rename it (**H**). I'm calling mine Watercolour Style.
3. Locate and copy some brushes over to that folder. In the Drawing folder there is a brush called Blackburn. Swipe left on that to duplicate it, then drag and drop the duplicate into your new folder (**I**).
4. In the Artistic section, there is a Brush called Old Beach – repeat the process above to duplicate and drag that over to your new folder also.
5. We just need a couple of other brushes to complete the set – Heavy Metal from the Industrial folder and Water Flicks from the Water folder. Let's also drag across a copy the 6B Pencil so we have everything to hand. Your new brush set should now look like this (**K**).

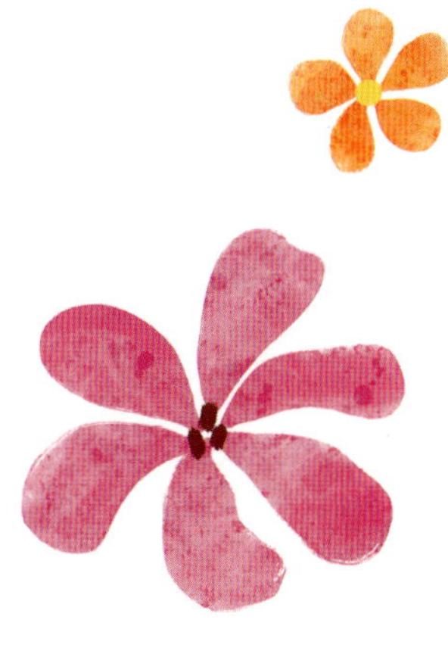

4. Using the Reference feature

I'm going to gather a few reference photos from the internet and save them to Photos on my iPad. I just need a few simple flower and leaf shapes to work from – nothing too complex.

An easy way to view this reference whilst sketching is by using a feature called... Reference! You'll find it in Actions (**L**). Just turn on Reference and a small floating window will pop up. Tap on Import, then Image, and you can choose from your Photo Library (**M**).

5. Painting silhouettes

I'm going to draw in the shape of my flowers and foliage with the Blackburn brush. This brush replicates an actual paintbrush really well – you can draw petals and leaves by varying the pressure while drawing. You can also alter the size of the brush for different shapes. Try a few strokes – you'll soon get the hang of it. I'm just concentrating on the silhouettes for now. You don't need to copy the reference photo perfectly, but try to keep the shapes natural looking (**N**).

USING LAYERS

Once you're happy with a motif silhouette, name it in Layers, then create a new layer. Keep each motif on a separate layer and try to vary the size and style of each element.

We're going to need one or two large flower shapes, two or three medium flowers and leaf stems, plus some tiny elements that can be scattered around. Arrange your motifs on the page so nothing is overlapping, ready for the next stage.

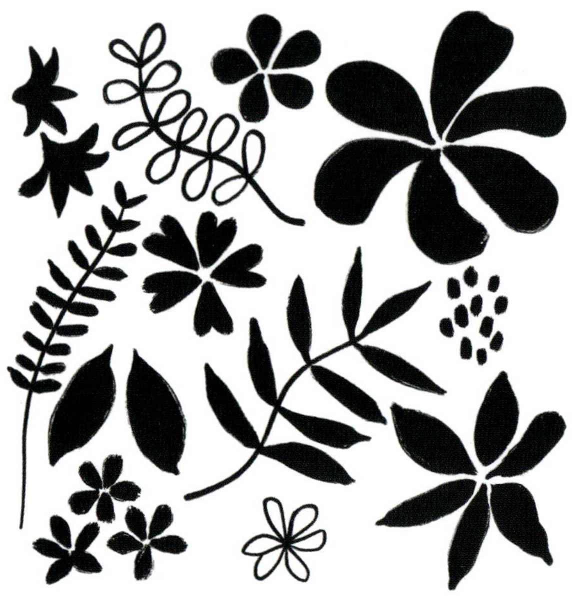

The blocked in shapes ready to be coloured.

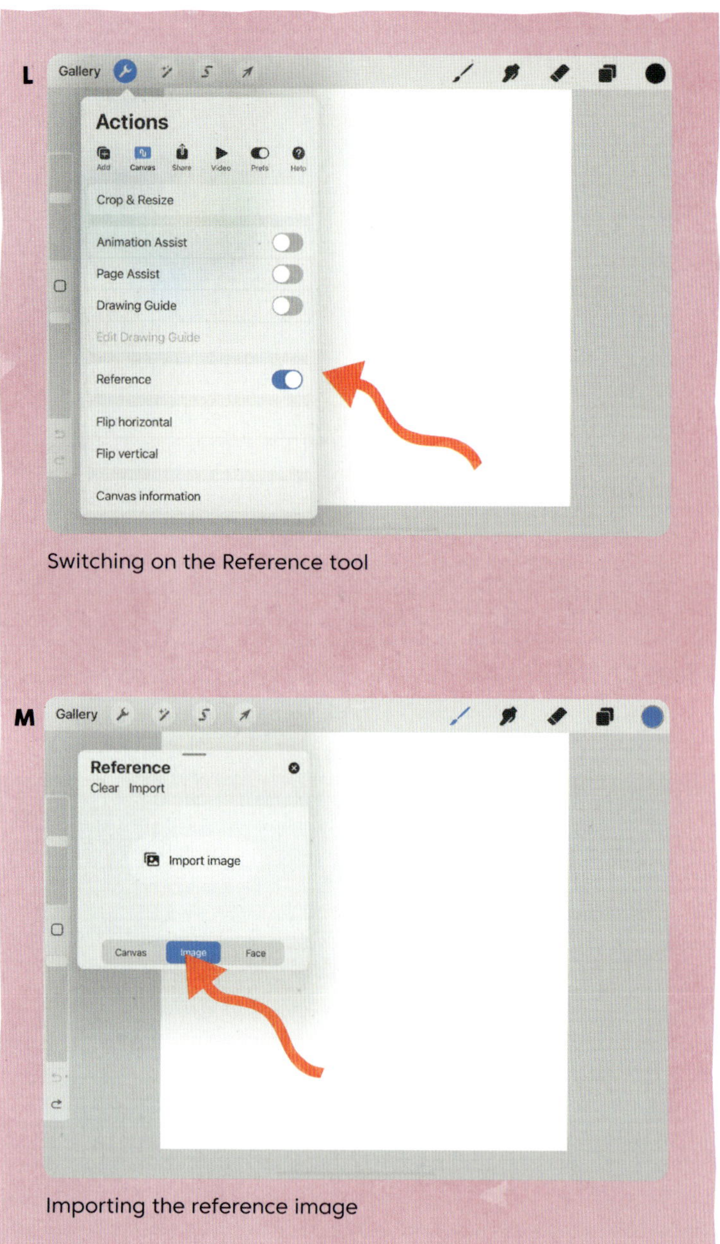

Switching on the Reference tool

Importing the reference image

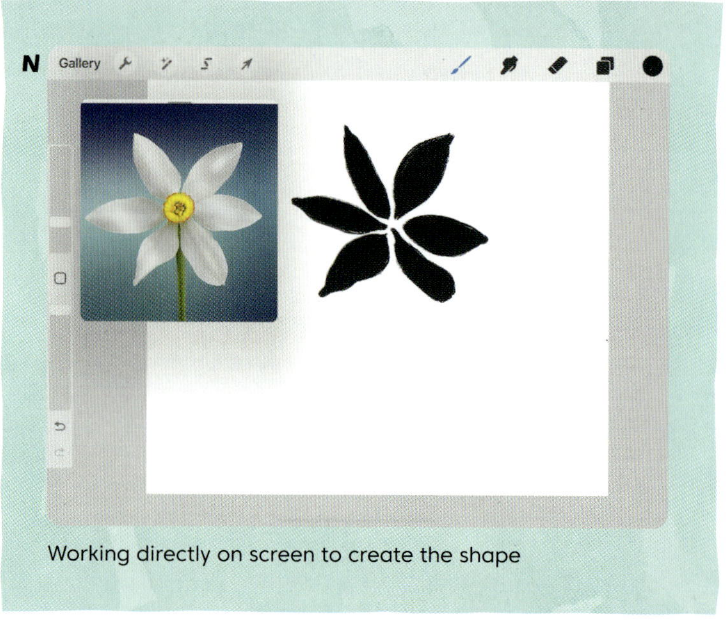

Working directly on screen to create the shape

O

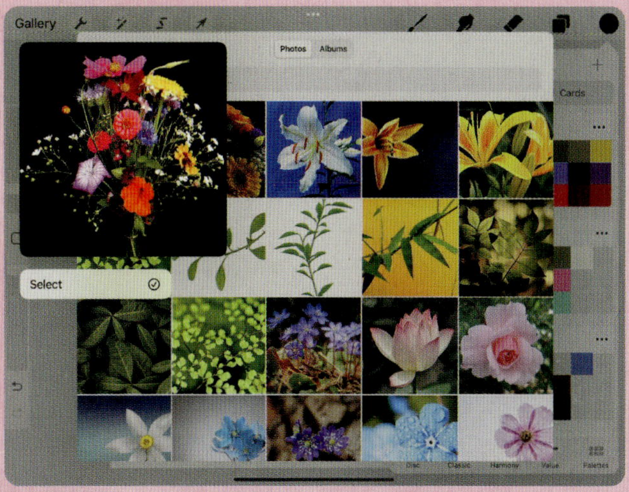

Selecting a reference image for the colour palette

P

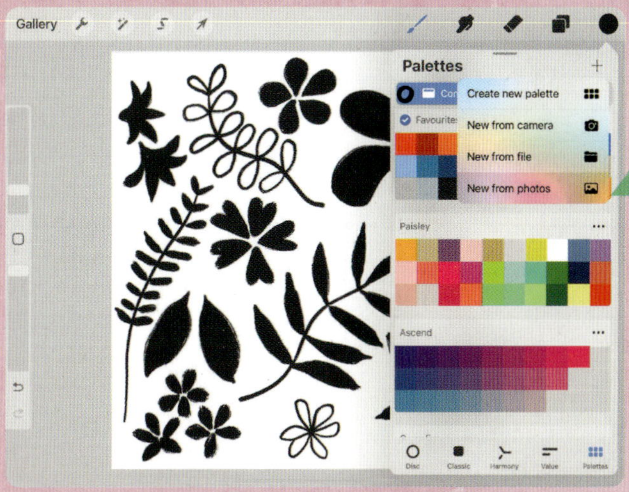

Creating a palette with New From Photos

Q

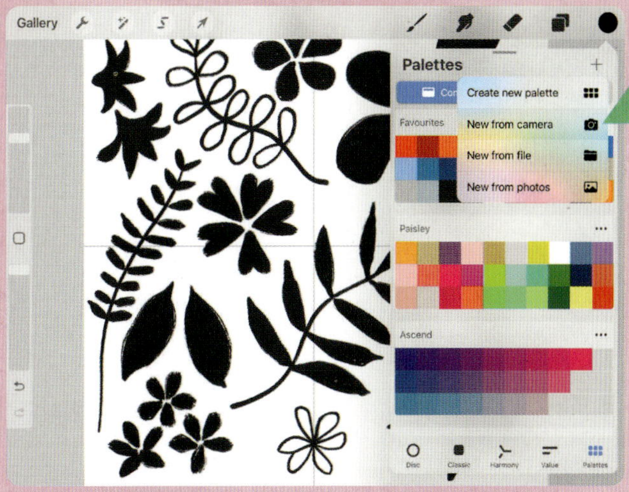

Creating a palette with New From Camera

6. Creating a colour palette

When I researched images for my floral shapes, I included a few photos of colourful bouquets. I'm going to select one of these (**O**) to create an instant palette that's both varied and cohesive.

PICKING A PALETTE FROM A PHOTO

To do this, we'll use a simple action contained in the Palettes menu. Tap on the + and choose the New From Photos option (**P**). Just tap on your selected photo and a new palette is instantly created. You can refine this as you go, adding and deleting swatches, but it's a quick and easy way to get started.

PICKING A PALETTE FROM A CAMERA

You can also create a palette directly from the camera, which is a really fun way to do it (**Q**)! Tapping on this option will open the camera and you can choose from two modes:

Indexed mode – whatever you point the camera at (i.e. the image shown across the whole iPad screen) will be broken down into the rectangular palette located in the centre of the screen.

Visual mode – this mode captures exactly what is directly in front of the rectangular palette area on the screen, using nothing from the surrounding area.

Try out these different modes for yourself now to see how simple they are to use. These options are great for capturing spontaneous palettes when you're out and about with your iPad!

7. Adding colour and watercolour texture

I'll now show you how to create the watercolour effect that will make up our floral motifs – there are a few simple steps to get the hang of.

ADD TEXTURE TO THE FIRST FLOWER

1. Let's start with the largest flower shape. Hold down two fingers on the layer to select the shape. Create a new layer above and hide the selected shape layer. We're going to work within the selection to create a coloured and textured bloom (**R**).
2. Select the Old Beach brush and a colour of your choice from the new palette. To add texture, increase the brush size to 50%. Brush lightly within the selection to create a painterly base layer. Keeping that selection active, create another layer above, make this a Clipping Mask layer and set the blend mode to Multiply (**S**).
3. On this layer, we'll use the Heavy Metal and Water Flicks brushes to add more texture. You can keep the same colour selected or choose something else. Try different combinations until you find one you like. I'm going to add another layer above and use the Blackburn brush to add details at the centre of the bloom (**T**).
4. When you're happy, group all the layers for this motif together and rename – you'll see further on that I named this Large Pink (**V**). Include the hidden silhouette in case you want to use it again for selection.

This is the basic formula for creating our watercolour flowers and foliage. Work through the rest of the motifs, grouping them as individual elements as you go along. You should now have a page that looks something like the illustration here.

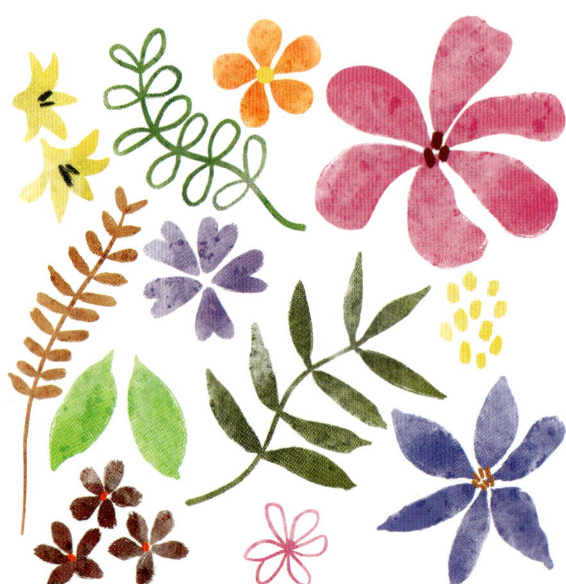

The coloured shapes with texture and details added.

R

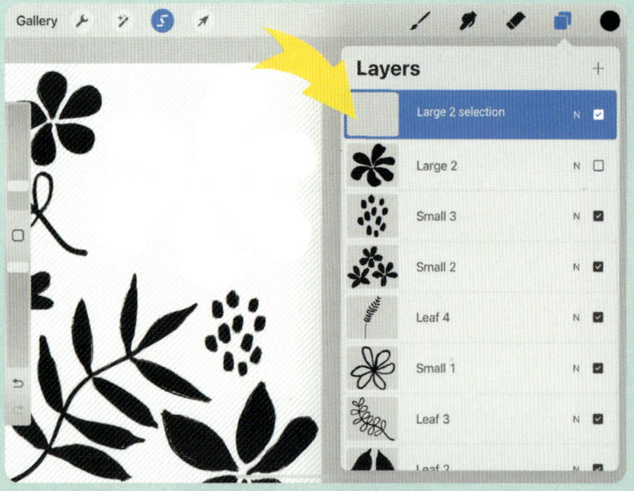

Creating a selection for the base colour

S

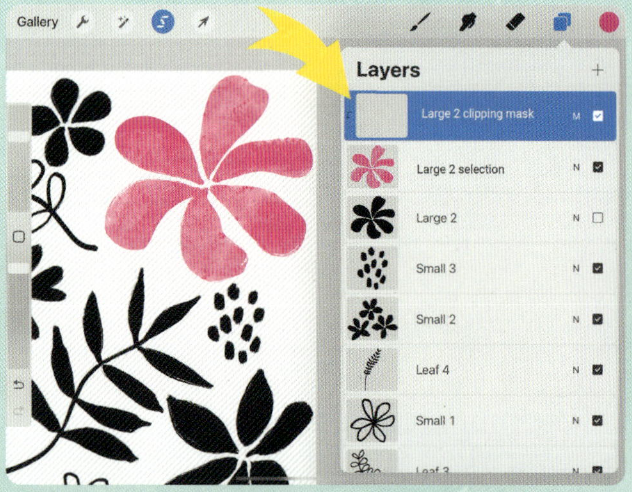

Creating a Clipping Mask for texture

T

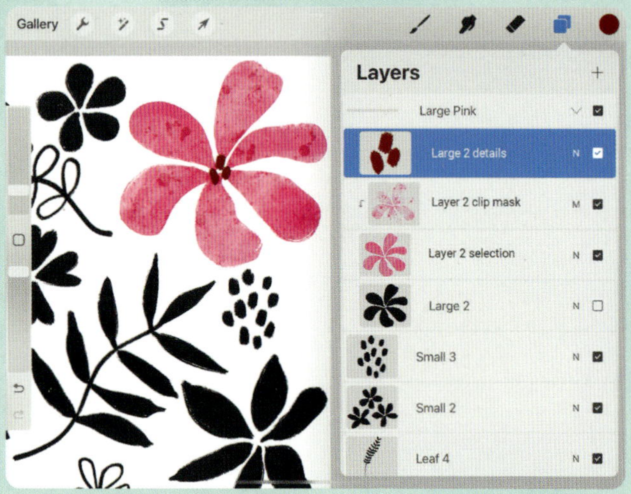

Adding details to the centre

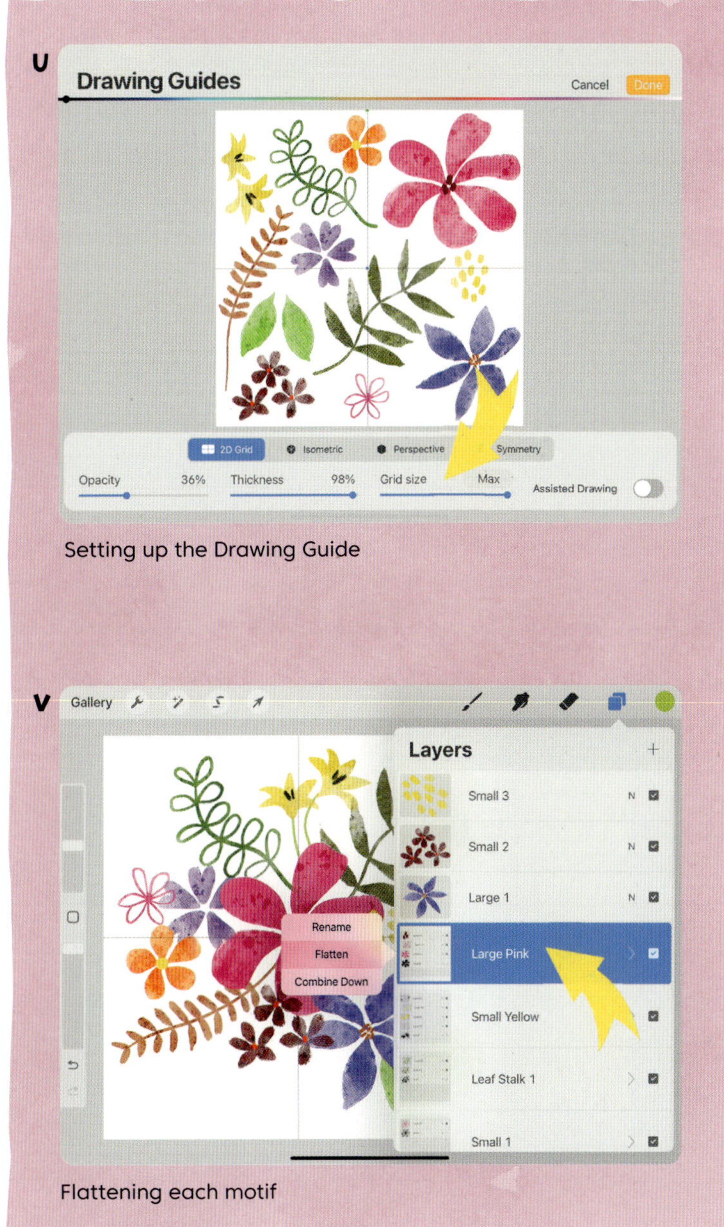

Setting up the Drawing Guide

Flattening each motif

8. Creating the pattern

Let's arrange our motifs on the canvas to create the pattern. Set up Drawing Guides to help us place our motifs (tap on Actions, then Drawing Guide, then Edit Drawing Guide). We'll also need the guide later to select the portions that will be flipped. Slide the Grid Size to Max to give us a horizontal and vertical guide (**U**). I'm also going to duplicate the canvas in the Gallery as a backup.

ARRANGING THE FLOWERS

The next step is like flower arranging, placing your motifs on the canvas in a visually pleasing way. Overlap, rotate and re-order your blooms and leaf stems, taking care to keep them on the canvas. You can go close to the edge but don't lose anything off the edge. It should look something like mine, as shown.

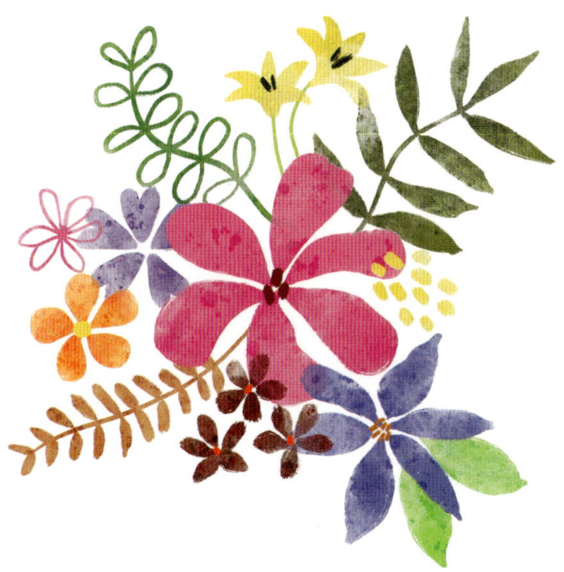

The design ready to be made into a repeat pattern.

PREPARING THE LAYERS

Let's go ahead and duplicate this canvas again to give us plenty of editable files to work with. In the new duplicate, merge the grouped layers. It will make the next steps easier, and also prevent us running out of layers halfway through! Just tap on each group and select Flatten (**V**). Be sure to keep each motif separate at this stage.

Select all the layers by swiping right on each one. Group them and duplicate the group. Hide the duplicate group at the bottom – we may need some elements from here later to fill in the spaces.

PRE-LOADED SELECTIONS

Now comes the part where we chop up the design into four equal parts and flip each quarter. Refer to the start of this project to go through the steps again if this seems confusing.

Let's set up a drawing guide to help us accurately save the selections. Tap on Actions, Canvas and turn on Drawing Guide. Tap Edit Drawing Guide and slide the Grid Size up to Max – this will give us the centre point of four quarters.

To help us do this accurately and efficiently we're going to pre-load some selections.

1. Add a new layer and fill it with colour (I've chosen purple). Tap on the Transform tool and make sure Uniform is selected.
2. Tap on Snapping and make sure Magnetics and Snapping is turned on. The Distance can be set around halfway but make sure Velocity is at Max (**W**). This is really going to help us place our selected shapes accurately on the canvas by "snapping" them exactly to the guidelines.

Let's try that now. Start to resize the selected coloured shape to the top left-hand corner of the canvas. When the bottom right-hand corner of the square reaches the centre point, the guidelines will change to gold and the shape will snap into place. You can check the sizing by looking at the pixel size box that comes up as you drag the shape. Since our canvas is 3000px by 3000px, the centre point will show up as 1500px by 1500px (**X**). Be careful not to nudge the position when you let go.

Select that top left-hand square by holding two fingers down on the layer. Tap on Save & Load. Save the selection by tapping the + sign (**Y**).

REPEAT FOR ALL FOUR CORNERS

You're going to repeat these steps for all four corners. Just go back to the layer, deselect, fill again with colour and repeat until you have all four quarter selections saved in this order: Top left, top right, bottom left, bottom right. You must make sure the selections are spot on to the guidelines to avoid hairlines in the design (**Z**) (**AA**).

You can now delete the colour block layer.

W

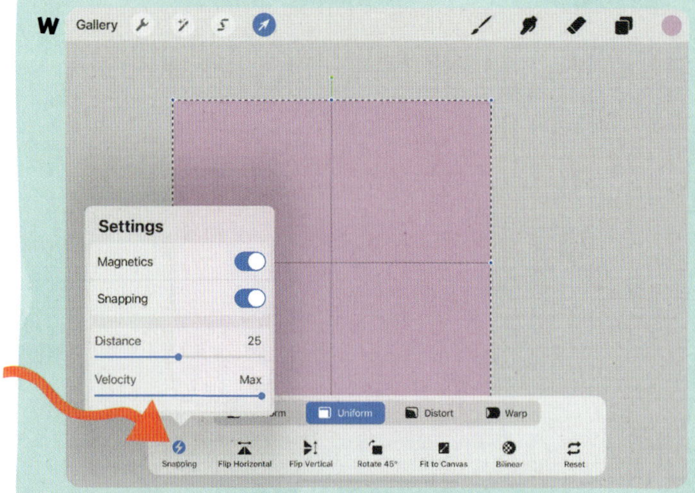

Preparing the canvas for the four quarters

X

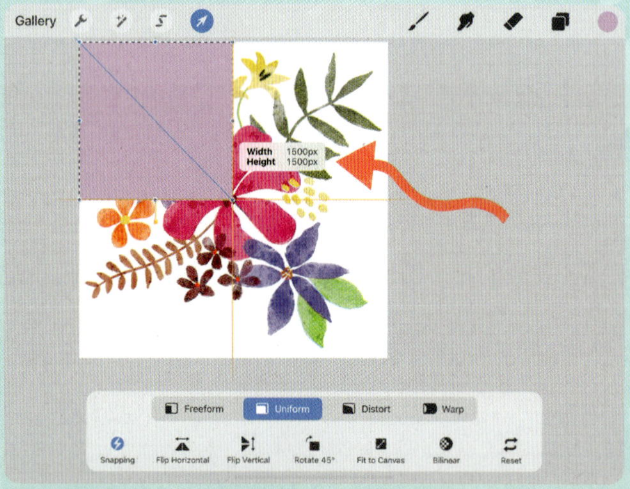

Resizing the square precisely

Y

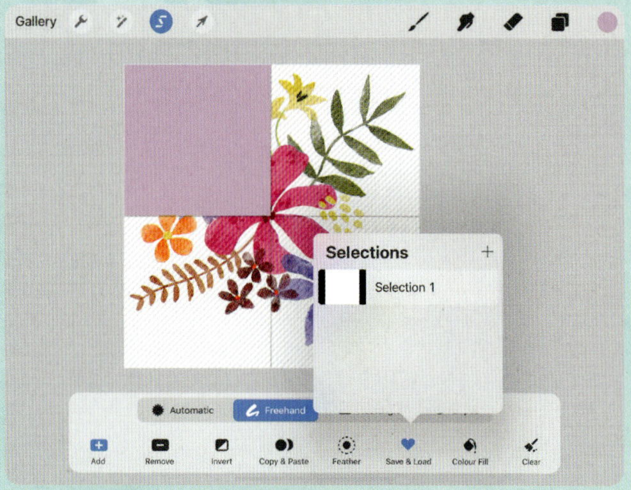

Saving Selection 1 – top-left quarter

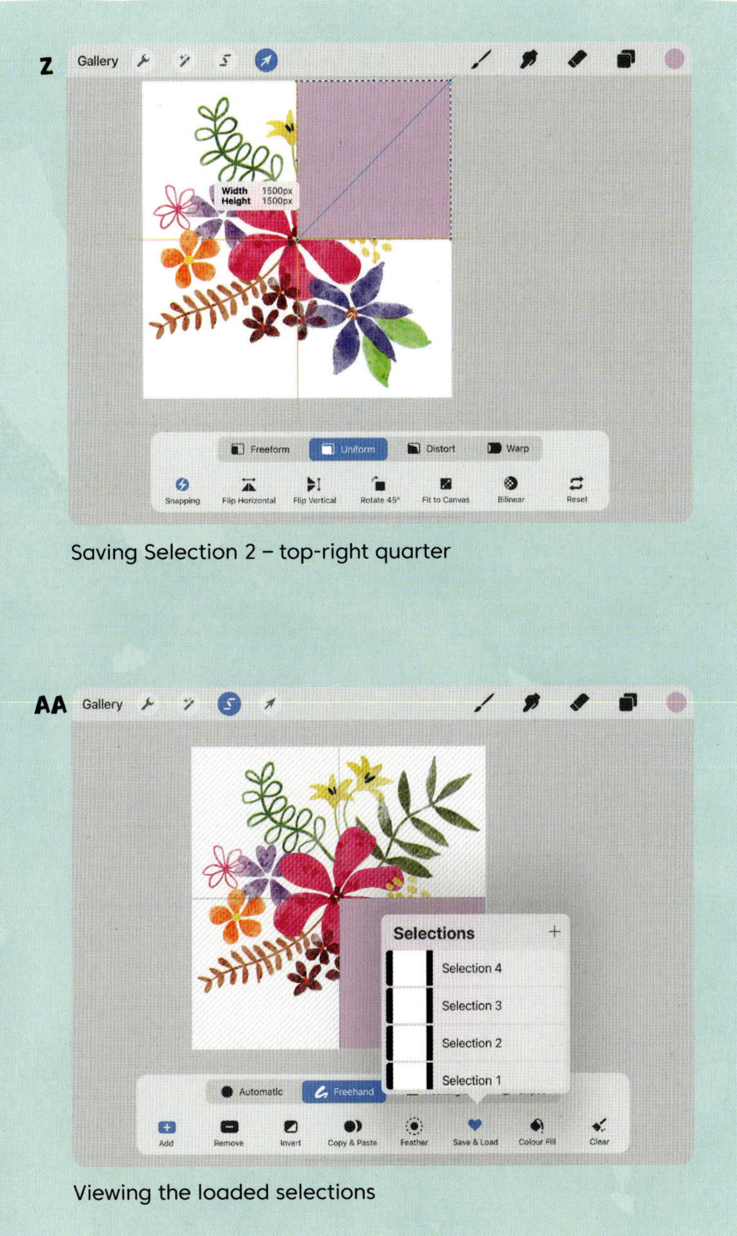

Saving Selection 2 – top-right quarter

Viewing the loaded selections

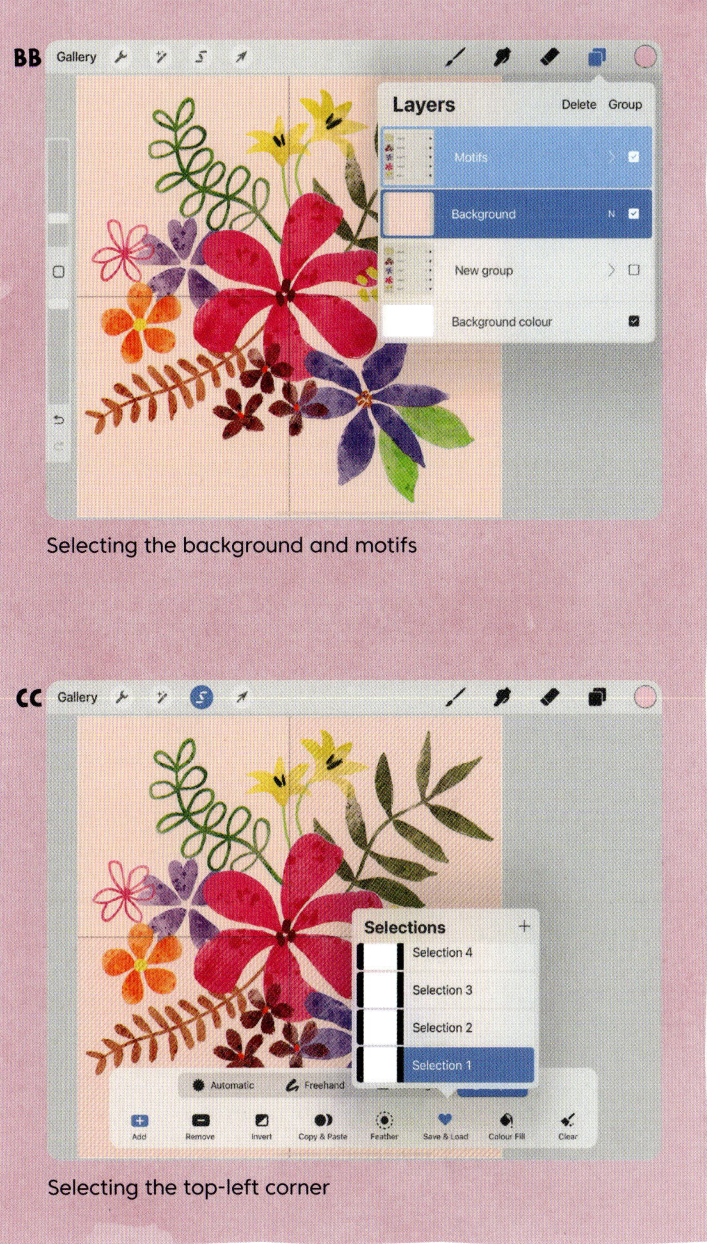

Selecting the background and motifs

Selecting the top-left corner

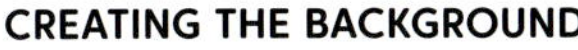

CREATING THE BACKGROUND

We do, however, need a background layer filled with colour to make this part of the process work. If you prefer your design on white, just make a new layer underneath your grouped motifs and fill it with white. You can of course try out some different colours, I'm choosing a pale but warm peachy pink colour.

KEEP YOUR TEMPLATE

Save a copy of this canvas with just a background layer, you can use it as a template for all future full drop repeat designs as the loaded selections will be permanently saved.

SELECTING AND FLIPPING THE DESIGN

Select the background and motifs layers by swiping right on both. We'll now select that top-left quarter of the design using our pre-loaded selections (**BB**).

Tap on the Selections tool, go to Save & Load, and tap on Selection 1. The top-left quarter will be automatically selected and we can flip that shape knowing the dimensions and position are exact (**CC**).

FLIPPING THE FOUR SECTIONS

With Uniform selected, tap on Transform. Tap once on Flip Horizontal and once on Flip Vertical (**DD**). The middle of your design is now transformed to the outer edges of your tile.

If you've never made a repeat tile before, this may be starting to look a little crazy but stick with it, all will become clear very soon!

Tap on Selections again to apply the transformation, then tap again to repeat the process with the three remaining sections (**EE**).

Your canvas should now look something like mine.

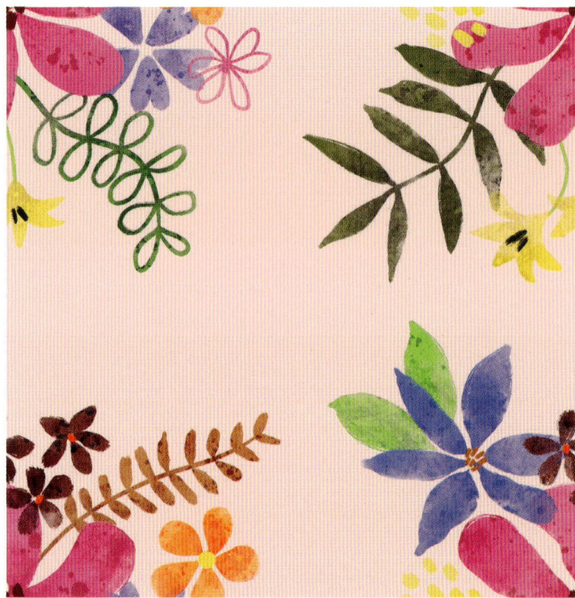

The quarters turned horizontally and vertically, ready for the space to be filled.

9. Filling the central space

As you can see, we now have a space to be filled in the middle of the design. You can draw new florals to fill this space or utilize the motifs we saved earlier on. I'm going to do a mixture of both.

USING PREVIOUS DESIGNS

Let's open the duplicate motifs group we hid earlier on. I want one of the large blooms from here so I'm going to drag and drop it above all the other layers. It's now visible above the other parts of the design (**FF**).

DD

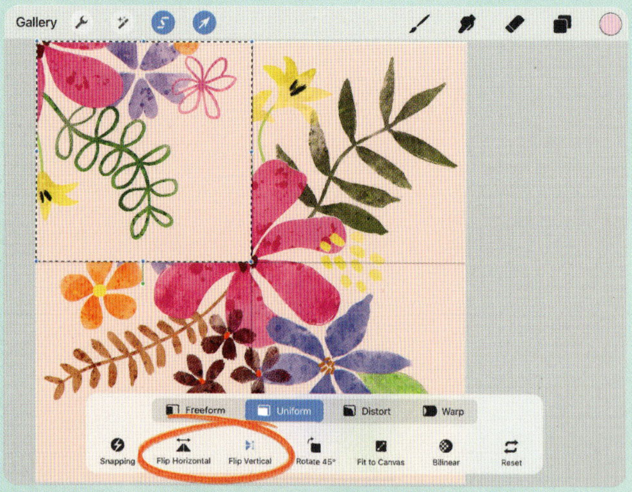

Flipping the top-left corner horizontally and vertically

EE

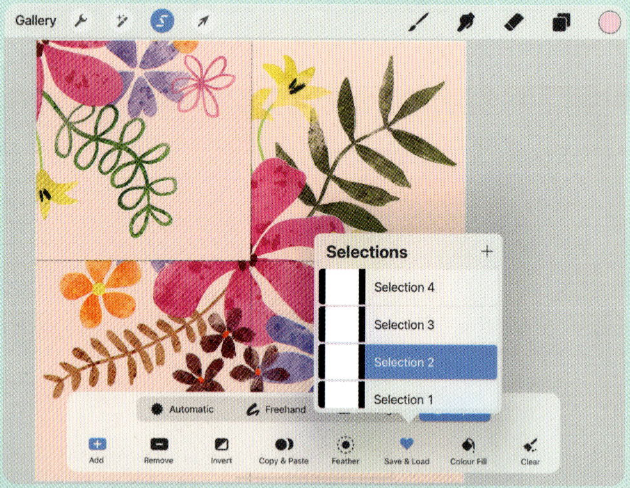

Applying the transformation

FF

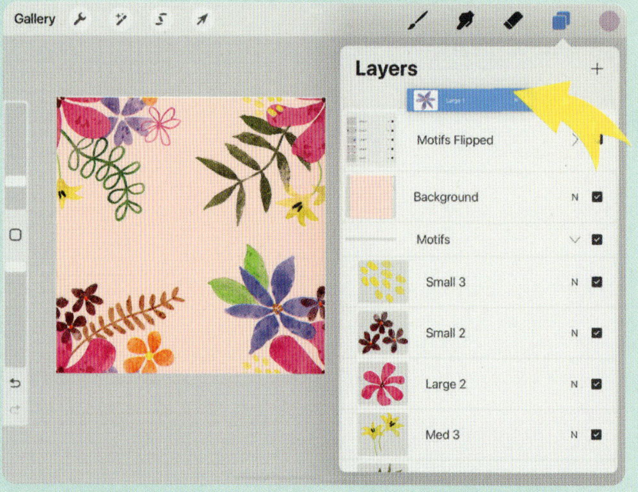

Dragging a hidden motif layer to the top

GG

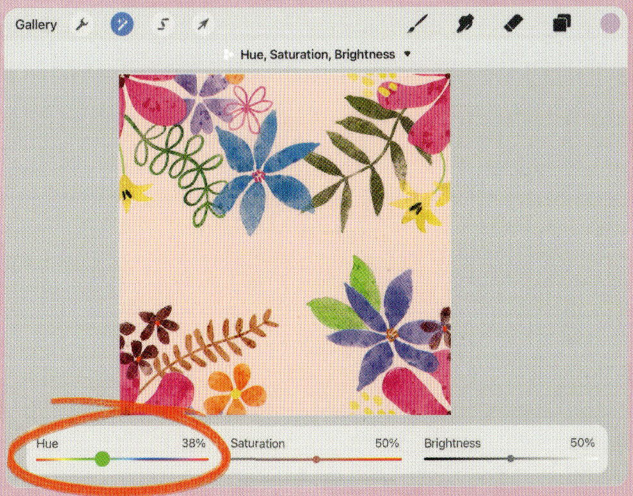

Varying the added motif

HH

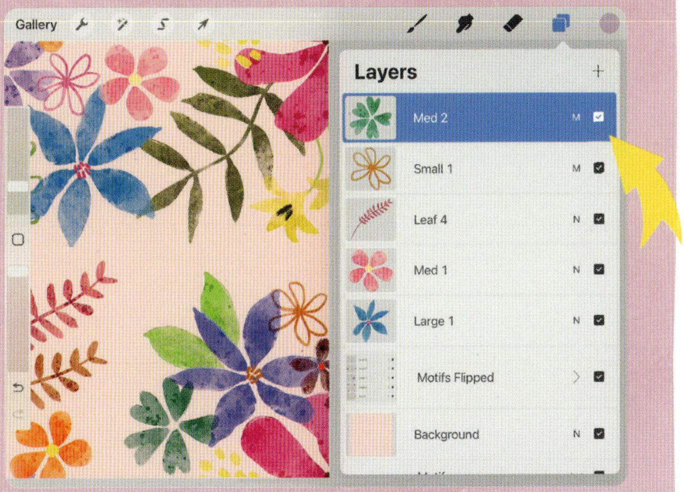

Setting some layers to Multiply

II

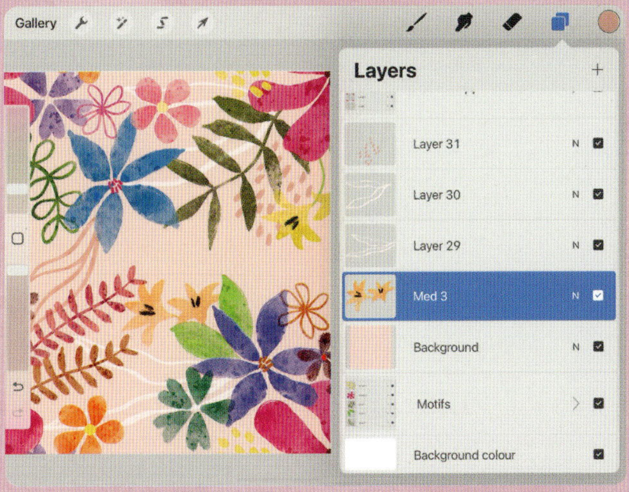

Layering more motifs

REFINING THE DESIGN

To vary the design, let's reposition and rotate the bloom, and play with the hue a little (**GG**). Turn off Snapping and Magnetics so you can position the motif more freely.

Repeat with some of the other florals, trying to make the composition natural and well balanced. Fill the spaces but be careful not to go over the edge with any parts of the motif. Everything should be contained within the canvas for this part of the design.

ADDING ORGANIC EFFECTS

Set some of the layers to Multiply to make the overlapping look more natural (HH).

You can also play with the layering. The floral elements we're using now do not need to be on top of the flipped design, we can drag them down underneath other leaves to vary the arrangement. It's also nice to have some of the more subtle motifs underneath everything else. Try using just outline shapes or dots. Experiment with mark making. This is where the magic happens (**II**)!

Once you're done adding in details, you should have something that looks like this. We can now test the repeat!

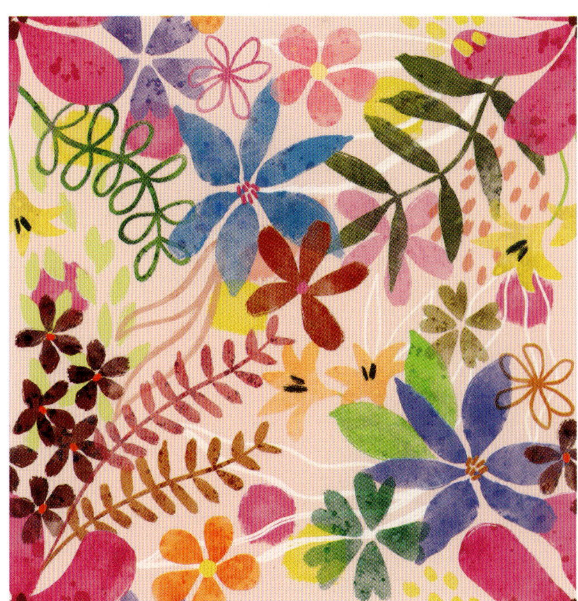

The finished tile, ready to be repeated.

10. Flattening the final design

Duplicate this finished canvas in the Gallery. Select all layers, group them and flatten the group. We're not pinching the layers together as we have multiplied layers and the effect can be altered by merging different layers. It's best just to flatten the image in one go (**JJ**).

Congratulations! You have created your pattern tile! Now let's test it to make sure there are no hairlines or errors.

11. Testing the repeat pattern

Ensure Drawing Guides are turned on and the grid is set to Max as before. Select the tile and turn Snapping and Magnetics back on. Resize the tile to fit exactly in the top-left square (**KK**).

Duplicate this layer and move a tile to each corner. As you stack the tiles together you should start to see the seamless repeat working (**LL**).

Here is my completed tile repeated four times – it all matches up. I can now save the tile and export it to upload to any site that will print fabric or wallpaper.

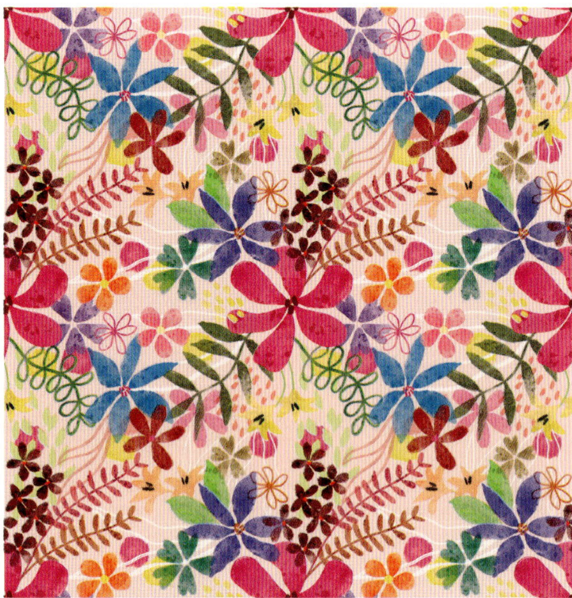

The finished tile, ready to export

PRACTICE MAKES PERFECT

If parts of your pattern are cut off in the middle or not lined up along the guides, something has gone wrong. Don't be discouraged. This used to happen to me often, and still does! Retrace your steps to discover where you went wrong. This is part of the process and unpicking your design is a great way to learn. Just keep lots of editable duplicates so you always have intact art to work with.

JJ

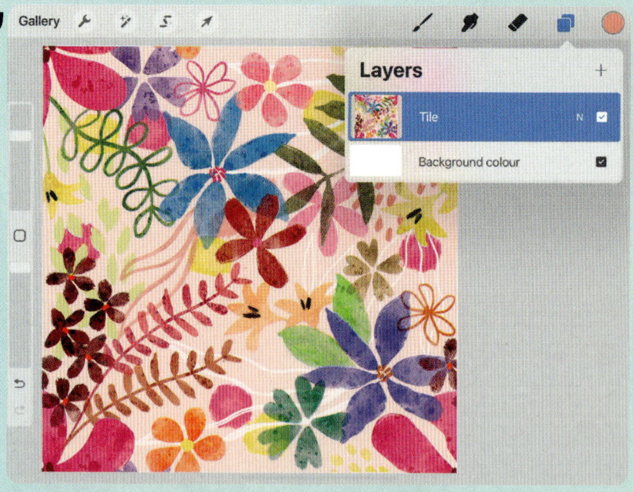

Duplicate and flatten the pattern

KK

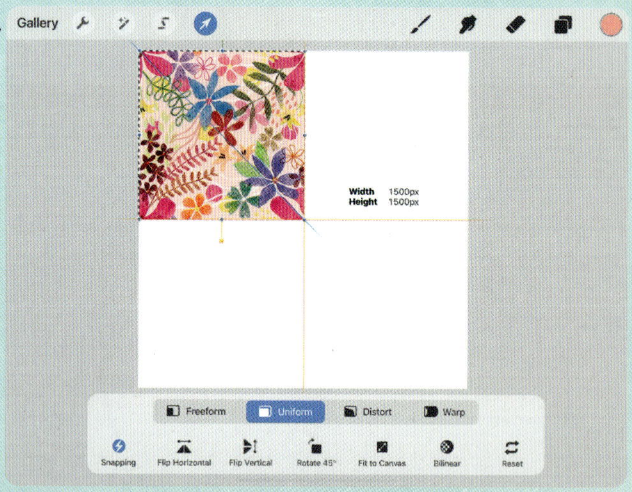

Resizing and inserting the pattern to be tiled

LL

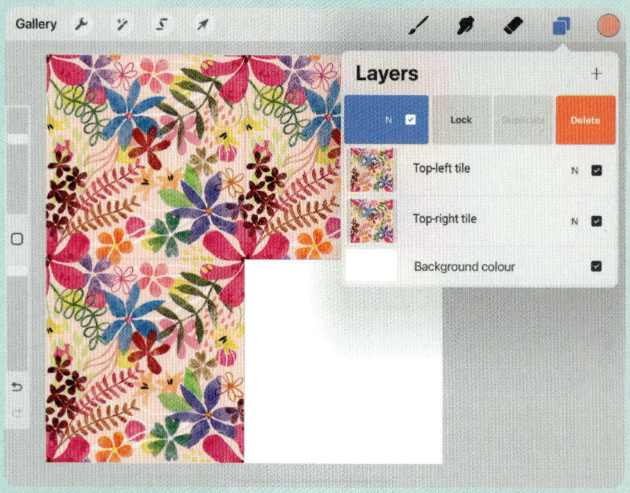

Stacking the tiles

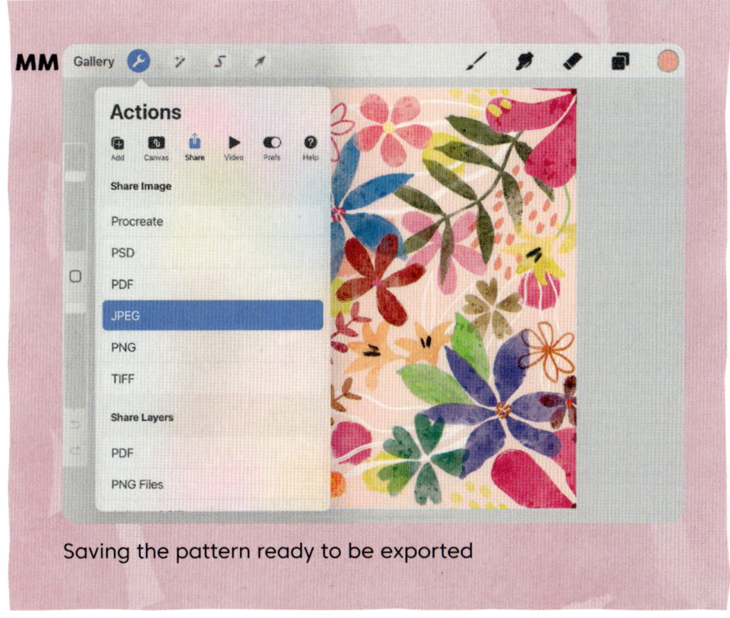

Saving the pattern ready to be exported

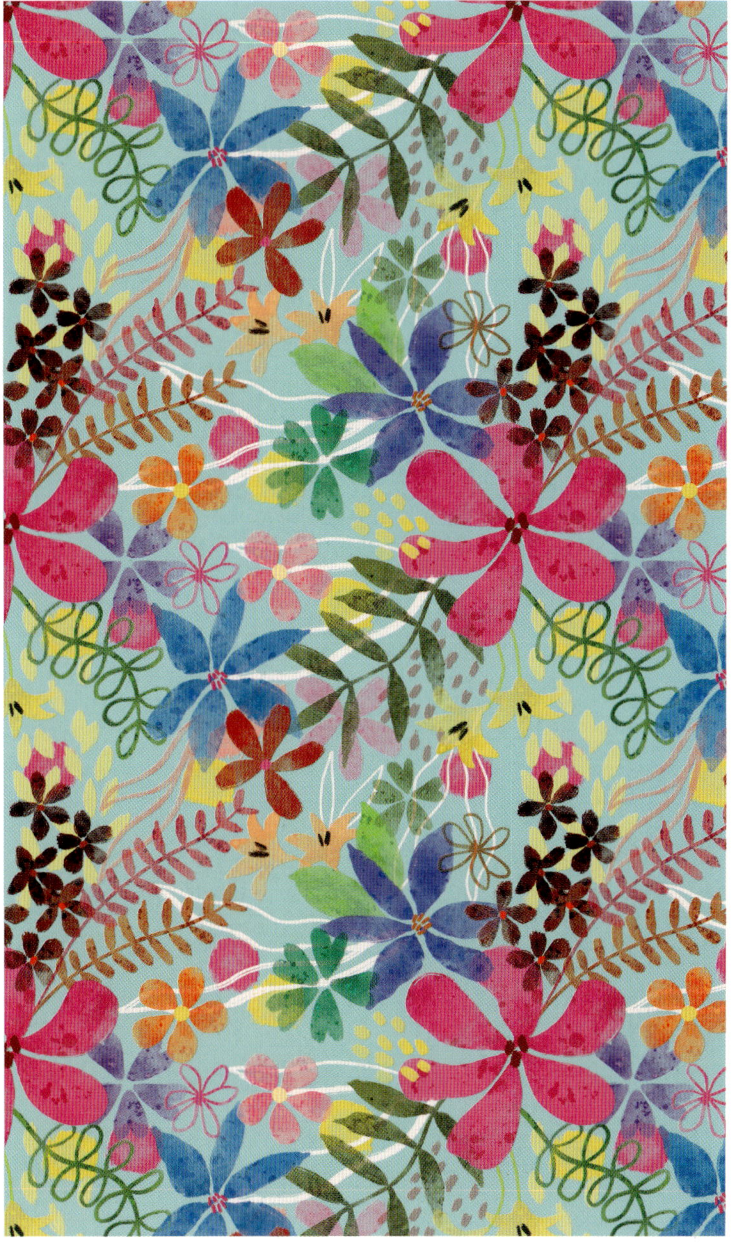

12. Exporting the pattern tile

Go back to your tile artwork canvas and export it as a JPEG. Tap on Actions, Share and select JPEG (**MM**).

Save the pattern to your files on the iPad, or AirDrop to a laptop or other device. You can also save to your Photos if that works for you. In my experience, a tile of this size – 3000px by 3000px, at 300 dpi – is more than adequate to upload to a digital printing site. Fabric-printing services such as Spoonflower usually print at 150 dpi, and will automatically resize the file you upload. Most sites have the option to print a test swatch, so it's a good idea to order something like that first to get an idea of the scale.

WHERE NEXT?

Now you know how to make seamless repeats, you'll have a lot of fun creating patterns. The options for printing on fabric and wallpaper are really varied these days. It's possible to create your own range of home decor or fashion products. Think about making collections with patterns of varying scale. Typically, you'll have a "hero" print (the main character!) with co-ordinating, simpler patterns that match or contrast. Do some research, have a trip to your local fabric store and immerse yourself in the world of surface pattern design!

BACKGROUND CHANGES

I'm going to save a copy of this tile with an alternative background colour. I've chosen a turquoise colour that makes the flowers pop!

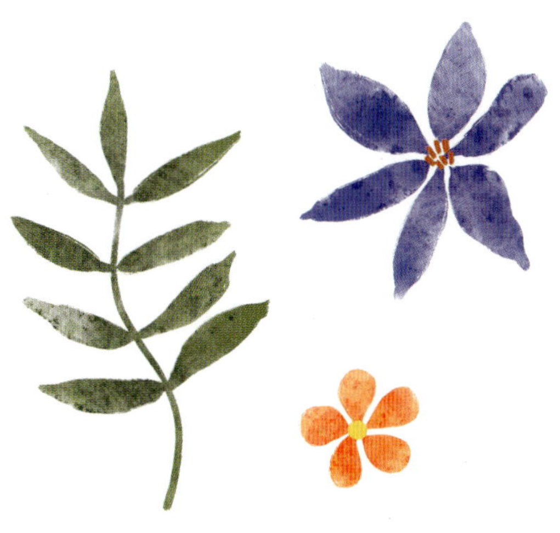

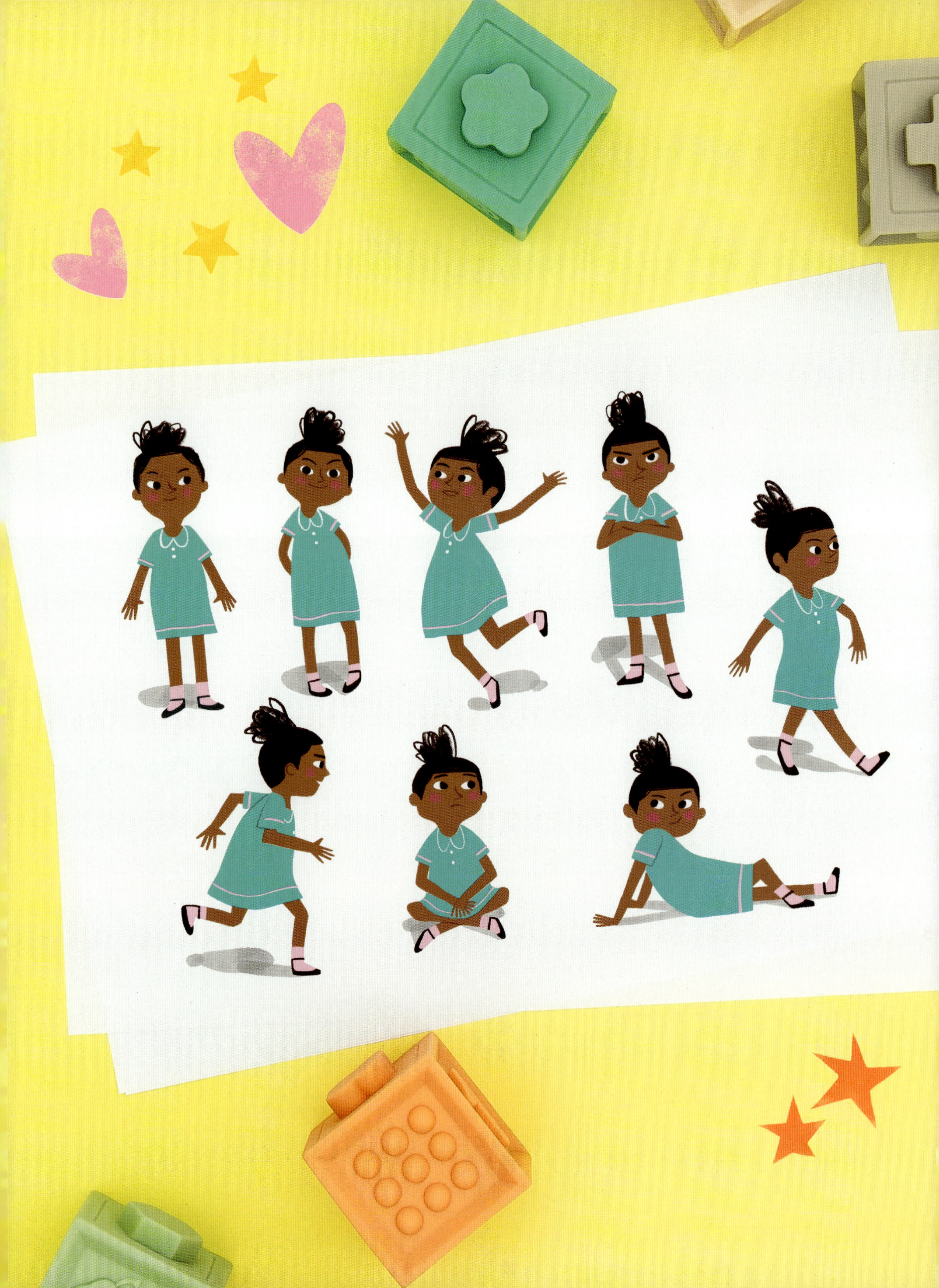

Children's Storybook Character Sheet

Creating the pictures for children's books is a dream job for most illustrators. The chance to create magical worlds and populate the pages with a cast of engaging characters is definitely one of the perks of the job! It is also one of the most difficult areas to break into and requires a lot of skill, time and patience.

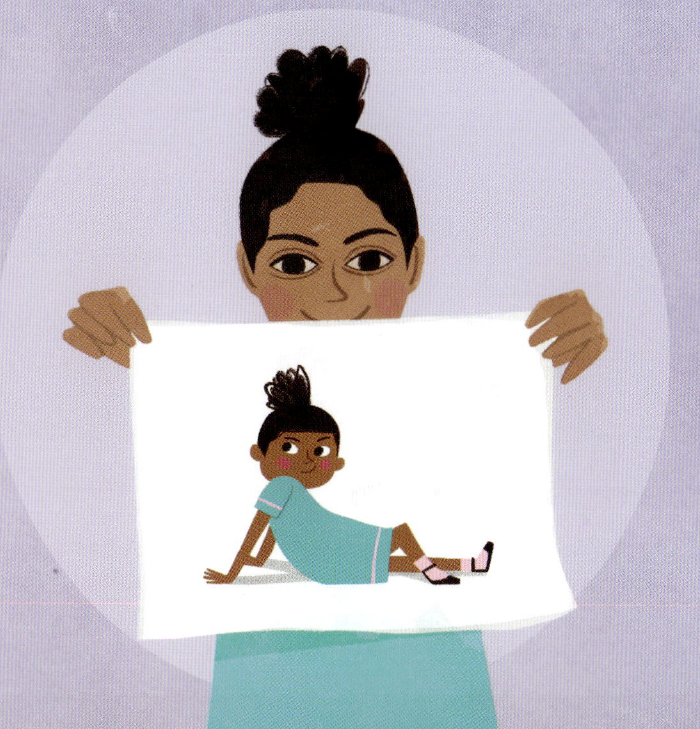

Identifying Your Audience

Creating a children's character typically involves observation, sketching and drawing from life. Being able to capture the movements and emotions of a child or childlike character is key, and most of the picture books you love will have been made by experienced and talented people who have worked in the field for years.

Children's books must be appealing to both the adults who are buying and reading them, and the children who are listening and looking at the pictures. The key to this balance is, of course, a good story that can be read aloud but also brought to life by lively and captivating illustrations.

Central to the artwork will be, in most cases, an adorable character. Someone or something that the child can relate to. Character design is actually quite a complex subject and there are many ways to approach this kind of project.

With all that in mind, here are some fun and easy ways to get started creating a lovable character or two. Have fun with these shortcuts – they will kickstart your imagination and help you on your illustration journey.

1. Researching the market

Have a look at some of your favourite children's books either from your own collection or take a trip to the local bookstore. Flick through the pages and study the characters for a while. Think about what makes them appealing, and jot down a list of what you think makes them successful, such as:

- Are the characters lovable or mischievous?
- How does the illustrator capture movement?
- How does the illustrator convey emotion?

2. Choosing the palette

Let's create a new A4-sized canvas at 300dpi. To get us started, we'll make a palette for a diverse range of skin tones. I searched online and saved this copyright-free photo to the photo album on my iPad (**A**). I used this with the New From Photo feature to give me an instant selection of natural colours to choose from (**B**). We can refine and edit these colours as we go along.

3. Creating the basic shapes

Next we need a light brush to create quick face shapes on the page. Since we're going to be drawing children, let's choose a medium that children might use themselves! Select the Soft Pastel from the Sketching section of the Brush Library and start to lightly sketch out some face shapes.

Try different shapes and colours. Don't worry about precision – we can go back in later and tidy the shapes. Fill the page with face shapes. Draw from your memory and imagination to create variety. Try to be childlike in the way you draw these shapes They can all be on the same layer for now, so leave a little space between each one so we've got room to add hair. You should now have something that looks like my layout.

A page of face shapes on a single layer.

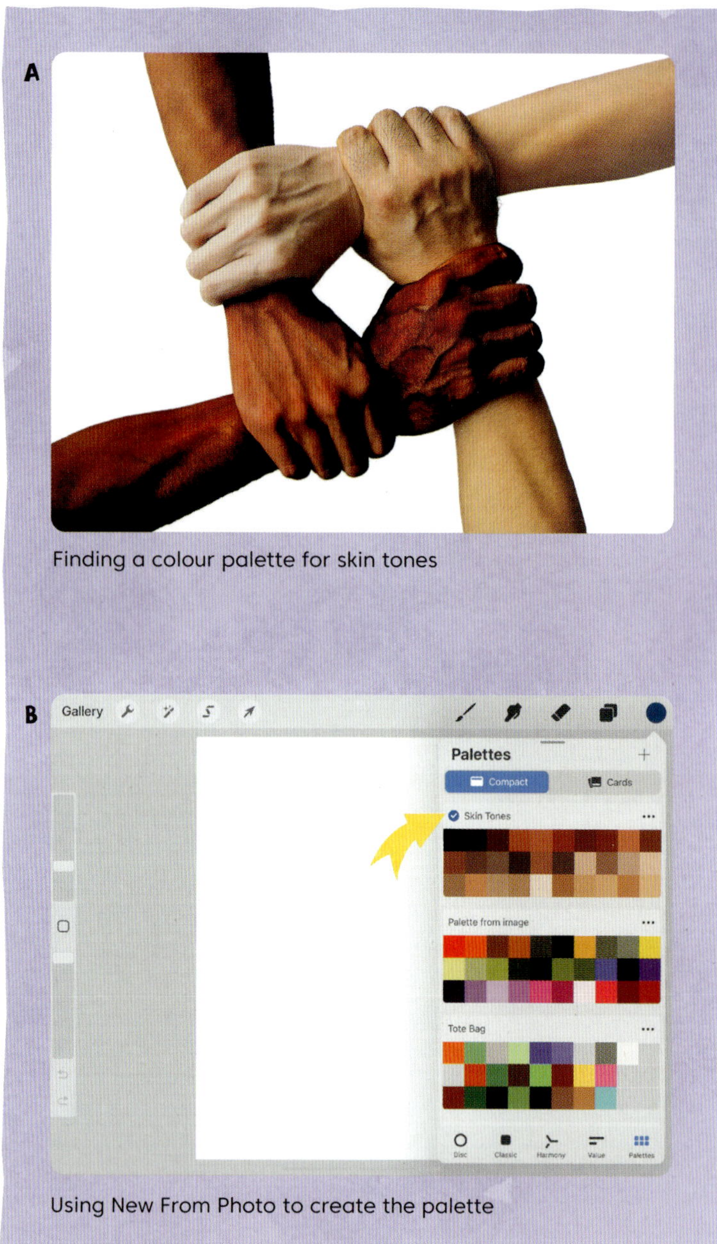

Finding a colour palette for skin tones

Using New From Photo to create the palette

4. Adding hair and noses

Let's start adding features, creating one feature at a time rather than one character. Working like this can help you try different approaches – you are forced to think of twelve different ways to draw a nose! if you finish one face completely, it will influence the way you draw the others.

ADDING HAIR

We'll add some hair first. It's fine to look at references, but don't get bogged down in details. I'm going to use the 6B Pencil tilted to the side to get the same effect as shading with a real pencil. You might want to add a layer behind the head shapes to add longer hair at the back of the head.

ADDING NOSES

Next up – noses! On a new layer, I'm adding a tiny, cute nose to each face. Sometimes it is just a line – experiment with different shapes. You can really start to see the characters forming now.

INSTANT CONNECTION

You'll be amazed at how much character you can create with just a few simple lines and dots. A perfect example of more being less!

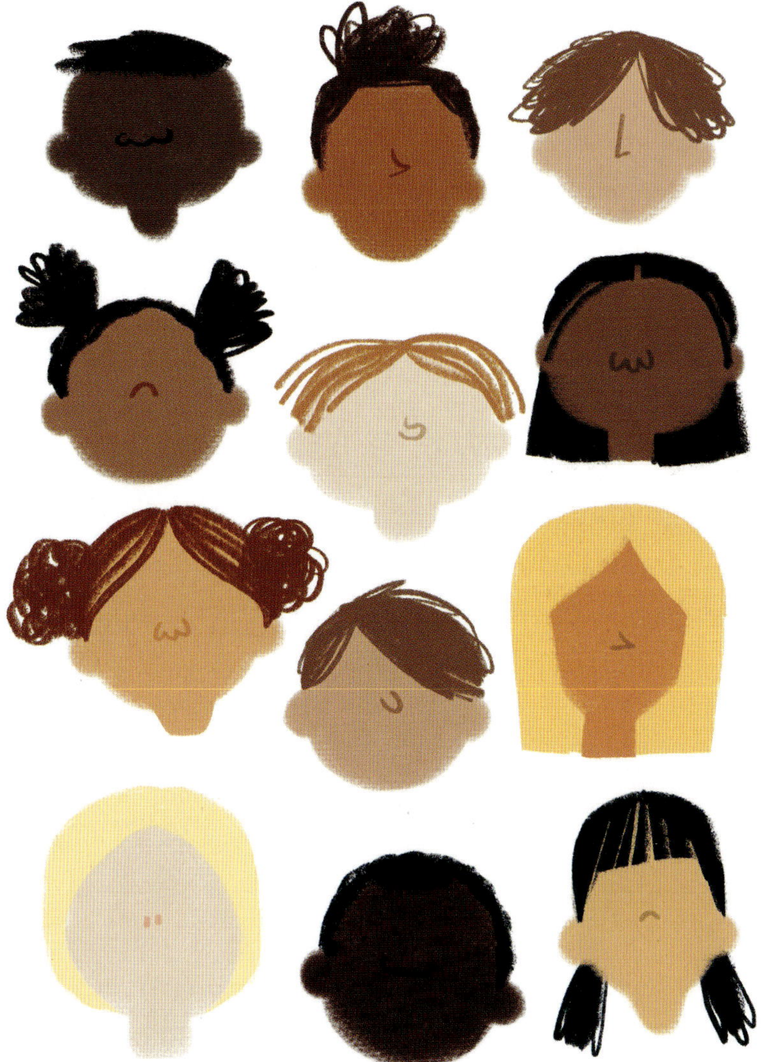

Even at this early stage, there is already so much variety between the characters!

5. Adding eyes, mouths and cheeks

Now that we have the central point of the nose, let's move on to the other features.

ADDING EYES

Create a new layer for eyes. There are so many ways to draw a character's eyes! Try different shapes and styles, but keep it simple for now. Create a dot, put white behind it, and change the shape for each character. Remember, we're playing, creating something that kids will love. The position of the eyes also makes a big difference. Try them wide apart then close together, looking up then to the side. Where are the eyes in relation to the ears and the nose? All these variations will not only make a difference to how your character *looks*, but also to their perceived personality and mood.

ADDING MOUTHS AND CHEEKS

Complete the face by adding another layer for the mouth, and another to add rosy cheeks to some of the characters (**C**). Looking at the completed faces, I can now see where I need to refine the shapes a bit. You can do this by erasing with the 6B Pencil. I've also redrawn some of the ears. Just use the 6B Pencil and try not to overwork anything. We want to keep the faces looking spontaneous and fresh!

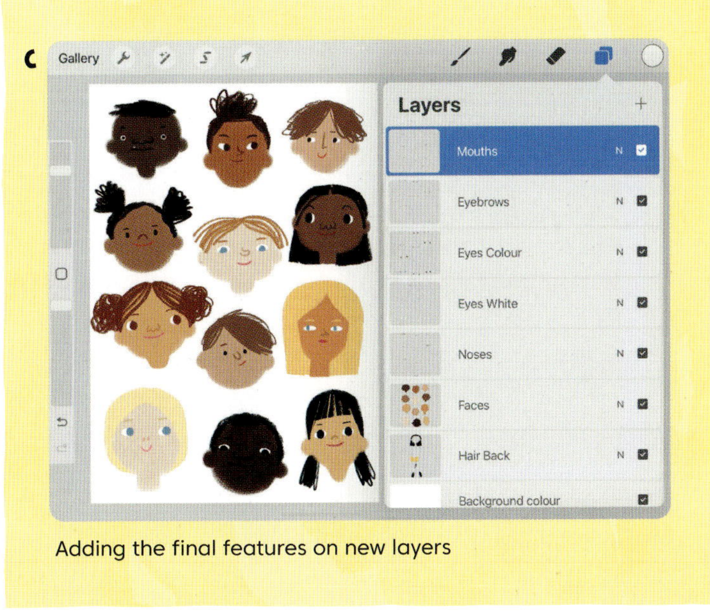

Adding the final features on new layers

6. Taking characters forward

Sit back and look at the faces you've created. If you've followed along, you'll have about twelve characters on your page waiting for their next stage of development.

CHOOSING TWO CHARACTERS TO DEVELOP

Pick your two favourites, the ones with lots of instant character and appeal. Give them a name, an age and a bit of a backstory. Jot this down, or keep a few made up facts in mind for the rest of this project.

MANAGING THE LAYERS

Duplicate the canvas and open the duplicate. We need to extract our favourite faces along with all the features. We'll keep everything on its own layer so that it's all editable – a bit time consuming but good practice!

When I need to repeatedly select a specific area of my artwork, I save a selection to make it quicker and easier to work with multiple layers. Follow along to ensure all our features are on separate layers, in the right order.

1. First, I'll roughly select my first chosen face with the Freehand Selection tool. Take care not to select parts of any other face.
2. Tap on Save & Load, then tap + to save the selection. You'll see a preview of the selected white-on-black space (**D**).
3. Select the faces layer, swipe down with three fingers to bring up the Copy & Paste menu and select Cut & Paste (**E**). You'll now find your selected head shape on its own separate layer (**F**).

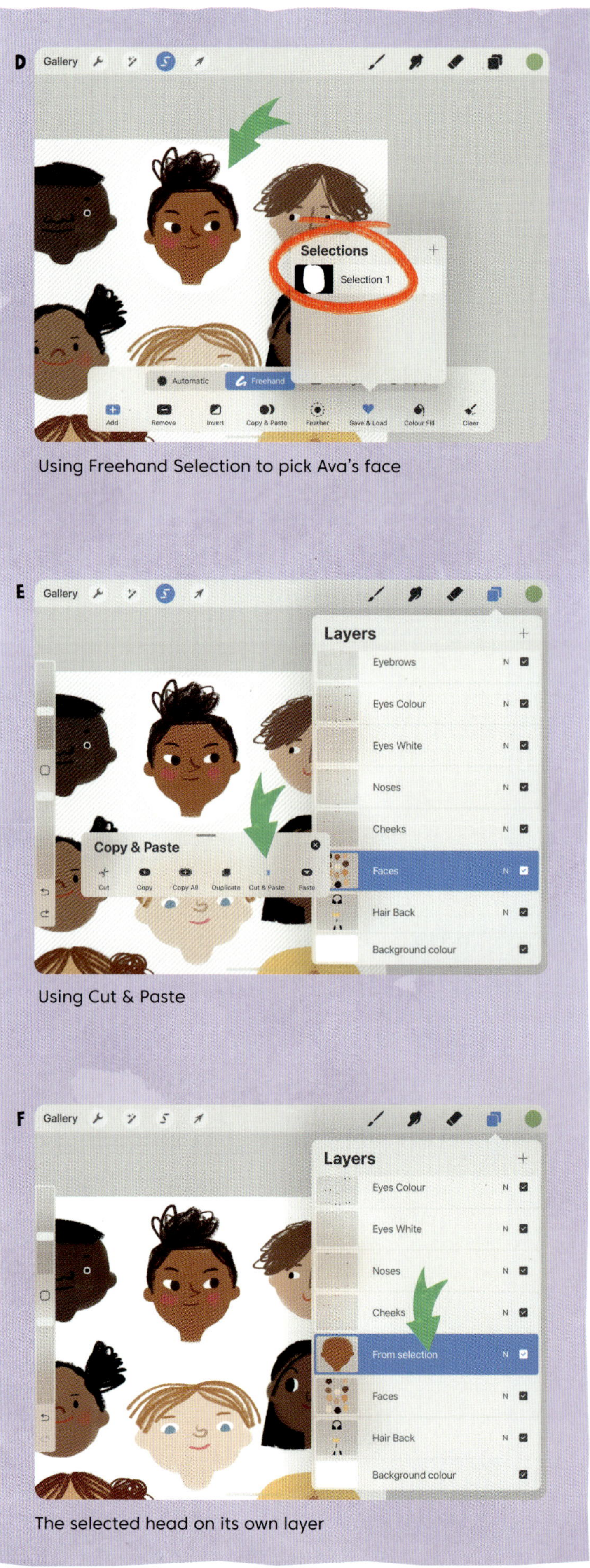

Using Freehand Selection to pick Ava's face

Using Cut & Paste

The selected head on its own layer

G

Pasting the character's features onto their own layers

H

Grouping the character's layers

I

Deleting the previous selection after starting again

7. Establishing a workflow

Return to the Selections menu – our selection is already saved so just tap on Save & Load, tap on the selection, then choose the next layer we need to extract from.

WORKING ON THE FIRST FACE

The first face I've chosen has rosy cheeks, so I'm going to cut and paste from this layer. It may help to hide the layers as you go along so you can see where you're at. The only face to stay intact will be the one you're working on (**G**).

Repeat this process until all the features have been selected, cut and pasted from the original layers.

THE WORKFLOW IS AS FOLLOWS:

Open the Selections menu, tap on Save & Load, select the selection, tap on Layers and select chosen layer. Swipe down with three fingers, tap Cut & Paste and hide the layer below the new pasted layer.

It seems like a lot of steps, but as you begin to work more on Procreate and understand how the app works, you'll develop your own ways of working. You'll solve problems and even find shortcuts by accident!

You can now go ahead and group all the new layers by swiping right on each one and tapping Group. Your first face and features are now organized and saved in their own group (**H**). I'm also going to hide the new group to avoid confusion when repeating the process.

WORKING ON THE SECOND FACE

We can now unhide the original layers and follow the same steps to extract our second face. When you save and load the next selection, you'll notice that the previous selection is still saved. You can swipe left on this and tap delete to avoid confusion (**I**).

Follow the above workflow closely. When you're done, delete the remaining faces and features to leave you with the two separate characters. Move them side by side to see how they look together. I think these two are going to be friends!

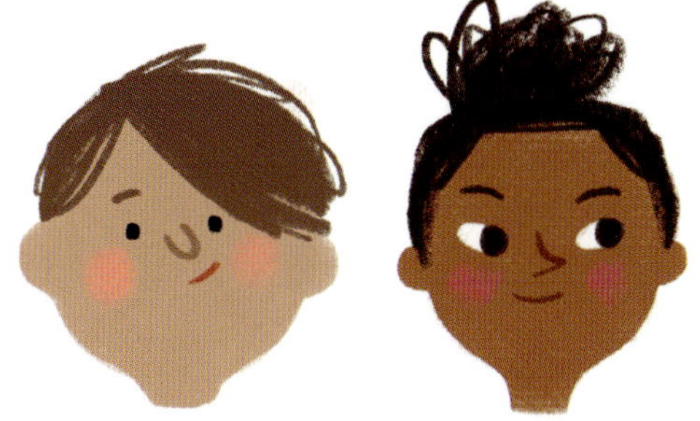

The selected characters, Frank and Ava, looking fun and mischievous!

8. Creating the bodies

We now have our heads so let's use them to construct a skeleton for our body shapes.

1. Make a new layer above the first head. We're going to sketch an upside-down bean shape following the size of the head (stay with me, I promise this will work out!). I've lowered the opacity of the head to show the sketched shape more clearly (**J**).
2. Once you have created the shape, flip it vertically, move it below the head and place at the neck to create a body shape (**K**).
3. On a separate layer, draw two lines a little longer than the body – these will be the guide for the legs. On another new layer, draw two lines the same length as the body – these will be the arms (**L**).
4. Using the Selections and Transform tools, place the arms and legs in position. You can rotate and move each line until you're happy. I also like to add a little circle or mark to indicate where the hands, elbows, knees and feet will be (**M**).
5. We now have a simple skeleton on which to build our body. Merge the skeleton layers together and lower the opacity. Take the 6B Pencil, select the skin colour and trace a body shape round the skeleton (**N**). Remember, we're drawing children so things like hands and feet can be small and dainty. I usually go in with the eraser to refine the fingers and feet.

KNOW YOUR RATIOS

To create a young looking character (3–5 years old) the head to body ratio should be about 1:3 or 1:4. For comparison, an adult's head to body ratio should be about 1:7 or 1:8.

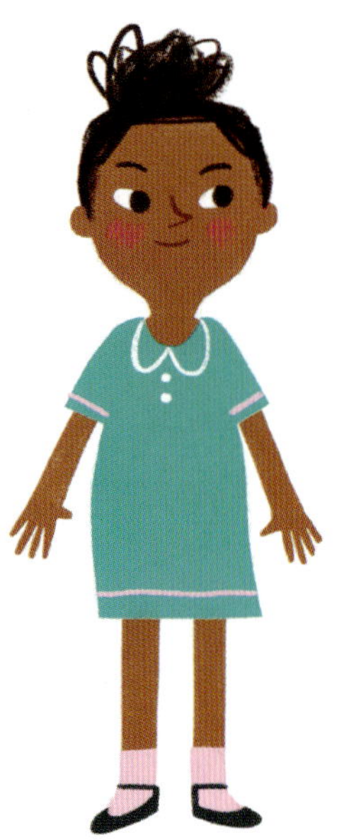

J

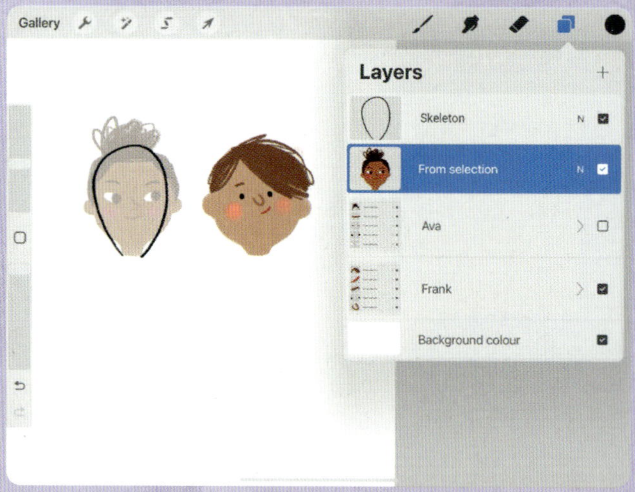

Sketching the head

K

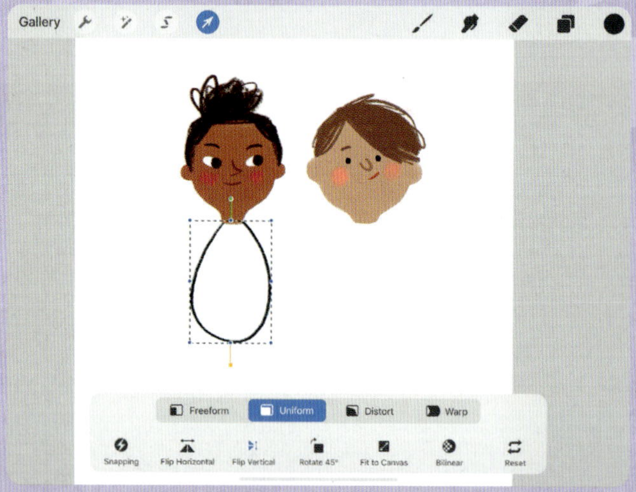

Creating the body shape

L

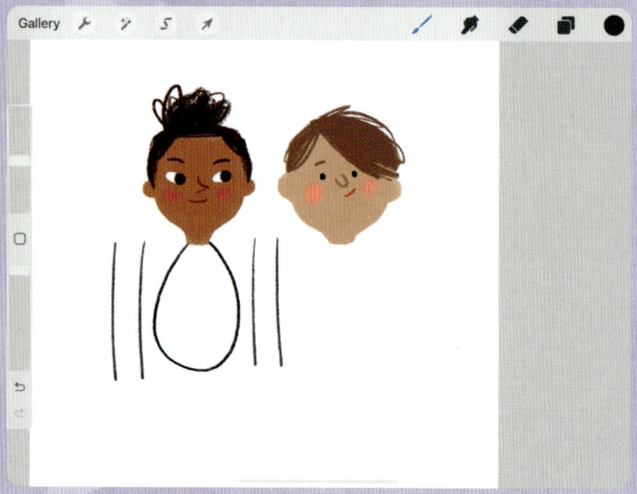

Preparing the arms and legs

M

Indicating placement of hands, elbows, knees and feet

N

Outlining the body with the 6B pencil

O

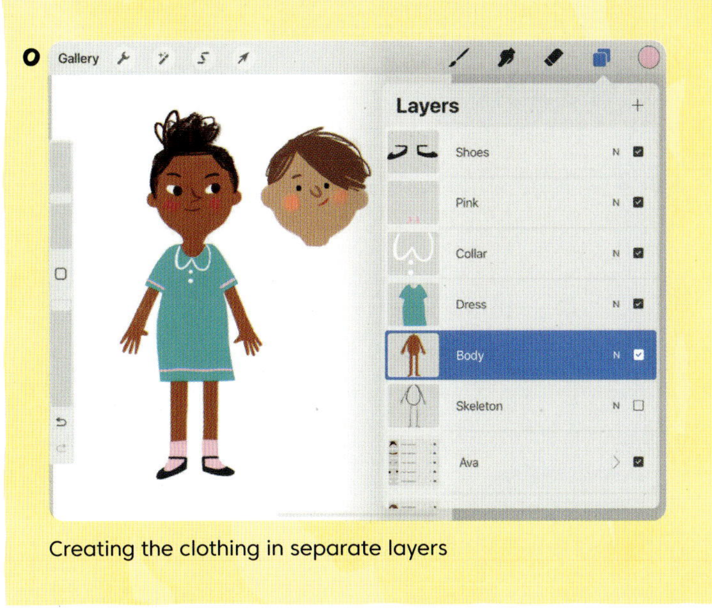

Creating the clothing in separate layers

9. Dressing your characters

It's time to dress the character – this is the fun part! Add details and try to keep everything on separate layers to make it easy to edit. I sketched and coloured the clothes using the 6B Pencil and the Soft Pastel. However, if you want to experiment with different brushes, go ahead! Hide the skeleton layer then group the layers together, not forgetting the head.

Congratulations, you have created a children's book character (**O**)!

Repeat the process for your second character.

PLAY WITH SCALE

You can afford to play with scale a little bit when creating young characters. Make their eyes bigger and their noses small and cute. They may have shorter legs and bigger heads with no neck. Play around with the shapes, keeping them soft and gentle.

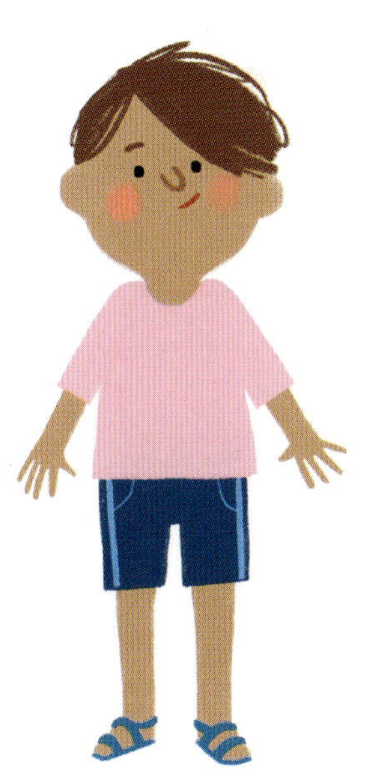

10. Bringing the characters to life

Our characters are looking great. I'm happy with the proportions, but they look a little stiff! Let's try now to bring them to life with different poses and expressions. I'm going to work on my first character, so I'll delete the other from this canvas for now to give me more room.

CREATING THE BASIC REFERENCE

I want to start by sketching out more skeletons using the original for reference, and also sketch the head shape. So let's flatten the layers for the head and lower the opacity a little. Find the skeleton layer and hide everything else (**P**). I'm going to sketch in a rough head shape for now – we'll be exploring movement in the body, so the position of the head and features will change along with it.

Now restore the opacity of the head, unhide the other layers and drag the skeleton sketch out of the group. Flatten the group and move the skeleton to the side. We now have a reference for the proportions, colours and features of our character.

PREPARING THE PALETTE AND CANVAS

Before we start to develop these character sketches I want to do two things: create a quick custom palette from the original, and resize the canvas so we have more room to work.

First, tap on Palettes, tap the + sign and select Create New Palette (**Q**). Pick the colours from the original by holding one finger on the drawing until the magnified circle takes on the colour and it appears in the top right-hand corner.

When cropping or resizing the canvas, move everything to the top left-hand corner so that no parts of your drawing are lost. I just want to increase the width of the canvas, not the height, so everything should be safe. Tap on the wrench icon and select Crop & Resize (**R**). Double the value in the first box and keep everything else the same (**S**). Tap Done to return to the canvas. I'm also reducing the size of the drawings a little bit to give us more room to work.

DON'T FORGET YOUR BACKUPS

Keep multiple copies of your artwork so you can go back in and find layers you may want to edit later on.

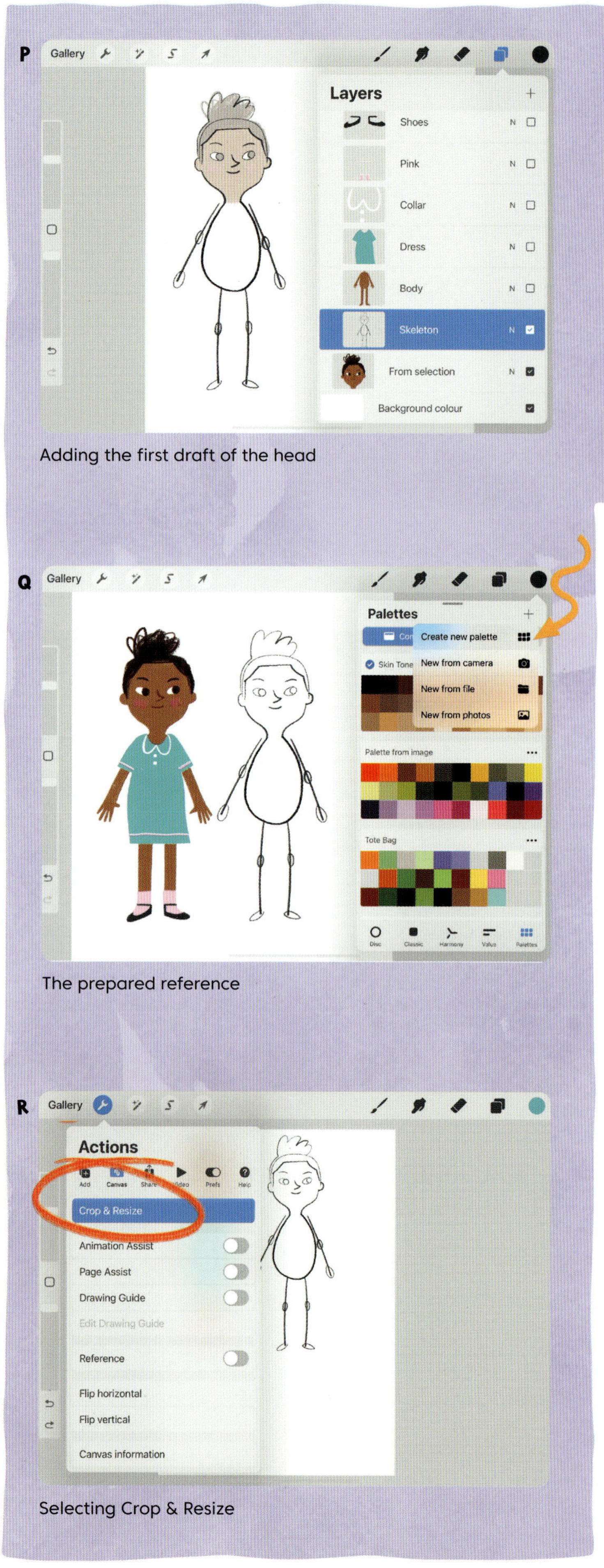

Adding the first draft of the head

The prepared reference

Selecting Crop & Resize

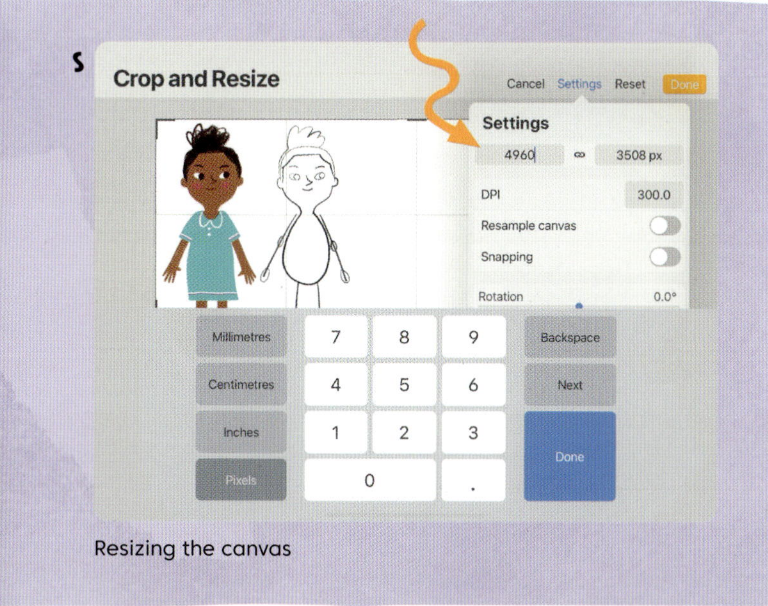

Resizing the canvas

11. Developing poses

We'll need references – as mentioned before, observation and drawing from life are essential for building up your illustration portfolio, and I encourage you to do that wherever possible. If you have work in your sketchbook, maybe you can use that for reference here. If not, you can search for images online to help.

SOURCING REFERENCES

We want to bring this character to life, making them walk, run, jump and sit. We'll also add emotions. Spend no longer than ten minutes finding reference photos. Try not to look at the work of other artists – your characters should be as original and true to your style as possible.

SKETCHING POSES

With the references, sketch quick skeleton poses. Keep the strokes light and spontaneous. Think about the body in motion and don't forget gravity. If your characters are still, they need to be firmly planted on the ground!

CREATING MOVEMENT

When you have a few poses you're happy with, start building up the body and clothing, referring to your original drawing. Keep in mind the three-dimensional forms of the body, but don't get hung up on having everything anatomically correct. Bring the spontaneity of the sketches into the finished poses and expressions.

You'll enjoy this part of the project and that will show in your work. Put on some music or a favourite podcast. Try to relax and bring a light touch to the drawings!

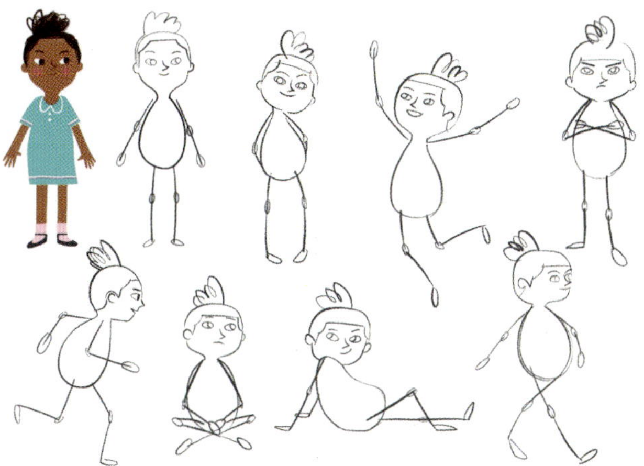
Sketching poses and movement using skeleton shapes.

11. Final presentation

Arrange the characters on the page with space around them – you can add a shadow underneath with a watercolour-type brush to add dimension. To develop these characters further, add shading and highlights to the skin tones and clothing, and even consider texture and pattern. This is something you can explore yourself.

You still have another character to develop, so go back to that when you're ready and have a play around!

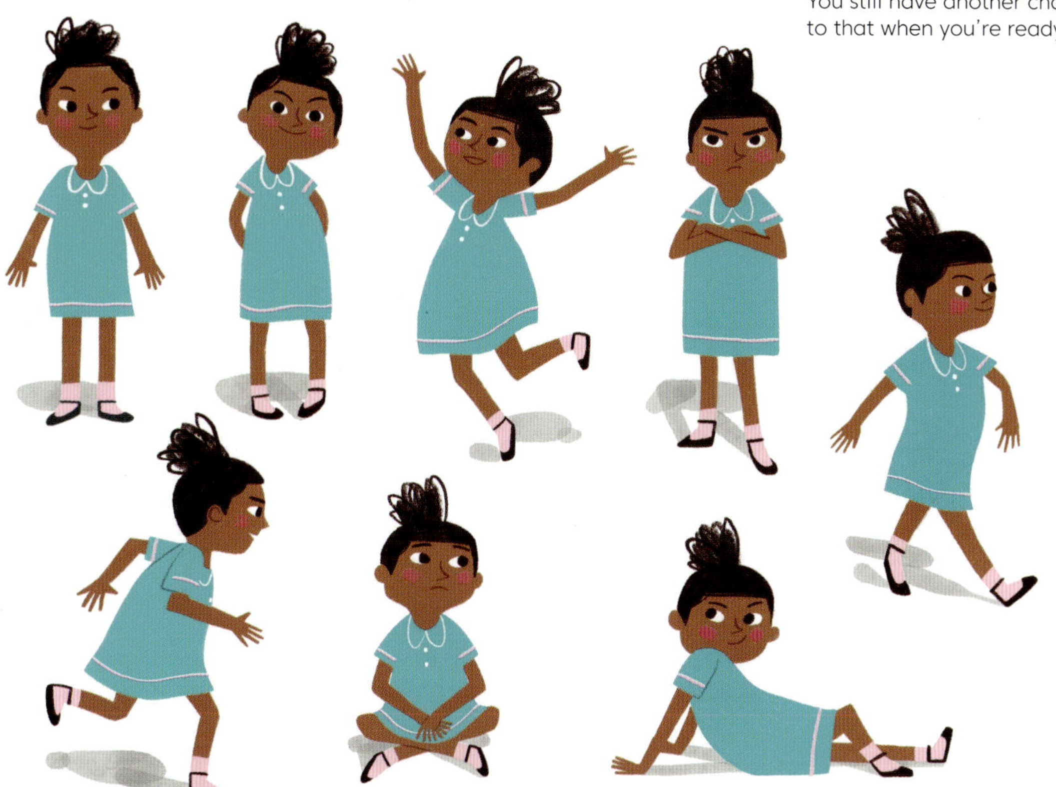
The final presentation of Ava, including anchoring shadows.

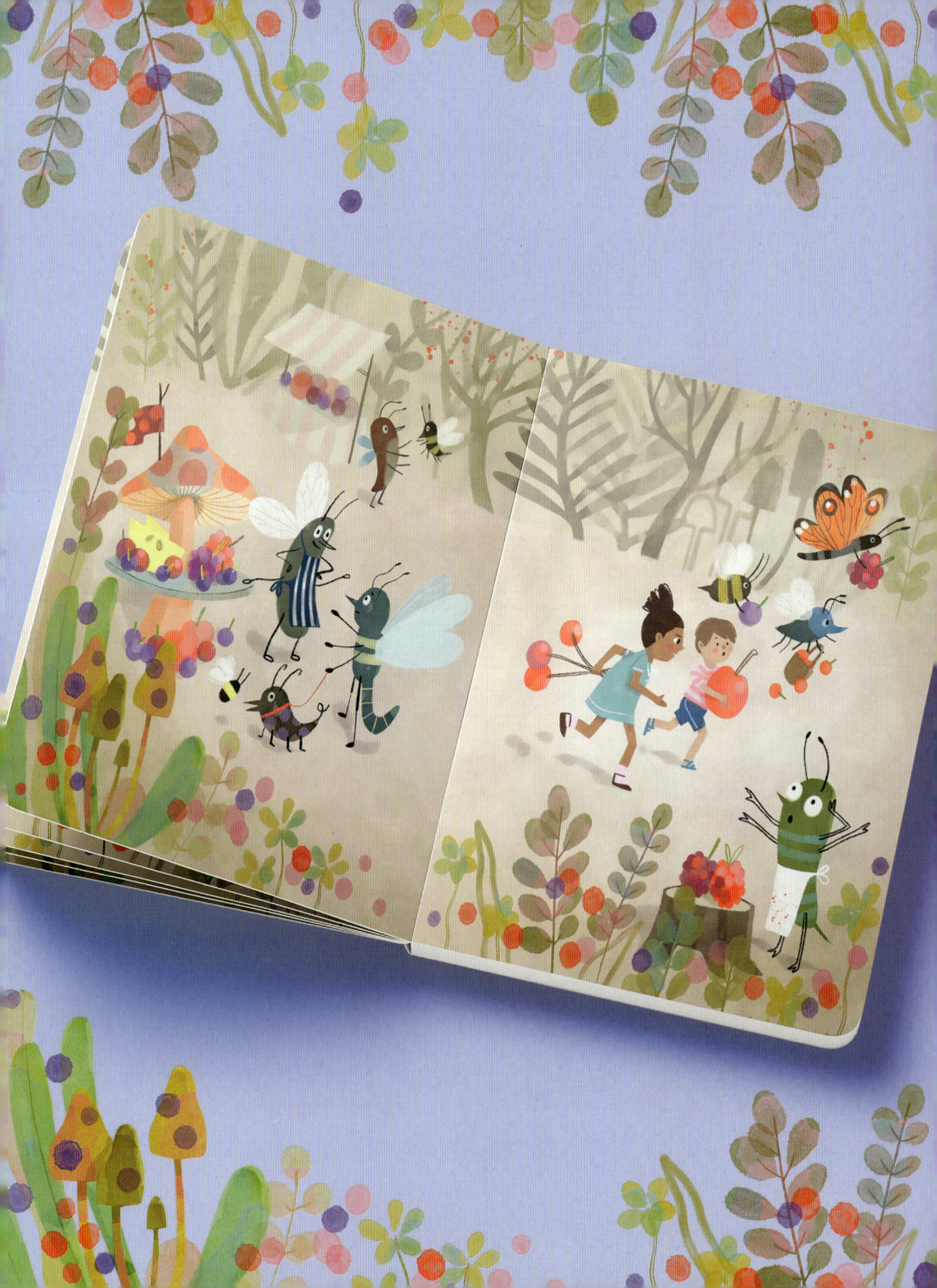

Children's Storybook Scene

By now you should have one or two fun characters in your gallery. However, at the moment, they are running, jumping, playing and generally looking for mischief on the white space of the canvas. Don't you think it might be fun to create a world for them? It won't be long before you've created a scene that really brings them to life!

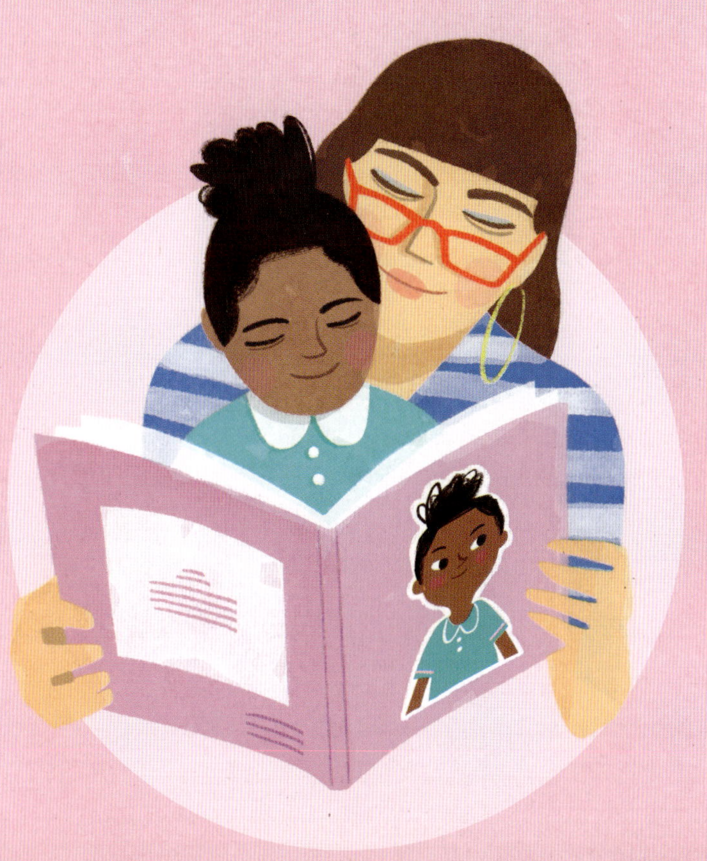

Setting the Scene

In this project, you'll use everything you have learnt so far to create a fun place for your characters to inhabit and interact with other characters. Let's imagine we're creating two pages – a double page spread – for a children's picture book. Another great piece for your portfolio!

A busy market scene gives us lots of scope to get creative. The illustration will be complex, and starting a project like this may be daunting for beginners and experienced illustrators alike. That is why we're going to break it up into bite-size pieces and treat each section as a problem solving exercise.

1. Understanding the workflow

We'll work through the project one stage at a time:

- Our prepared canvas will be a double page spread with a bleed and margin. This allows us to make sure the important elements of our illustration are not cropped off or too close to the edge of the page.
- We'll then brainstorm and think about the theme and content of our illustration. What elements do we want to include, and how can we make our illustration lively and amusing? We'll sketch some of the elements and start to look at how the scene will be laid out. Is there a focal point? Does the illustration lead the reader's eye through the scene?
- Once our scene is sketched, we'll choose a colour palette and block in the main shapes, thinking about light and shade as we go.
- Lastly, we'll add some line, texture and detail to bring the artwork to life.

You can follow along with the same theme or you can use the workflow of this project to create your own original artwork.

2. The anatomy of our template

Picture books come in lots of different formats, so if you're working with a publisher or art director, they will specify exactly what size of canvas to use. Most print publishers will give you the dimensions using metric measurements, hence the use of centimetres here.

Let's start by setting up the double page spread (DPS) template with guidelines to help us with the layout of the illustration. In this project, our book page is 23cm wide and 27cm high, so we need to double the width to create the DPS. We'll then create guides for a bleed and safe-space.

A quick guide to the features:

- **DPS:** Page area created by two pages facing each other when the book is open, separated by the fold.
- **BLEED:** The extra space that extends beyond where the paper will be cut to avoid white edges on your printed artwork.
- **SAFE SPACE:** The area where we want to keep all the important parts of our illustration.

Procreate does not have the exact tools to set up bleed and margins so this workaround will enable us to set up a workspace that is as accurate as possible. With this in mind, let's go ahead and set up our canvas.

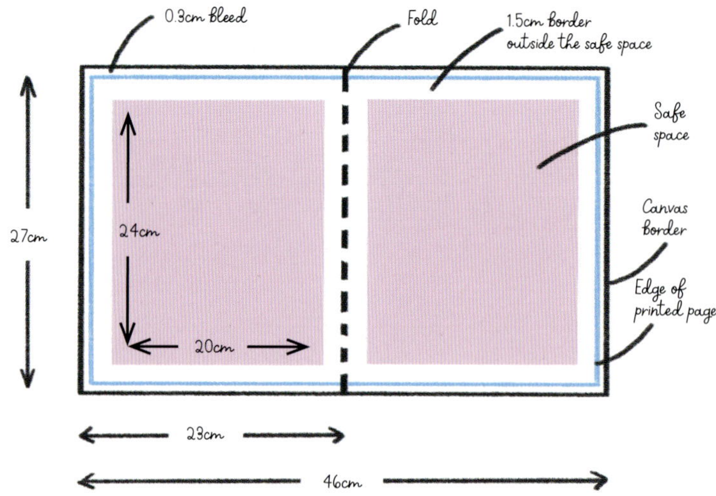

The template will ensure none of the detail or important parts of your illustration get lost.

3. Creating the layout template

Tap on New Canvas and add the dimensions 46cm wide and 27cm high – the total area of the printed DPS.

ADDING THE BLEED

We'll first add bleed to the spread using layers.

1. Fill Layer 1 with light blue. Then go to Canvas, and select Crop and Resize.
2. To add a bleed of 0.3cm all around, tap on Settings and add 0.6cm to the total width and the height of the canvas. A white border will appear at the bottom and right-hand side (**A**). Tap Done.
3. Tap Transform and turn on Snapping. Centre the block to give us a white border of 0.3cm around the canvas.
4. Hold two fingers on the layer to select the centred block, and tap on Invert to select the 0.3cm border. Create a new layer and fill the selected border with dark blue (**B**). Delete Layer 1, rename the bleed layer and lower the opacity. Our illustration will extend into this border.

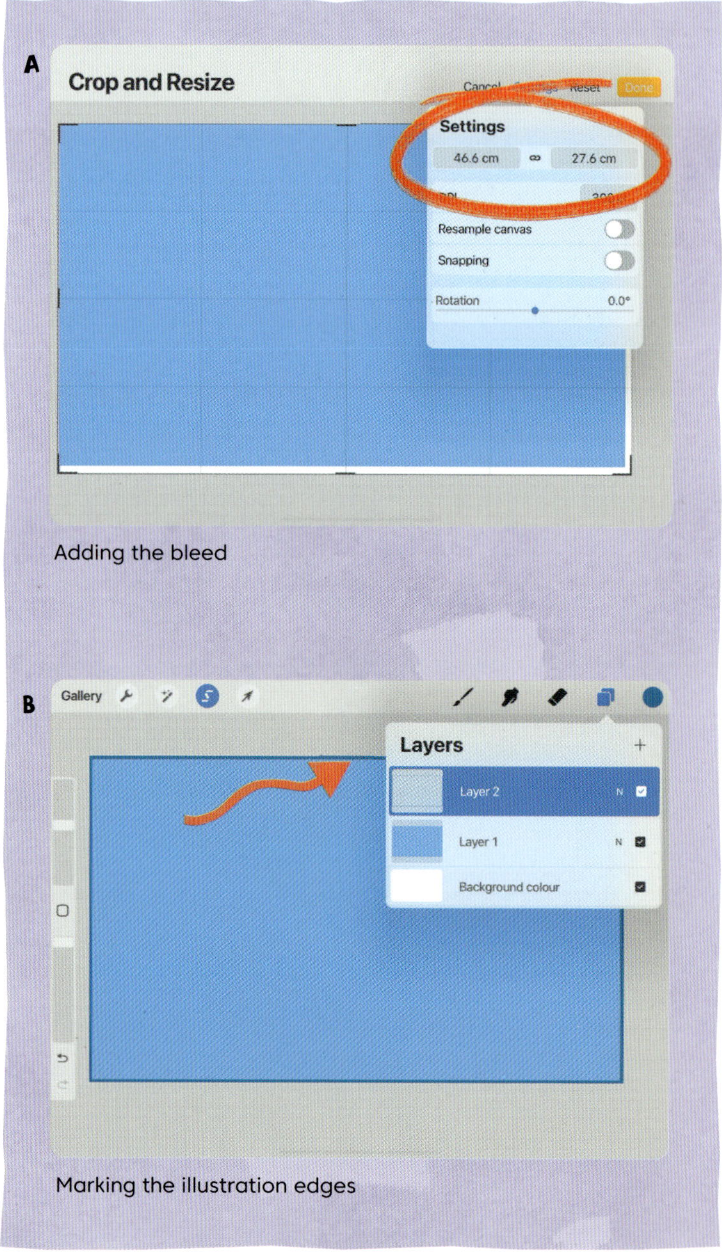

Adding the bleed

Marking the illustration edges

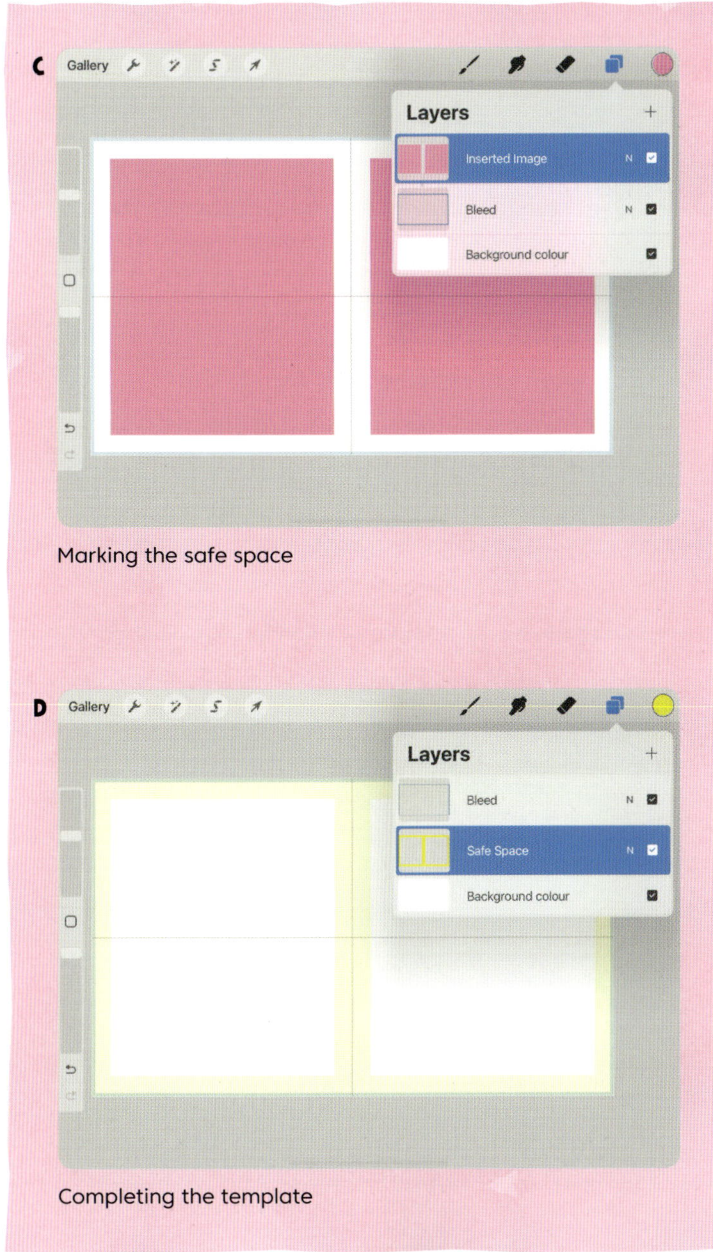

Marking the safe space

Completing the template

MARKING THE SAFE SPACE

We'll now add another guide to the canvas, this time to show where the safe space on each page will be.

1. Turn on the Drawing Guide. Set the grid size to Max to reveal the horizontal and vertical centre lines.
2. Go back to the Gallery and create a new canvas the same size as our safe space (20cm wide by 24cm high). Fill this new canvas with pink, then copy and paste it back into our DPS on the left-hand page. We'll place this by eye – it's just a guide so don't worry if it is not centred exactly on the page.
3. Duplicate the shape and move this to the opposite page, then merge the two layers together – you should now have a pink block on each page (**C**).
4. Select the pink blocks, invert the selection and drop yellow into the border on a new layer. Delete the pink blocks and lower the opacity of the new border. You can also pinch the two border layers together (**D**).

KEEP A COPY

Save a copy of this canvas as a template for future reference. You can use it again as is, or duplicate and tweak the dimensions for a different book or magazine page size.

This may seem like a lot of preparation before we begin brainstorming and sketching, but it will ensure that your illustration is well laid out across the page spread. Having these guides will also help with the composition of the illustration. I usually keep the drawing guide on so I can see the page in quarters. You can always turn it off if you find it confusing.

Now let's get on with the fun part!

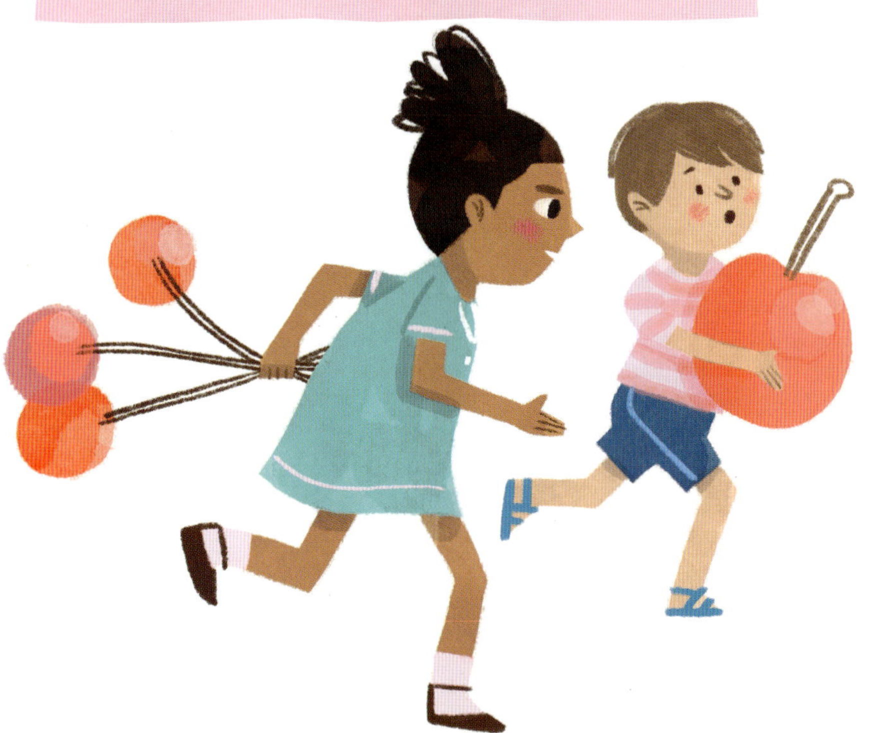

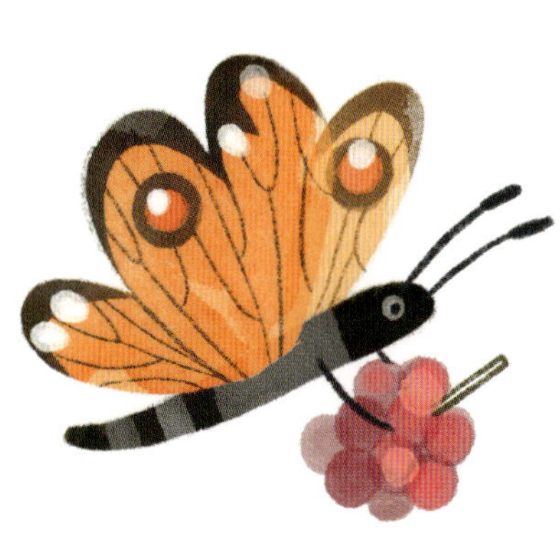

4. Brainstorming and sketching

To illustrate a lively scene, let's write down ideas for a busy market. What might we find there? What objects will we need to include? It's also great to have a twist to make the illustration more interesting – maybe a play on scale. The stallholders are all animals, the market is floating in outer space! Think outside the box to make things magical and exciting.

SPARKING YOUR IMAGINATION!

There are many different ways to find ideas. Maybe go for a walk, watch a documentary, look at vintage books, visit a museum. Leave your drawing tools at home and take inspiration from the world around you.

In this case, I took my dog for a walk in the woods and let my imagination run wild while observing ordinary things along the way. At home, I jotted down ideas, then narrowed down the theme to something fun and interesting, but simple and easy to draw. I condensed my thoughts into three sentences as my starting point!

- The characters are shrunk down to the size of insects.
- The stallholders are friendly and colourful bugs.
- The market is located on a woodland floor amongst the ferns and fungi.

WHAT OBJECTS DO I NEED TO SKETCH?

Now we need to create a visual shopping list of items we need for the scene. Feel free to use a sketchbook for this – you can photograph and drop them into the canvas later. I'm going to sketch straight onto my Procreate canvas. I sketch bugs, plants, fruits and cute little stalls!

COMPOSITION

Now free to think about the composition, I'll sketch a few lines and shapes on a duplicate canvas to see how this might work. I want the action to flow from left to right. When the reader turns the page, I want them to look at the top left-hand corner and follow a path through the market to the right-hand page where my main characters will be.

I'm not going to worry about perspective for this illustration, as I want to work in a more flat style. I'll use shape and shading to bring the characters and objects to life, and create depth with colour and scale. It is an imagined world so can have a non-realistic style.

I want to work quickly and spontaneously for the first rough sketch, so I'm switching from my usual 6B Pencil to the Dry Ink brush from the Inking section. My library of reference sketches allows me to work at speed – the ideas are already there!

Friendly bugs

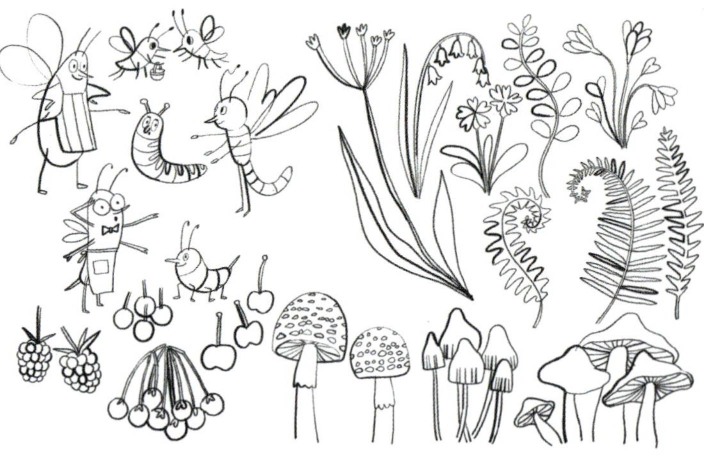

Woodland fruits and berries

Plants, ferns and fungi

Quirky woodland inspired market stalls

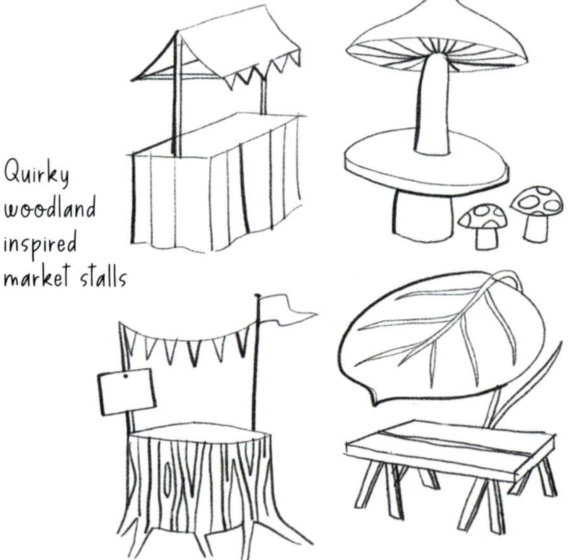

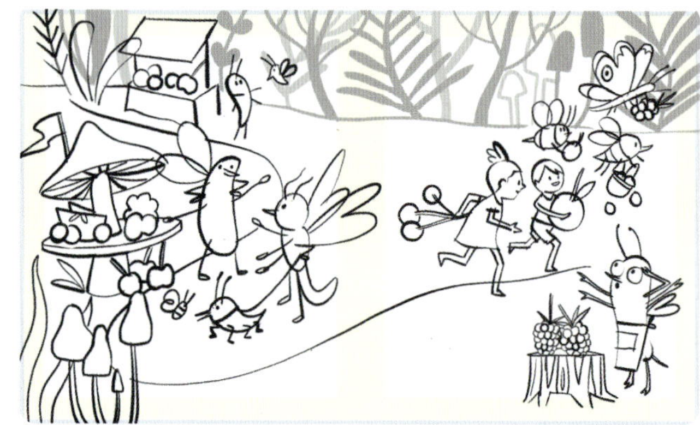

I want the action to flow from left to right.

E

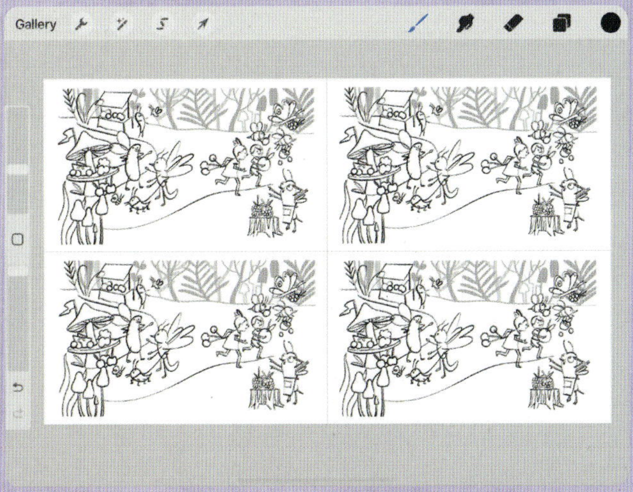

Preparing to test four colour palettes

F

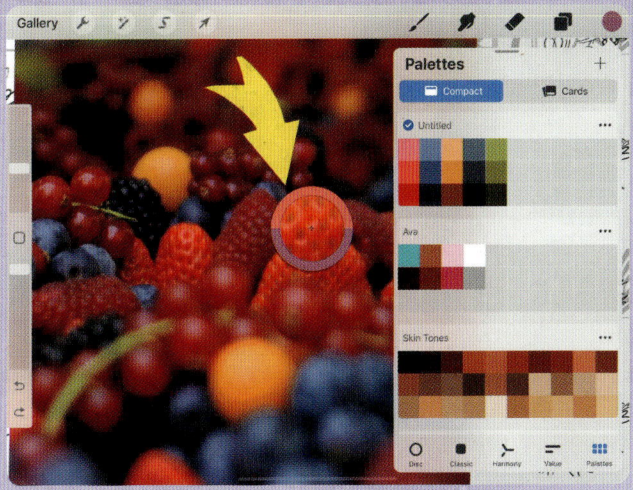

Using the Colour Picker to create a palette

G

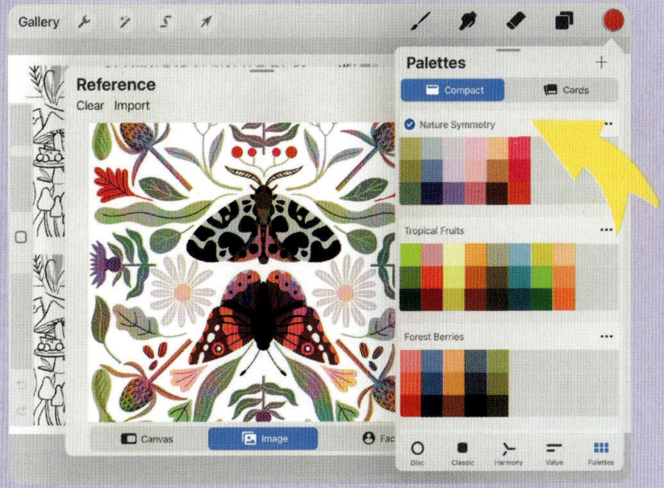

Lifting colours from a previous project

5. What's the story?

Since we don't really have a story to work to for this project, you can let your imagination run wild again. I want to have my characters running in the scene to add action and movement, so they are running from the market with the fruit. Hopefully this tension will make the reader want to turn the page to see what happens next!

If you're following along with your own scene, take a moment to sit back and look at what you've created.

- Is there a flow to the composition?
- Have you added some depth with background items?
- Are your characters interacting?
- Is there movement and detail to engage the reader?

Add or cut elements of the illustration until you're happy. Keep the guides layer on to check that the important parts are within the safe zone. Anything that bleeds off the page must extend into the bleed area.

6. Creating colour palettes

Duplicate this canvas in the Gallery and merge the sketch layers on the duplicate. Hide the guides and scale the sketch down to one-quarter of the canvas. Duplicate the layer three times (**E**) to test colour combinations.

I often find myself returning to my favourite palettes – bright and bold, with lots of warm colours. I often start planning softer, neutral colours, but the brights creep in and... another vivid palette! Here, I'd like to use colours that I'm not usually drawn to. Let's make four palettes and see what variations we can come up with.

- **Forest Berries:** For the first palette, I'm going to insert a photo of forest berries that I found online. I'm then using the Colour Picker, holding down one finger and dragging it around the photo to select colours I like (**F**). I'm building up a palette with light, medium and dark tones. I try not to think too much about where the colours will be applied exactly, but more the overall mood of the piece. I'm keeping this selection quite limited and renaming the palette Forest Berries.
- **Nature Symmetry:** I'm creating a palette using previous artwork – design from the *Natural Symmetry Tote Bag* – as a reference photo and lifting colours from it (**G**).
- **Tropical Fruits:** I'm choosing colours directly from a photo of tropical fruits. Go to the Canvas, tap on the wrench icon, and turn on Reference. Tap on Image, and import it from your Photo Library. The Colour Picker works in exactly the same way here as it does on the canvas. This is useful if you want to pick colours from the photo you are using for drawing reference.
- **Campfire:** For the final choice, I'm using a default palette included with the Procreate app called Campfire. It has a nice range of soft, natural colours.

7. Testing the colour palettes

I've dragged the palettes together in Compact view, ready to start the colour thumbnail studies (**H**).

WORKING INTUITIVELY

We're going to approach this stage quickly using the Dry Ink brush again. Set the sketches to Multiply and lower the opacity so you can work underneath the sketch with colour. I used only a few layers to sketch out the different areas underneath, and stuck mostly to the palettes (but added in a couple of lighter and darker tones where needed). Use simple, bold strokes – don't get caught up in the details. When finished, zoom out and look at all four thumbnails. I know immediately which one I'm drawn to. It may take you a while to decide on your own, but I'm guessing you'll have a favourite.

AND THE WINNER IS...

I love the top right-hand thumbnail – the Tropical Fruits palette. The neutral background and pops of red and pink for the berries appeals, and I have some green in there. The original colours I chose for my characters from the last project also fit nicely, with no changes. It looks like I added a very light turquoise blue to pick out some of the insect wings, so I'll keep that and add it to the palette also.

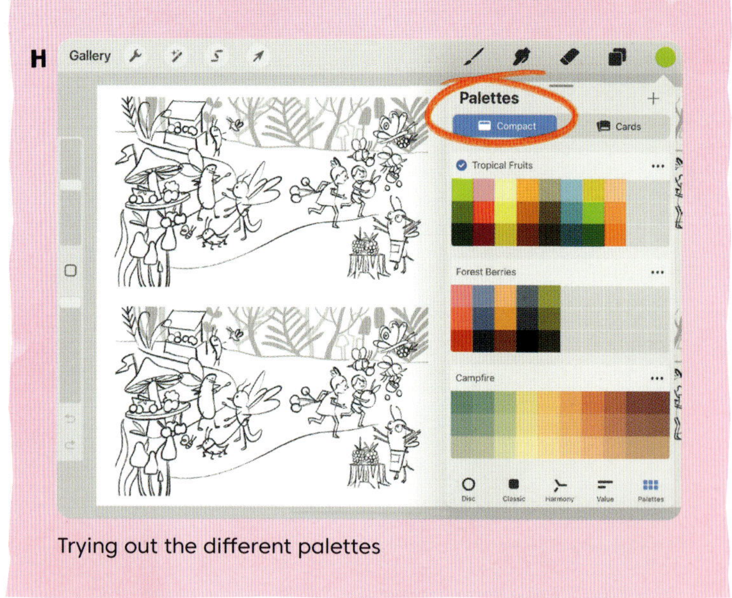

Trying out the different palettes

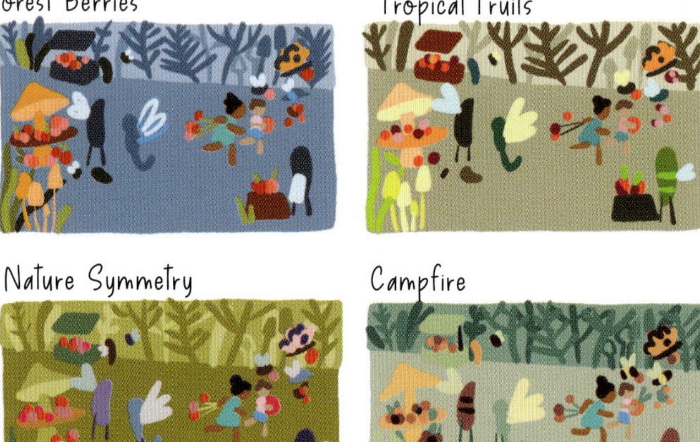

The result of testing each of the four palettes.

8. Starting the final spread

We have our characters, sketch library of objects, composition with page guidelines and colour palette, so let's prepare for the final spread.

1. Duplicate your original sketch canvas in the Gallery. Pinch all the sketch layers together, set to Multiply and lower the opacity.
2. Hide the guides layer, but don't delete it. You can view it at any time to make sure you're not losing details on the edge of the page or in the fold.
3. Keep your colour study on a separate layer so you can view or hide it for reference when necessary.

I've also decided to scale down the sketch a bit. I want to move the insect wings away from the fold, so I'll spend a few minutes chopping and resizing things.

I'm going to use my favourite brush – the watercolour brush I used in the *Print & Cut Stickers* (part of a set bought online). Use something similar if you have it and follow this workflow, but I also encourage you to use your own favourite tools and workflow. I'm starting with the neutral background colours, looking at my colour reference but tweaking here and there. Next I'm blocking in the objects and characters in the middle ground.

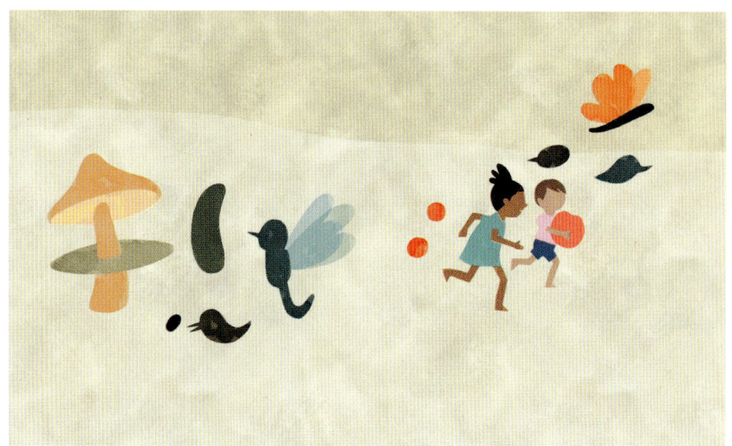

Blocking in middle ground objects and characters.

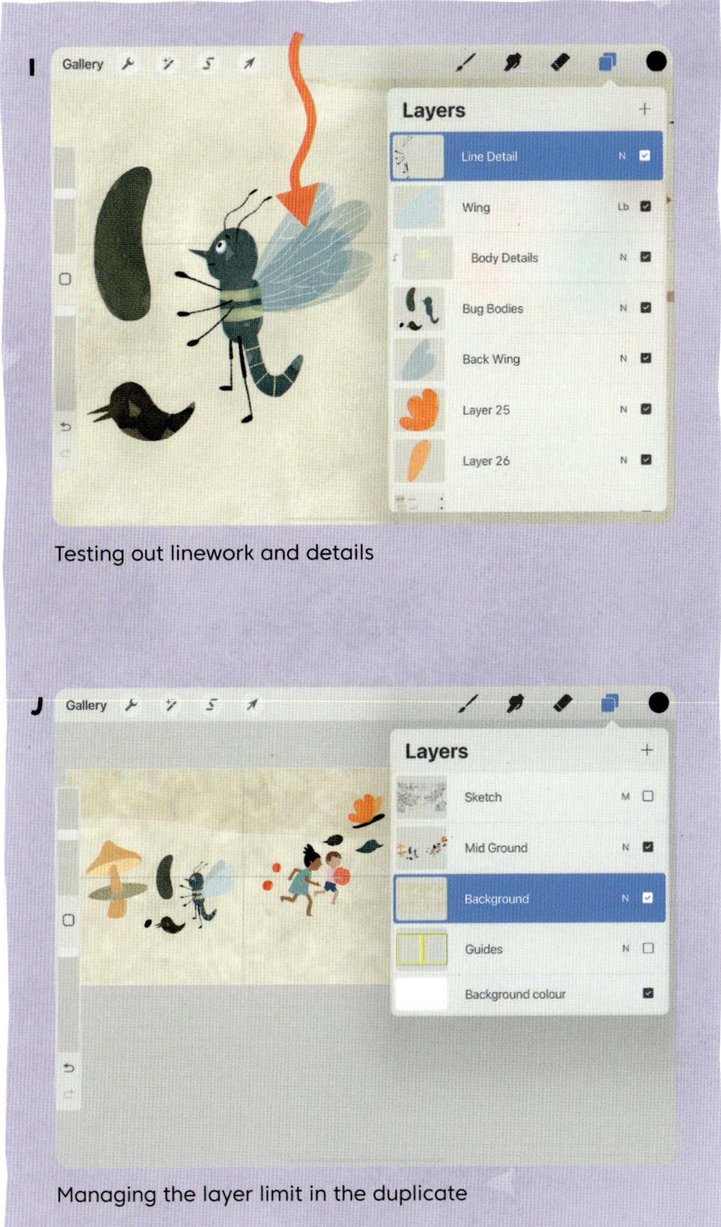

Testing out linework and details

Managing the layer limit in the duplicate

9. Giving my plan a test-drive!

At this point, I start to get nervous. I've spent a lot of time on preparing and planning how I want the finished artwork to look, but I begin to doubt if I'm on the right track. To avoid this, I usually develop part of the illustration a bit further, adding line and details to see how it will look when finished (**I**). Once I'm satisfied with the way it looks, I can move on with the process confident that the illustration will be a success.

10. Troubleshooting the layer limit

I have reached my layer limit, but I want to keep all my characters and objects highly editable. There are a couple of things I can do to put my layer allowance back in credit:

FLATTEN AND MERGE

I'll go back to the Gallery, duplicate my canvas, and flatten and merge where possible. I'll be coming back to these earlier versions later on.

GIVE SIMILAR ITEMS THEIR OWN LAYER

Another trick to save on layers is to keep similar items together, just as we did for the group of faces in the *Children's Storybook Character Sheet* project. For example, I can keep all the insect bodies together on one layer but I'd like the wings to be separate. I have the front wings of the dragonfly and butterfly on the same layer and the back wings on another layer. It can get complicated but naming the layers and keeping everything organized will help.

You can see here how I've merged the layers in the duplicate. I should now have enough layers to block in the other shapes, objects and characters (**J**).

11. Adding details

Now, I'm turning my attention to all the details of the drawing.

THE BACKGROUND

I'll paint in the background ferns and plants. I'm keeping them the same tone for now as I'd like them to fade into the distance (**K**). This will add some depth to the illustration.

THE MID-SECTION

I'm working on legs and antennae for the insects, and eyes and clothes for the characters. I'm working on just a few layers, some with Clipping Masks, others set to Multiply for shadows. I've also started to add in the fruit, and the linework on the wings (**L**). I'm pretty happy with the detail on the mid-section now, so I'm going to duplicate the canvas and merge most of the layers together.

THE FOREGROUND

I'm now building up layers in the front section. I'm working mostly from my imagination now, and am no longer referring to the sketch. This stage is more about resolving the scene. Helping it come together in a balanced way (**M**).

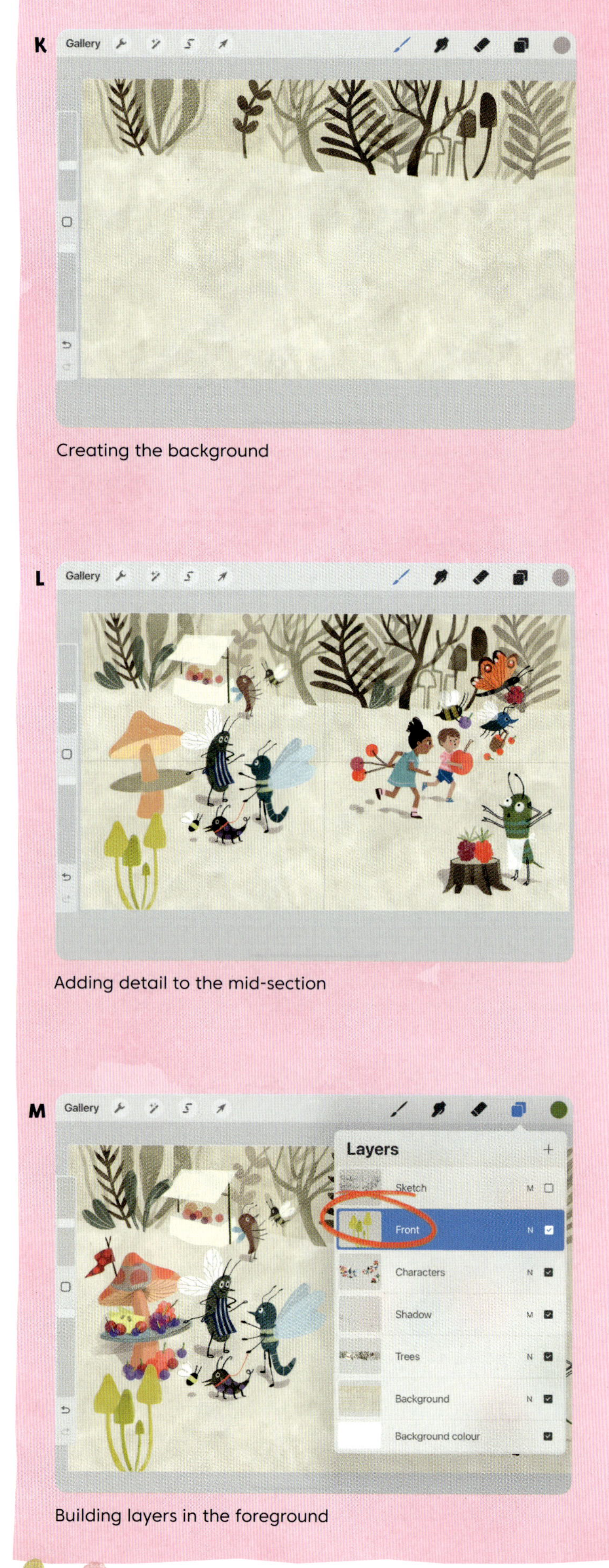

Creating the background

Adding detail to the mid-section

Building layers in the foreground

BALANCING LIGHT AND DARK

As I'm adding to the front, I see the mid-section and background are too dark, so I'm lightening up both sections and taking some detail out of the forest to make it look further away (**N**).

I want the details at the front to be darker and more vibrant, so I'm adding an extra layer by duplicating the Front group, flattening the duplicate and setting that Front Copy layer to Multiply (**O**). I can then slightly lower the opacity of this group to help blend with the original group directly underneath. This is a really subtle and quick way to add more vibrancy.

I feel very close to finishing now so I'm just making an extra layer to add some lighter areas in the mid-section and another layer to brush in some darker areas in the corners to give a vignette feel (**P**). I've also added a pink fill layer underneath the background texture to warm up the whole scene – you can see the effect of this on the finished piece.

CHECKING AGAINST THE GUIDES LAYER

Let's turn on our guides layer one last time to check that everything important is contained within the safe space.

As you can see, building up a complex illustration like this is quite complicated and there are a lot of decisions to be made during the process. Procreate provides us with the tools and the technology to create work like this in an organized manner. It stores and holds everything we create so we can make the decisions about what to keep and what to let go.

N

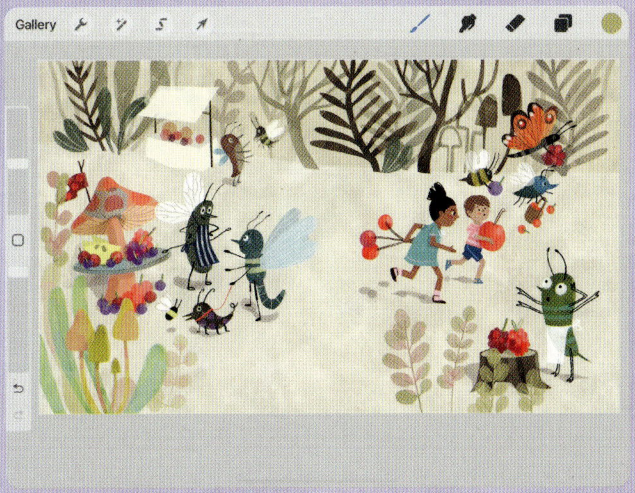

Playing with light and shade

O

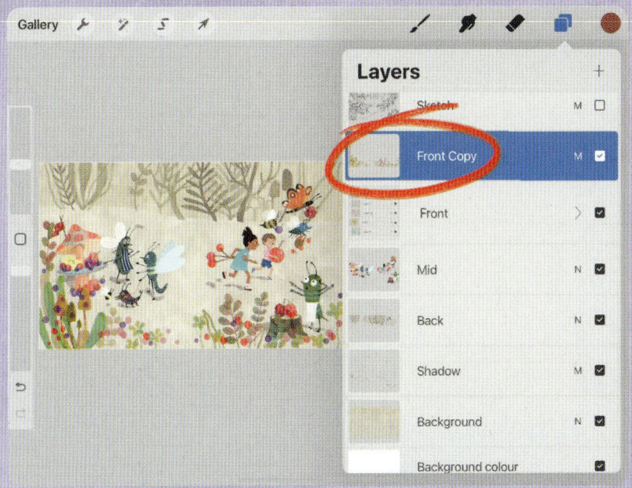

Adding vibrancy to the foreground

P

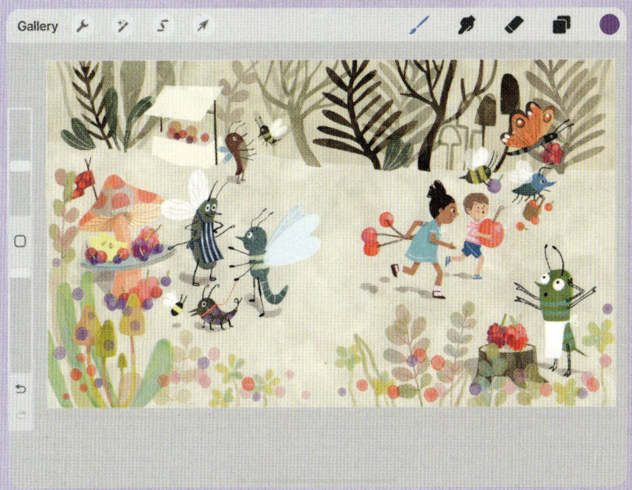

Lightening parts of the mid-section

The finished piece sitting under the guides. All the main detail and action have been placed within the safe space so will be fully visible to the reader on the page.

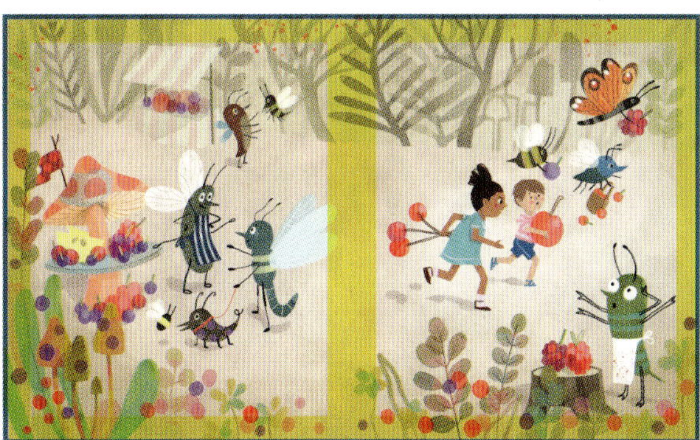

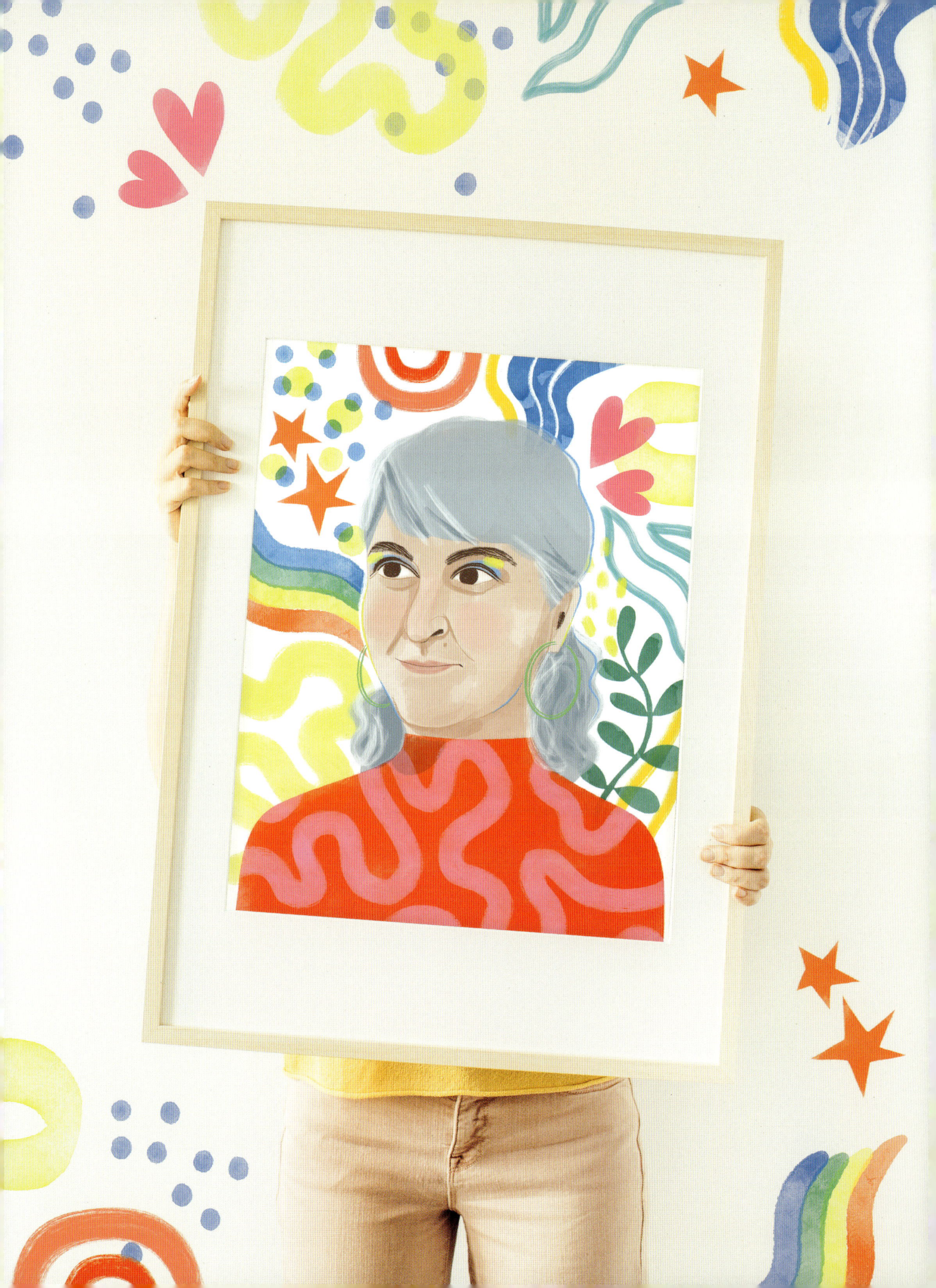

Colourful Portrait Wall Art

Drawing and painting faces in a convincing manner is a great skill if you're thinking about illustration as a career. It is also something that most people will say they can't do. It does take a lot of practice and if you're drawing from life, there are many things to consider such as proportion, form, light and shade. If you're a skilled painter, you'll be able to paint a portrait on Procreate using your own modified brushes, overlaying and blending layers, just as you would on a traditional canvas.

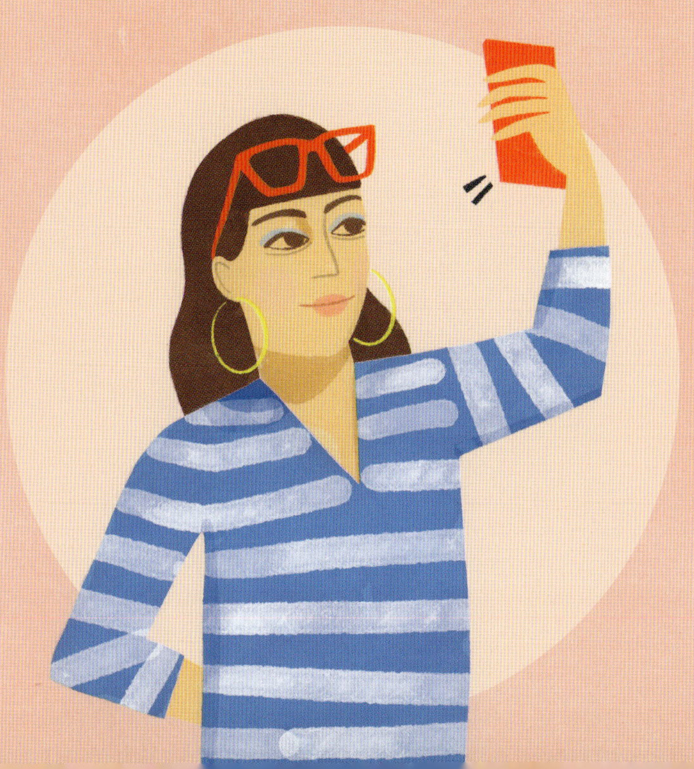

Time to Experiment

If you're looking for a simpler way to capture your friends and family, it might be nice to try an illustrated portrait style that allows the use of line, stylized features and an alternative colour palette. The struggle to capture a true likeness often prevents aspiring artists from experimenting with portraits. Sometimes the success of a portrait comes from finding the essence of the subject rather than an exact copy of their facial features.

Practise drawing faces whenever you get the chance. Sketch from life, take a selfie or use online reference. It's sometimes fun to draw people from history or old black-and-white photographs. Whatever the subject, have fun and illustrate the way you want!

1. Choosing a style and subject

In this project, we'll look at the way I build up a portrait in my own personal style. You're welcome to follow along closely. By now you may have a favourite brush or technique you want to use, so follow along in your own style. Techniques include working with a reference, sketching, blocking in colour, defining with line and looking at ways to bring the portrait to life!

So, who will we capture for this artwork? The answer is... *you*! You might not like the idea to begin with, but working on a self portrait is a great way to get started. Reference material is to hand – simply look in the mirror or take a selfie. If the nose ends up wonky, the only person who will be offended is yourself. You can also use this project as a chance to refine your features and make yourself look ten years younger!

FAMOUS FACES

If you want to illustrate a portrait of a celebrity, chances are you'll be looking at reference images online. Try not to copy exactly, look at a few different images and draw that person in your own way.

2. Sketching from the selfie

Take a couple of selfies, or ask someone to take it for you – they don't need to be perfect. I turned my head slightly to the side and looked away from the camera. I also sat near an open door, so there is natural light on one side of my face. I'm not wearing makeup and my hair is a mess, so I'm going to correct all that in my drawing and make myself look fabulous!

Use the sketching stage to solve the problems of the portrait. I'm only using this reference to get the shapes and proportions roughly sketched out, so study your reference and use light strokes to divide up the face and place the main features. If you're struggling with the proportions, it might help to add your selfie to the canvas, lower the opacity and mark out the position of the hairline, eyebrows, nose, mouth and chin on a separate layer. Try not to trace too much detail though – we are looking for a characterful, stylized piece.

PREPARING THE CANVAS AND BRUSH

I'm setting up a new canvas with the measurements 2550px wide by 3300px high. This will give us plenty of room for a head and shoulders portrait. I'm diving straight in with my 6B Pencil, lightly sketching the shape of my head and the main features.

LAYING THE FOUNDATIONS

We're just a few strokes in and I'm cheating! I've lowered the line of my shoulders and probably drawn my eyes a little larger than real life, but let's keep going and see how it comes out (**A**).

I'm sketching quickly, erasing and redefining areas that need work (**B**), using a thicker brush to pick out lines that seem important. I don't have a true likeness but I can see myself in the sketch somehow. I'm going to stop, before it becomes overworked, and think about colour.

3. Starting to add colour

I'm using the Palette From Image option to create a palette, selecting my selfie to give me some idea about skin tone (**C**). It's just a good place to start.

Set the sketch layer to Multiply and lower the opacity. Make a new layer underneath to start painting on. You can start filling the skin tone with your chosen brush on this layer – I like to use the Freehand Selection tool to select the area I want to paint. I'm using the Gouache Brush set to 12% size, brushing lightly and leaving spaces where the light is hitting the face (**D**). I'll then pass the brush lightly over again, this time catching the white space. I like to create this patchy surface to work on; it may look a little strange to start with but will add character to the finished piece (**E**).

When I'm finished with the initial colour, I'll refine the outline with the eraser set to 6B Pencil.

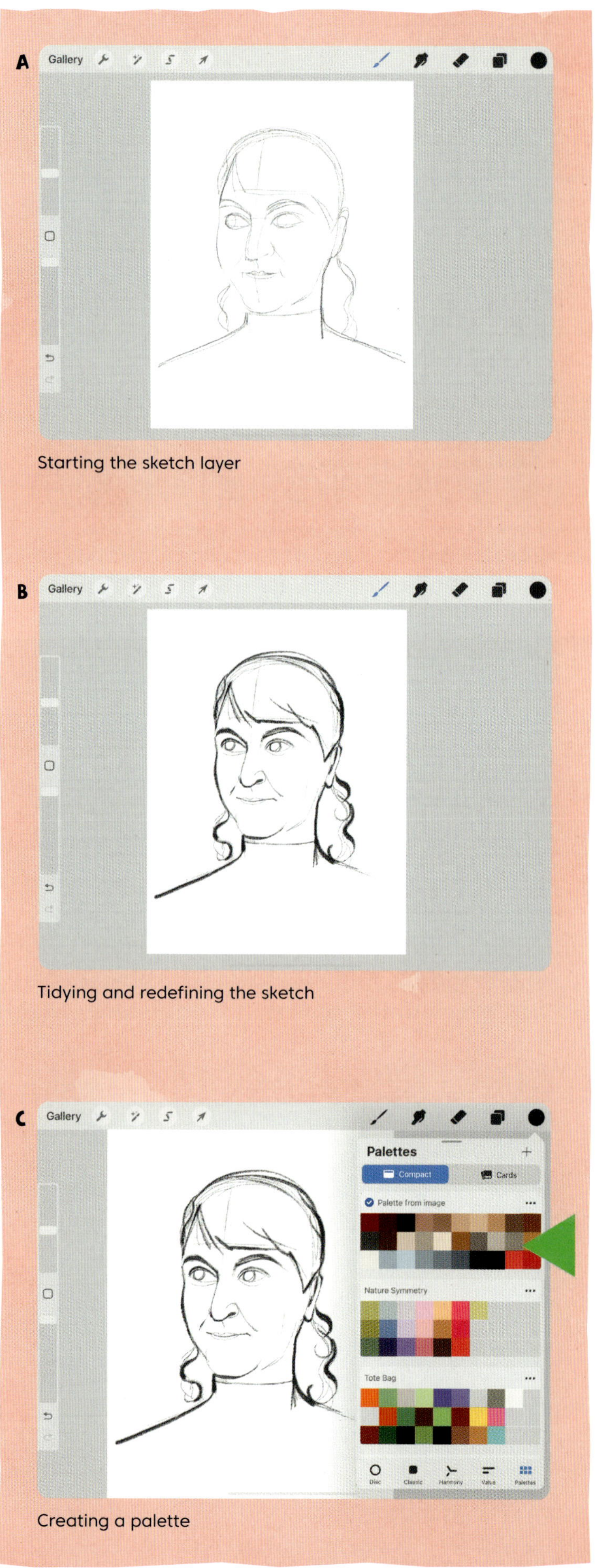

Starting the sketch layer

Tidying and redefining the sketch

Creating a palette

4. The hair and sweater

Create a new layer above the face layer but below the sketch and we'll paint in the hair using the same process. Every time I trace with the Selections tool, I'm making the shape slightly *bigger* than the sketch so I can refine with the eraser afterwards (**F**).

Once the hair layer is filled, and depending on your hairstyle, you can cut and paste part of it behind the face layer, as I've done (**G**). I'm also adding in a smart turtleneck at this point (**H**).

The base of the illustration is now complete and I can start work on building the features.

D

Adding the first layer of colour

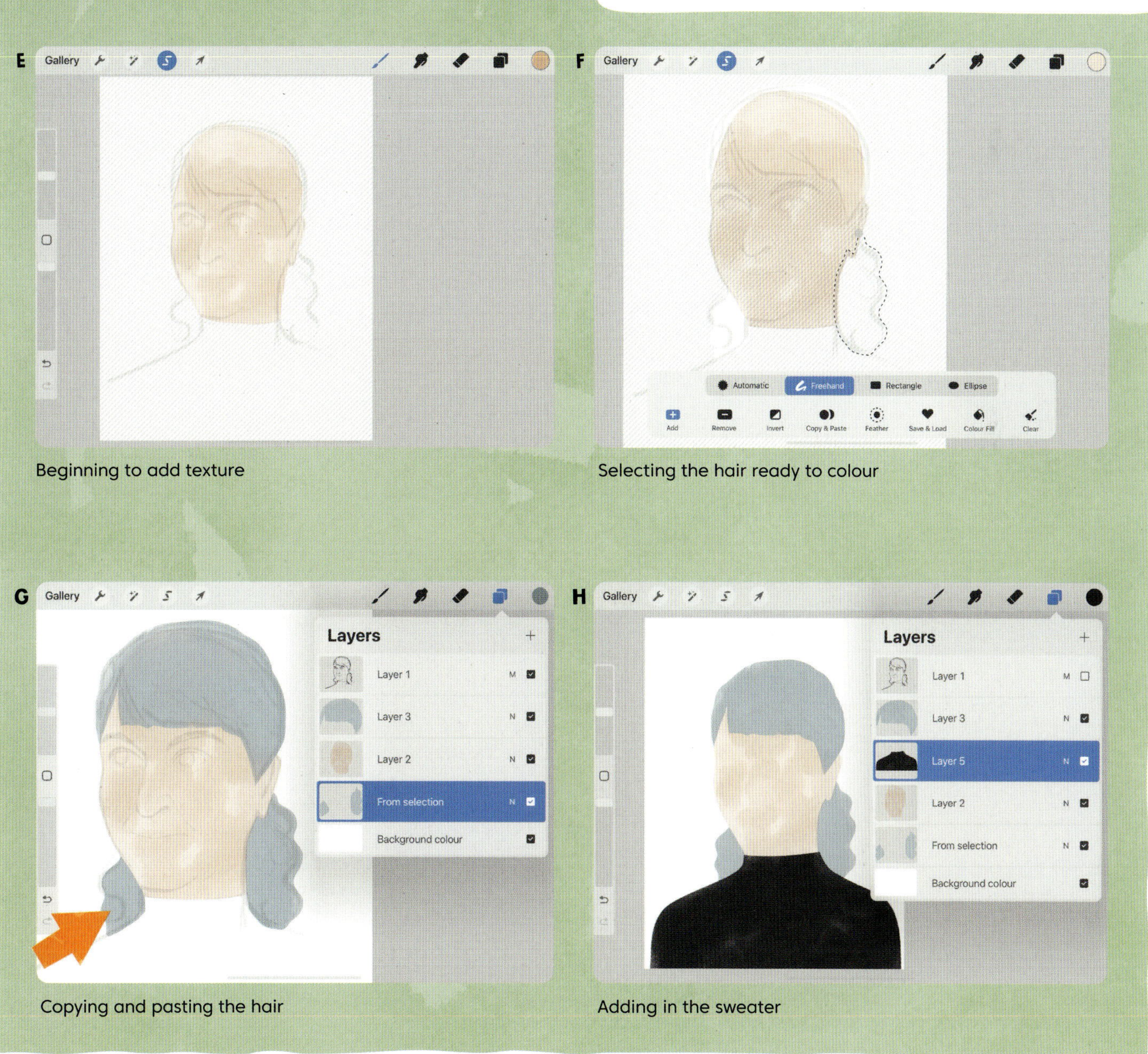

Beginning to add texture

Selecting the hair ready to colour

Copying and pasting the hair

Adding in the sweater

5. Adding features

First, I've made a new layer above the face but underneath the hair and sketch.

DRAWING SIMPLE LINES

To draw in the features, I'm choosing a colour that's a shade or two darker than my skin tone. Then using the 6B Pencil, I'm drawing in features using simple lines. It's a nice idea to also choose a thicker brush to add some variation.

DEVELOPING YOUR STYLE

This is where you can start to stylize your portrait if you want to. You might want to use a black line or something smoother than the 6B Pencil. Try out different brushes and play with the thickness and quality of the line. You can trace all the lines from the sketch, or only the ones you think are necessary to tell the story of the face (**I**).

I'm also using a darker colour in some areas to define shapes and add shade (**J**).

ADDING FURTHER DETAILS

Once you feel there is adequate linework, create layers underneath for the features and details, including:

- A layer set to Multiply to add shade
- A layer for lips
- A layer for the whites of the eyes
- A layer for rosy cheeks (at least for me!)

The level of detail is up to you but keep everything on separate layers so you can edit, delete or hide later if you're not happy with the outcome (**K**). I'm brushing in all of this detail with a very light watercolour brush with the opacity lowered. I'm using the original palette from the selfie image and adjusting colour on the Colour Disc when necessary.

I've also added in a layer for some hair texture (**L**). I'm not adding much detail here but if you have curly or textured hair you might want to make a feature of that. It's all about choices and balance – decide which bits of the portrait to have fun with and which bits to keep simple and more true to life.

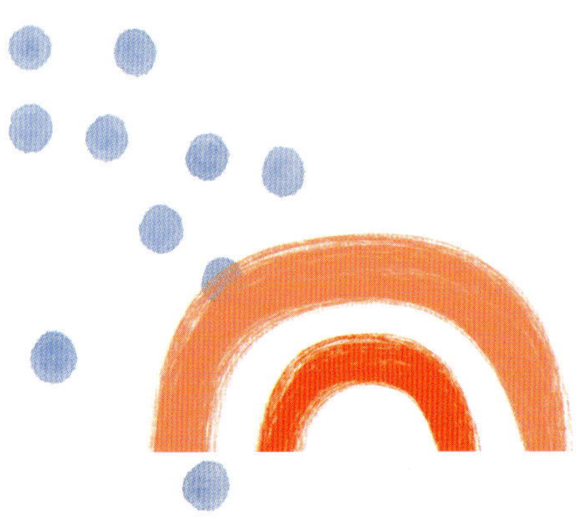

I

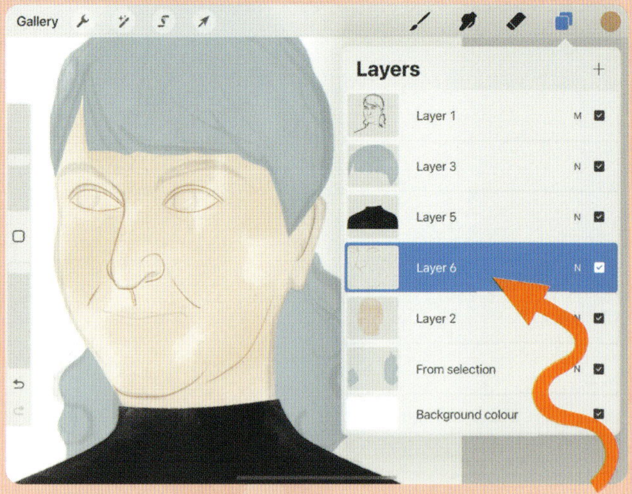

Choosing which lines to define on a new layer

J

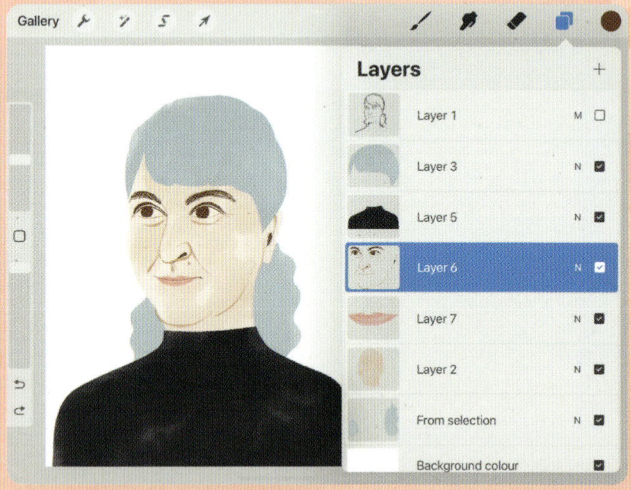

Defining and shading features

K

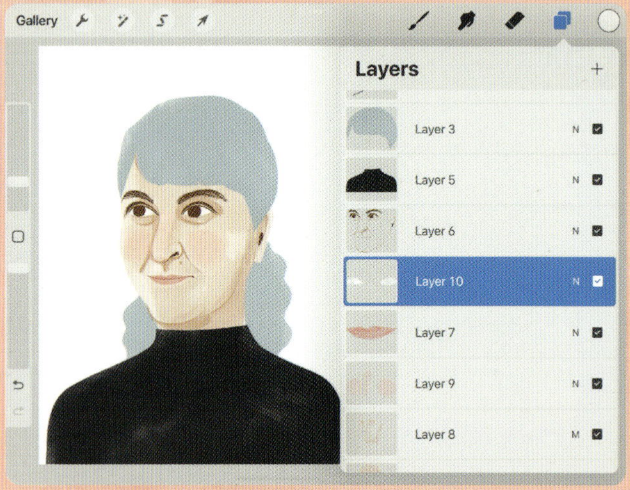

Using layers to allow for editing

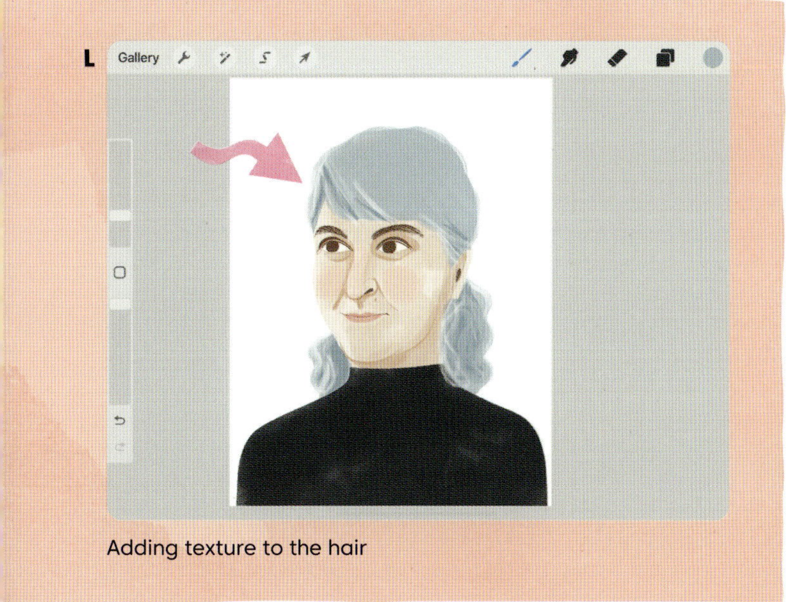

Adding texture to the hair

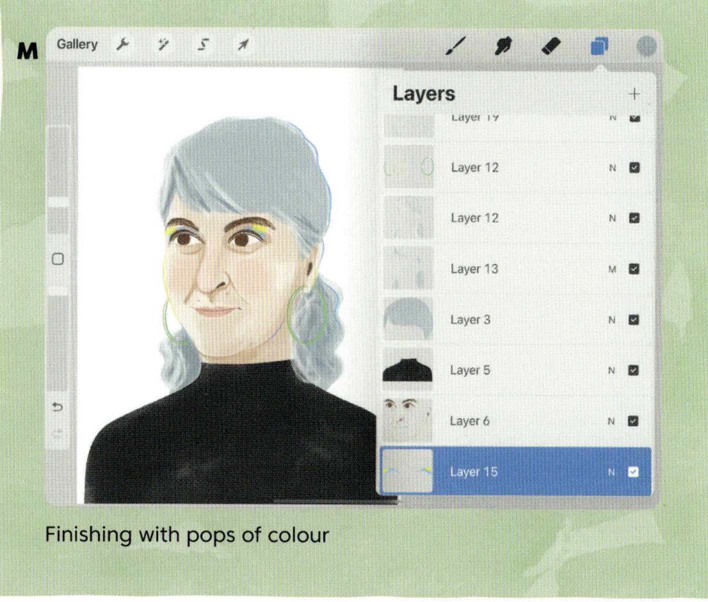

Finishing with pops of colour

6. Adding personality

If I wanted a simple self portrait, I would probably stop here. But since it's an illustration, I'd like to add a few details to make it stand out and say something about my personality.

POPS OF COLOUR

On a new layer, I'm going to add subtle pops of colour using line on top of the drawing. Not too much – I don't want it to be a cartoon – but I'm also adding some crazy eyeshadow and neon earrings! (**M**)

CREATING THE BACKGROUND

To finish the piece, I'm going to create a background using some of the motifs I use frequently in my work. I'm also updating the plain black sweater by dropping a red colour directly onto the layer, adding a Clipping Mask above and sketching in a pattern.

At this point, I'm happy with the portrait, I hope you've followed along and realized how easy it is to put something like this together. It's important to not get hung up on the details and not spend hours trying to create an exact likeness of a photo. I started this project with the intention of capturing the spirit of Ruth, and I'd like you to approach your self portrait with the same mindset.

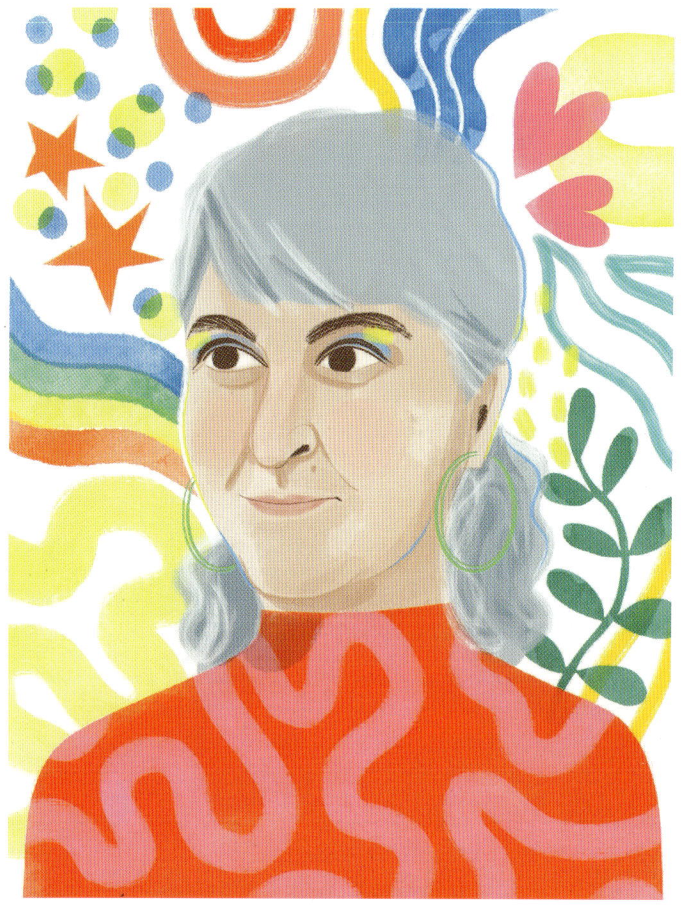

Creating the background and changing the sweater!

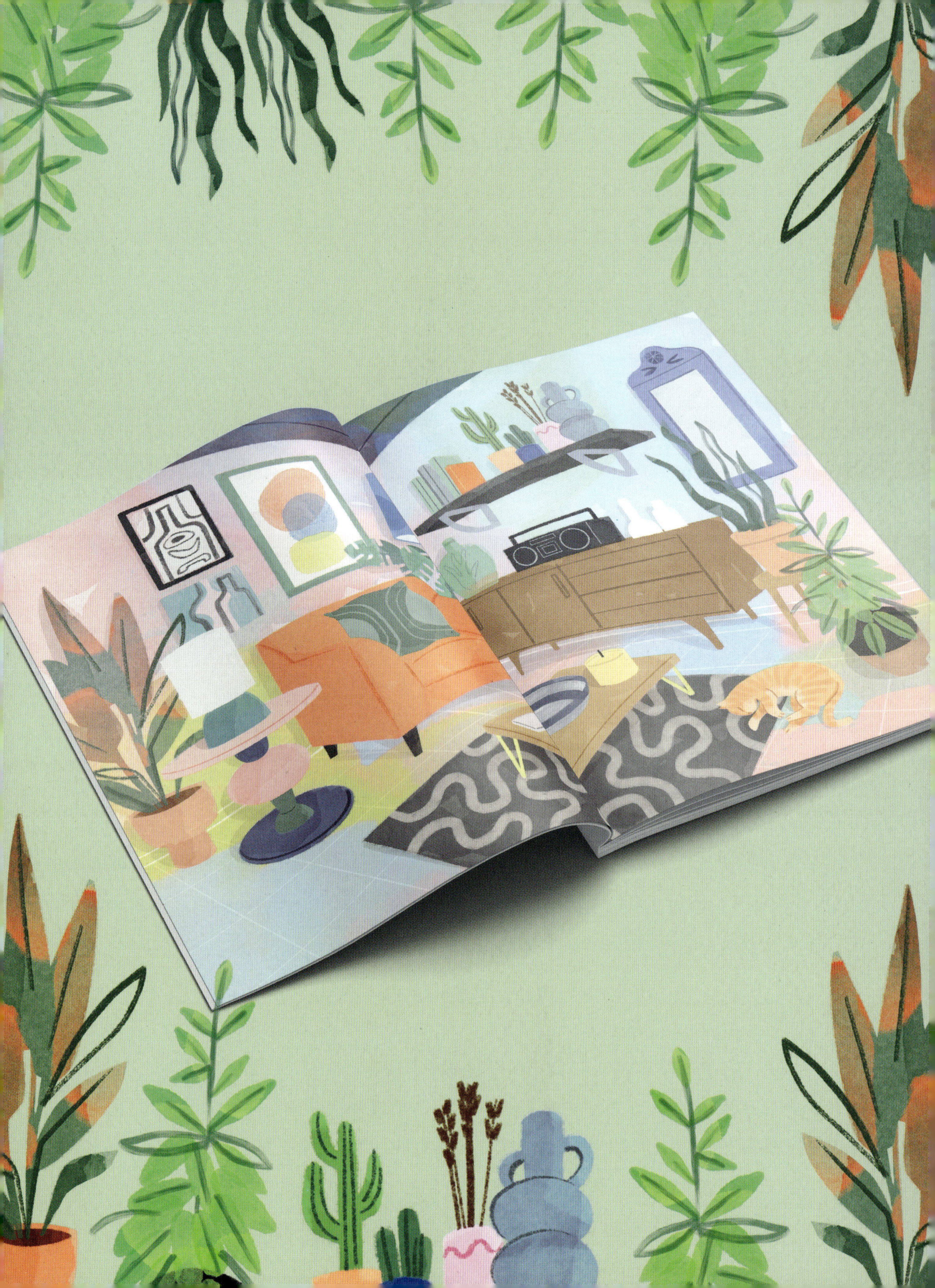

Interior Design Magazine Spread

Most creative people live and work in creative spaces! Their surroundings may be minimalist and uncluttered, with statement pieces taking pride of place. Or cosy and stacked to the rafters with curious objects and dusty books. Whether it's actually where you live or somewhere you *dream* about living, the space you create will tell a story about your personality. Remember – you can afford anything in this illustrated interior!

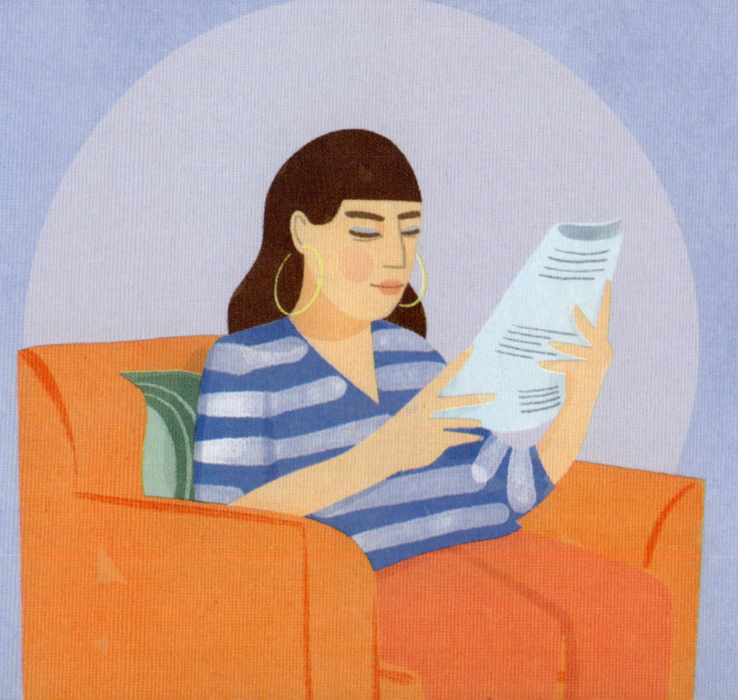

Blueprint for Creativity

Here, we'll look at how to illustrate your dream interior in Procreate. Being able to draw convincing spaces dressed with home accessories is a great skill to have. It's useful for both editorial and storybook illustration, as well as actual architectural-style drawings for interior design. As with all the projects in this book, we'll be creating for fun, but you can put these skills to use in other areas of your life and art.

This project provides the perfect opportunity to look at another amazing, in-built feature from Procreate. The Perspective Drawing Guides will help us sketch out our room with ease, creating the framework for a space with depth and believability.

1. Planning your illustration

Jot down ideas and do picture research, starting with favourite items already in your home. Pinterest is great, and I also look at contemporary online lifestyle stores and mix their ideas with vintage furniture shapes and historical textiles. Save all your references in one place in your Photo Library or a folder on your iPad. By now, you know how to view references while working. I mostly keep my reference on a separate device and view it on a larger screen, but do whatever is most convenient and comfortable for you.

Here's a list of items I want in my room and have included in my picture research:

- Mid-century style shelf unit or sideboard
- Statement armchair and quirky side table
- Colourful, patterned rug and unusual lamp
- Wallpaper and abstract wall art
- Large plants and vases
- A cat

You can sketch these items out as we did for the picture book spread in the *Children's Storybook Scene*. It's a good warm-up exercise and gives you some knowledge of the shapes before we begin to place them in our room. You can also set up your colour palette in advance by picking from your reference photos as we have done previously. I'm going to make up my palette as I'm working through the piece. I want it to be bright, unexpected and unlimited.

2. Setting up the workspace

Once you have gathered all your references, open up Procreate and create a new canvas 3000px wide by 2000px high. This size will give us plenty of layers to work with.

We're going to create a framework for our sketch using the Perspective Drawing Guides, so tap on the wrench icon to open Actions, turn on Drawing Guide, tap Edit Drawing Guide (**A**). Turn on Assisted Drawing and Perspective, then tap once near the centre of the canvas to add a vanishing point (**B**).

3. Establishing perspective

I've jotted down a quick introduction, or refresher for some of you, about simple perspective.

BASIC PERSPECTIVE

Single-point perspective, or parallel perspective, means you're looking straight on at your subject. Imagine you're directly facing the back wall of your room – that wall is a rectangle, with nothing distorted. However, the edges of the side walls that meet the ceiling and floor will be angled upwards or downwards, running towards the four corners of the back wall (**C**). If those four lines continued, they would eventually all converge at one point in the distance – the vanishing point.

The blue horizontal line represents the horizon line.

TWO-POINT PERSPECTIVE

Now imagine you're standing in the *corner* of the room, looking at the back wall from an angle. The ceiling and floor edges run off in two different directions towards two vanishing points, hence the name: two-point perspective (**D**).

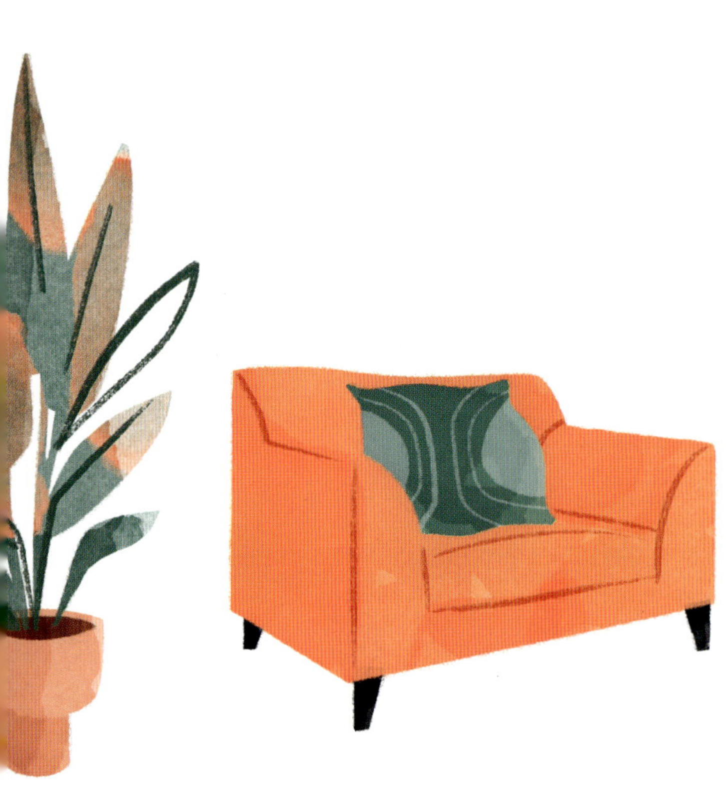

A

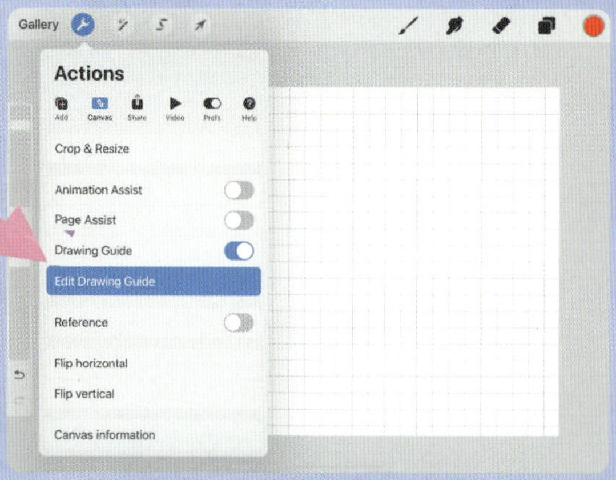

Using the Drawing Guides

B

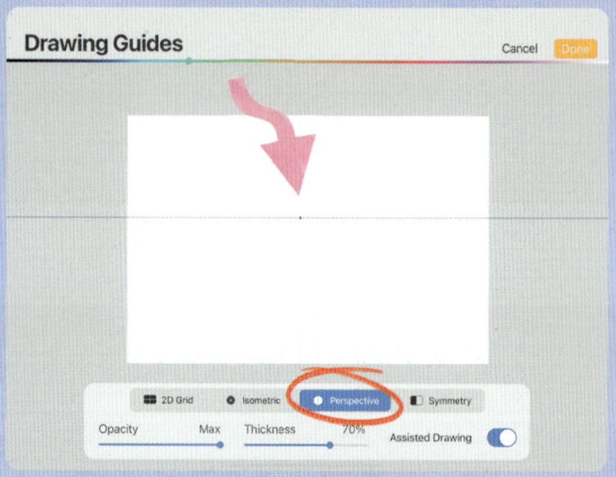

Turning on Assisted Drawing and Perspective

C

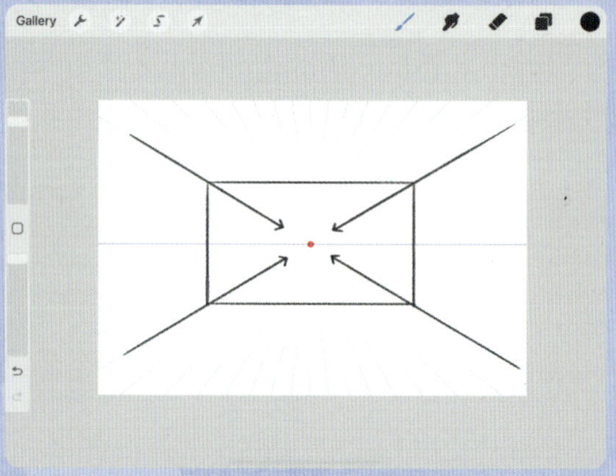

Lines converging at a single vanishing point

D

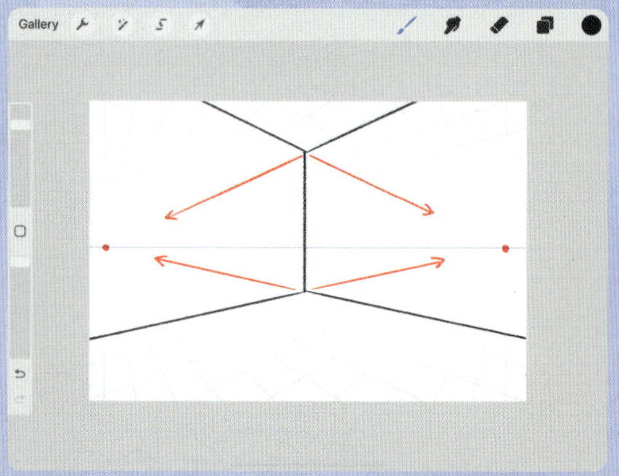

Lines converging at two vanishing points

E

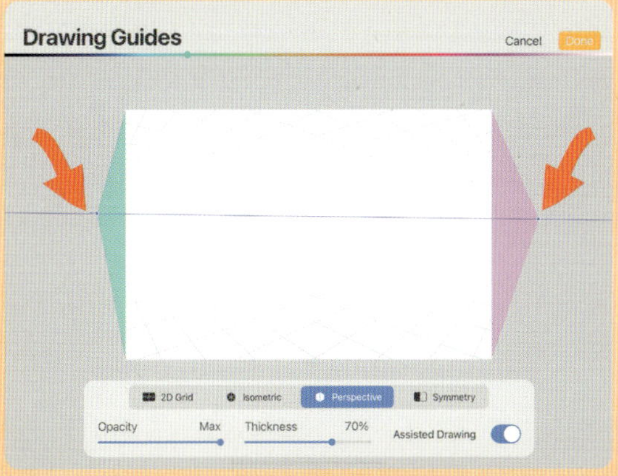

Dragging the vanishing points off the canvas

F

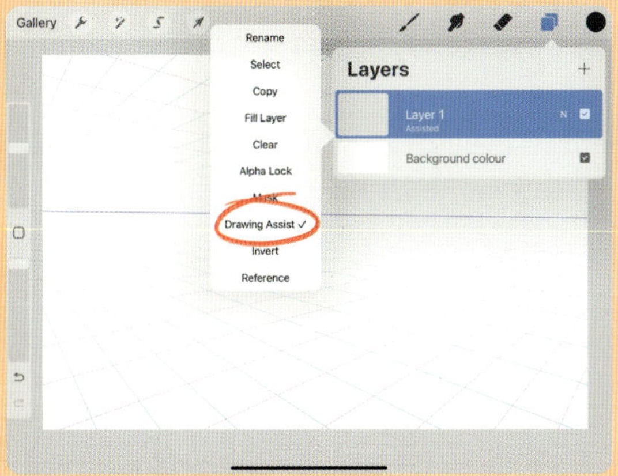

Setting up Drawing Assist

G

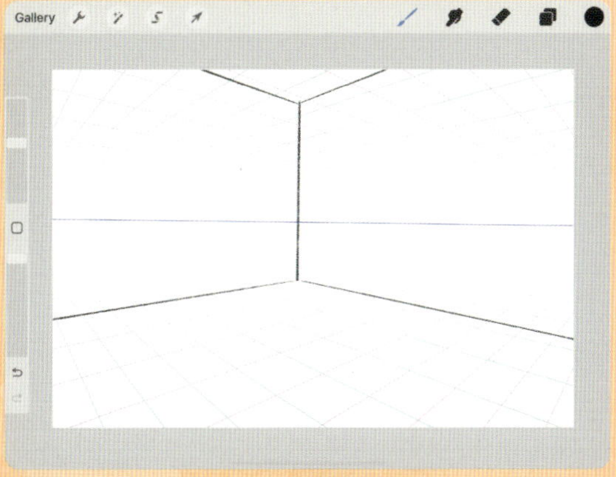

Sketching the basic lines of the room

H

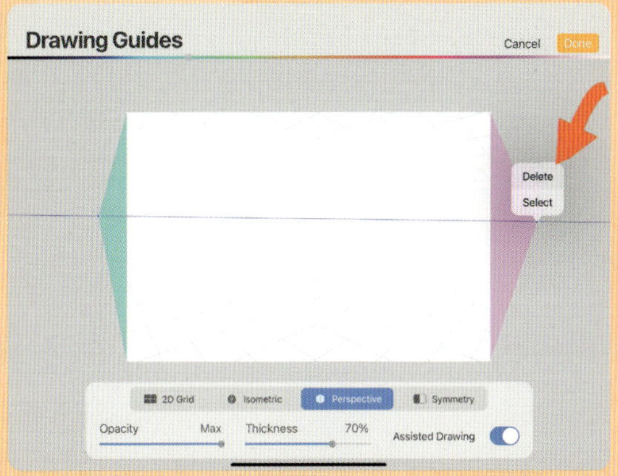

Editing the vanishing points

USING PROCREATE TO ESTABLISH PERSPECTIVE

For our interior illustration, we'll use two-point perspective. Don't worry if you're starting to find this confusing. Procreate is just about to give us a very big helping hand!

1. Tap on the vanishing point you have just created and drag it all the way to the left and outside the drawing (**E**). Tap and drag to create a second vanishing point on the horizon line. Drag this off the right-hand side of the drawing. Try to keep the blue horizon line parallel to the edge of the drawing. Then tap Done to return to the canvas.
2. Make sure Drawing Assist is turned on for Layer 1 (**F**). This means your lines will automatically adjust to follow the drawing grid. Go ahead and try it out. Notice that in this mode, we can only draw straight lines that snap to the Perspective Drawing Guide. It helps us understand the space by telling us what will be seen and what will be hidden from view.
3. Now imagine the corner of your room and sketch in the lines for the ceiling and floor (**G**).

It may take a few tries to get this right at first. You're aiming for plenty of floor space and adequate room on the walls to place the furniture and pictures. It's not necessary to show too much ceiling.

Feel free to go back and edit the vanishing points in the Drawing Guide menu (**H**). To start over, tap on a vanishing point and select delete.

Keep redrawing until you're happy with the space. The Drawing Guides make this process very fast, so you can afford to produce a few versions before you hit on the best view for you!

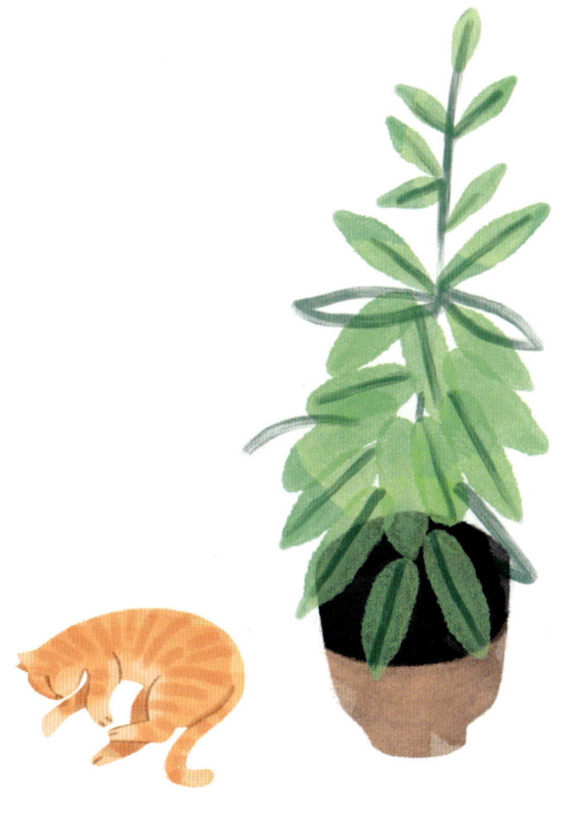

4. Planning the layout

Once we're happy with the space, we can start thinking about the placement of our items. Sketch out a floor plan of where you want the larger items to go (**I**). I've drawn in a space for chair, sideboard, side table, coffee table, plants and rug.

STRAIGHT AHEAD

You can't draw curves with Drawing Assist on. If you want to add something circular, like a plant pot, add the shape as a block for now and we'll sketch over it later.

We can now start to "grow" the items up from the floor! I like to imagine I'm reserving space for each item using a cube or block. Are you starting to see your dream room? Add in the pictures and block in space for the smaller accessories like candles and bowls. Continue until you feel you have everything in place (**J**).

5. Sketching the items

We're now ready to start sketching in the items from our research using the blocked-in layer as a guide. Lower the opacity of Layer 1 and add a new layer. Leave Drawing Assist off for now. This means we can sketch in the actual furniture and accessories, some of which may be curved. (We will turn Drawing Assist back on later to help us with some of the straight lines.)

Free to draw curved shapes and ellipses, sketch in the larger items first (**K**). The Drawing Guide will help you understand the space. For example, we can see the soil in a plant pot that is on the floor, but we can't see the soil in a pot that's high on a shelf. This is a great exercise for understanding perspective and the volume of objects in a space. I turned on Drawing Assist for this layer to help with the shelf and the sideboard. Keep adding items until your interior is full of your favourite things.

ADDING EXTRA LAYERS

You can also add layers to sketch in the "softer" things like plants and cushions. Relax and enjoy the process!

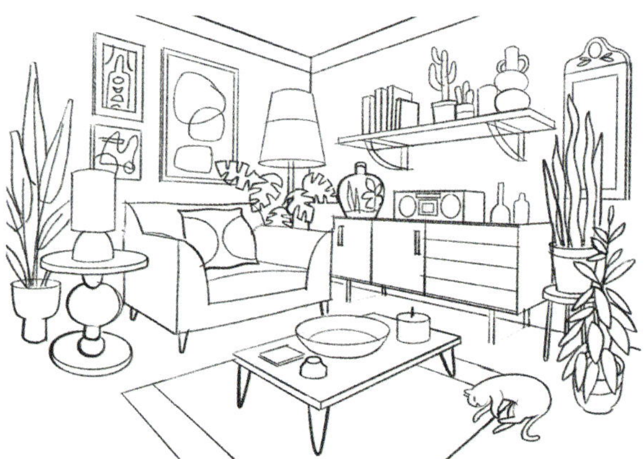

The finished sketch, ready for colour!

I

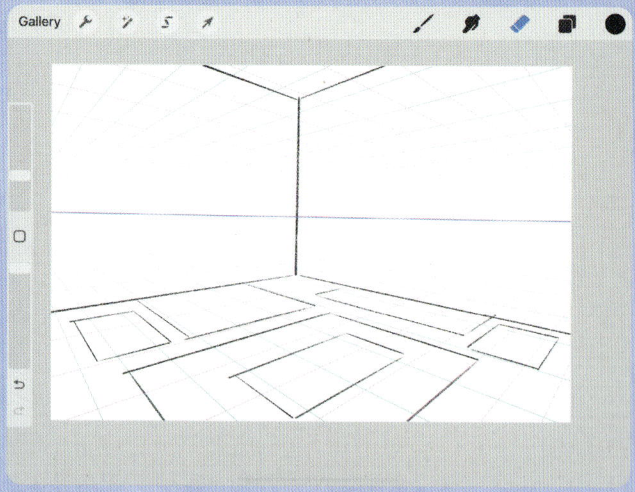

Placing the furniture with Drawing Assist on

J

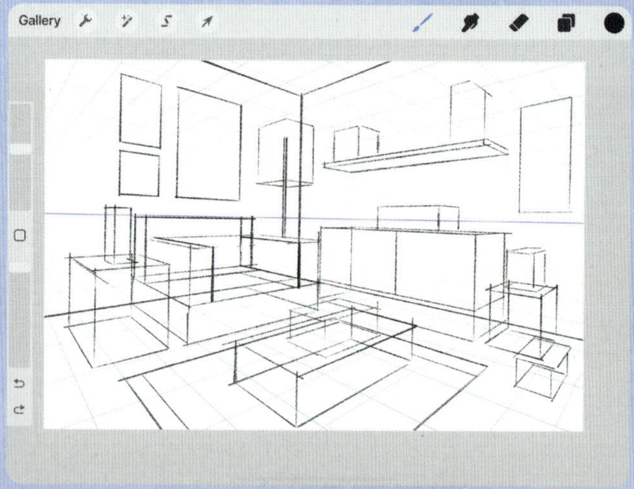

Building up the furniture with Drawing Assist on

K

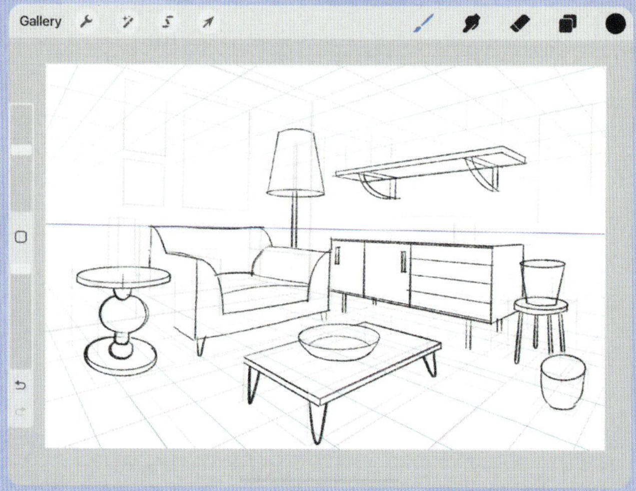

Sketching furniture and curves, with Drawing Assist off

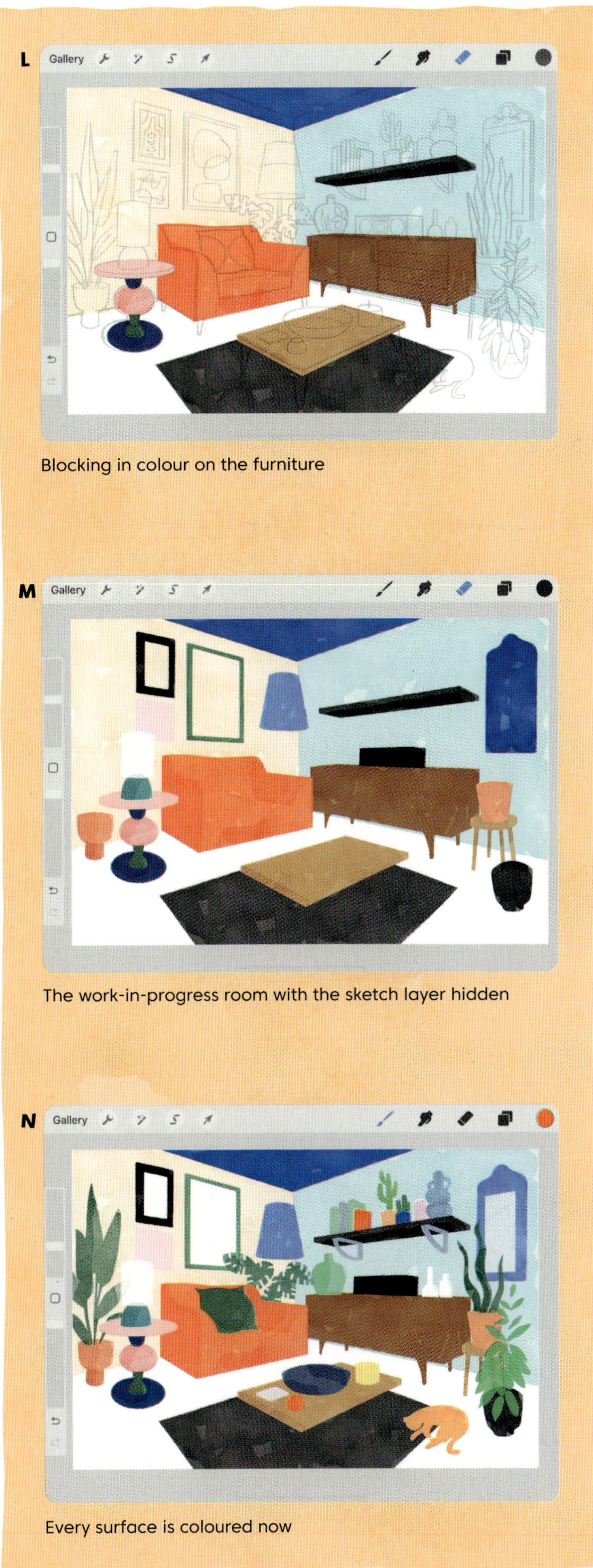

Blocking in colour on the furniture

The work-in-progress room with the sketch layer hidden

Every surface is coloured now

6. Adding colour

As always, I'll start work on a duplicate of this sketch – pinch all the sketch layers together, set to Multiply and lower the opacity. I'm turning the Drawing Guide off, and adding a new layer underneath to start the colour.

THE PALETTE

As mentioned, I haven't planned a palette for this piece. I'm looking at my reference images and picking out colours I love. I want the scheme to evolve as I go along. I also want a light touch for this illustration. I'll be using watercolour and gouache brushes as well as some line for details. The sketch is tight and detailed so I can afford to work more intuitively on the coloured final.

WORKING IN LAYERS

I have plenty of layers in this file so I'm keeping everything separate, blocking in colour for the largest areas. I'm starting with the ceiling and walls, then moving on to the larger items such as the armchair, rug and sideboard (**L**). Because each item has it's own layer, they will be easy to edit if I change my mind later.

USING REFERENCES

You can hide and view the sketch as you like, and turn on the Drawing Guide if you want to create precise lines and edges. As far as colour goes, I'm using my reference photos and tweaking to suit the interior as it grows (**M**).

At this point, I have colour on all of the surfaces. I've started to sketch in the plants and add accessories, but I'm leaving line and detail until everything else is done (**N**).

7. Adding details

I always enjoy this stage of working on the illustration. This is the time when it really starts to come to life, and you can add in unexpected details. I added some extra layers with Clipping Masks to overlay extra colours on the plants (**O**). I also used a Clipping Mask layer to add a crazy pattern to the rug. Drawing the artwork on the walls is also fun!

LINEWORK

When it comes to adding line, it's a good idea to zoom out and assess just how much detail you need to tell the story. One of the few downsides to working digitally is the tendency to zoom right in and add detail that may not be necessary. Keep taking a step back from your work – sometimes less is more.

SHADING

I'm not adding any shading to this piece until the end. By using the Perspective Drawing Guides, we have added a lot of form and depth to the illustration already. This accurate perspective has already given the image a very believable sense of dimension and depth, so I don't want to overwork it by shading every object on the canvas.

O

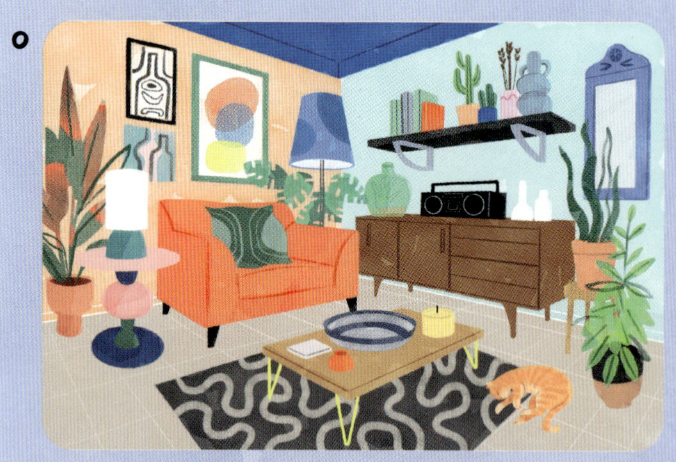

Adding details to the furniture, walls, and floor

8. Testing out some effects!

This is a bit of a lucky dip moment and one of my favourite parts of finishing an artwork. Everything is in place and almost perfect. Then I drop in a random colourful hand-painted texture and test a few Blend Modes to see the different outcomes!

TEXTURE

I'm going to add some texture. I have a rough painted page from another project that I want to try as an overlay in the background, just to break up the blocks of colour and add some visual interest. If you have something similar, take a photo and add it to the canvas. I'm inserting the image on a layer above the wall, floor and ceiling layers, but below everything else. I flip it and resize it to find the best placement (**P**).

BLEND MODES

The photo actually looks pretty good dropped in like this, but I'll try a few different blend modes to see how they compare, starting with Overlay (**Q**). Subtract also gives an interesting dark mood (**R**), but the one I really like for this piece is Colour (**S**).

P

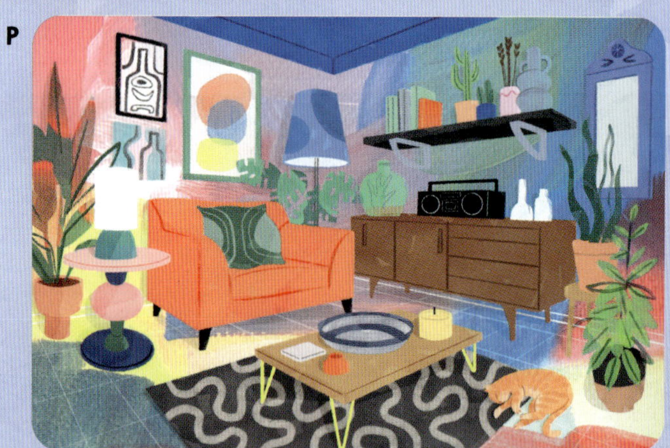

Adding texture using a painted layer

Q

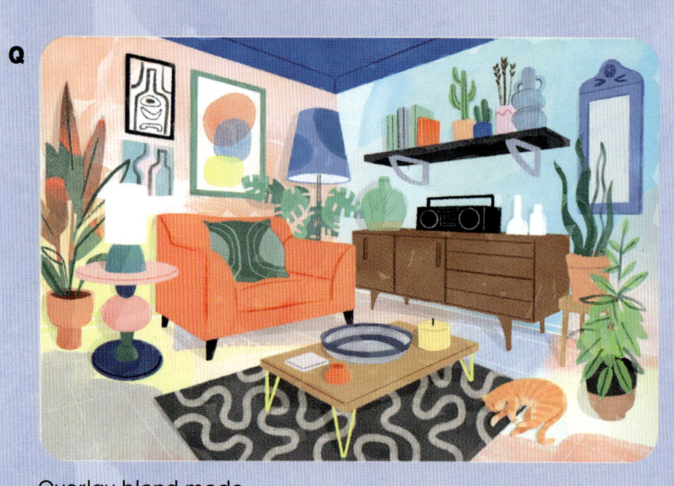

Overlay blend mode

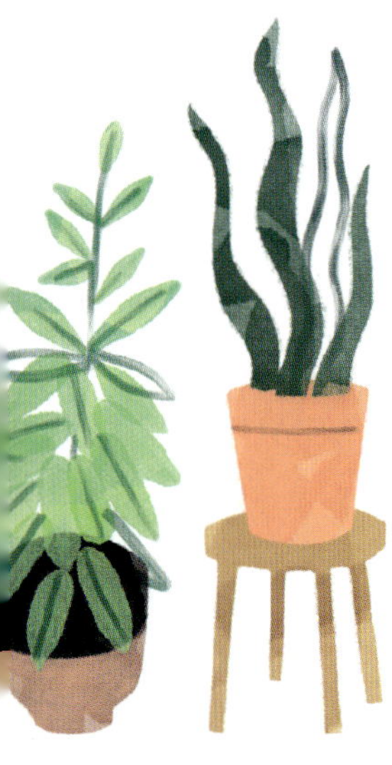

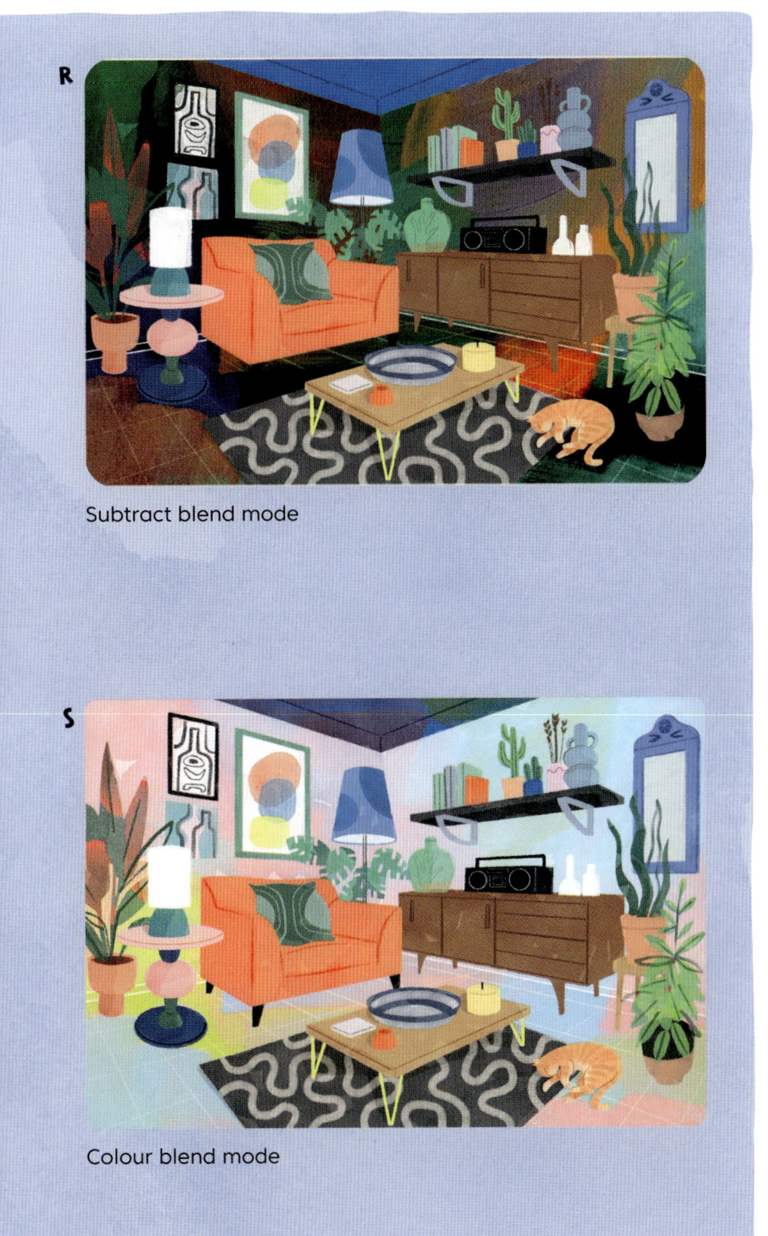

Subtract blend mode

Colour blend mode

9. Finishing touches

The last thing I'm going to do is add a couple of layers set to Multiply for shadow. A little bit under the tables and chair, and a light stroke or two under the cat – nothing too solid or dramatic.

LINEWORK

I always like to step away from a complex illustration like this for a while before committing myself to say it's finished. I may come back and add something in, change a blend mode or take something out.

10. Creating a mock-up

It's also a good idea to test out the design by printing it out at home or at a copy shop. For a theme like this, it would be fun to make a magazine-type mock-up. I found a free blank mock-up online and downloaded the file to my iPad. Try to find one with a transparent or separate background. I inserted my work into the mock-up like this:

1. You'll need to duplicate your illustration and flatten it to one layer. Tap on the layer, select Copy & Paste to the mock-up file.
2. Set the layer to Multiply so the shadows of the fold will show through.
3. I'm using the Distort option in the Transform menu to drag each corner of the image independently to match the corners of the magazine. It will not be exact – just place them as closely as possible.
4. I then tidied up the edges by using the Monoline Brush as an eraser to follow the shape of the magazine (**T**).

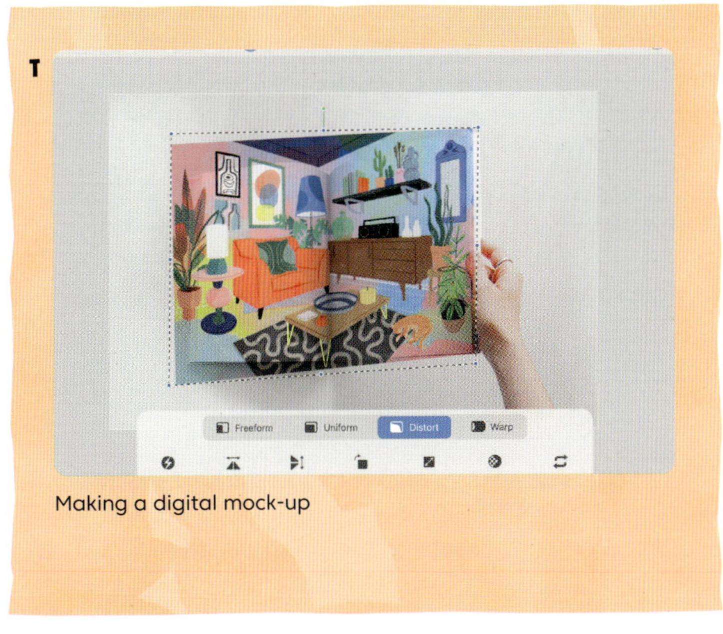

Making a digital mock-up

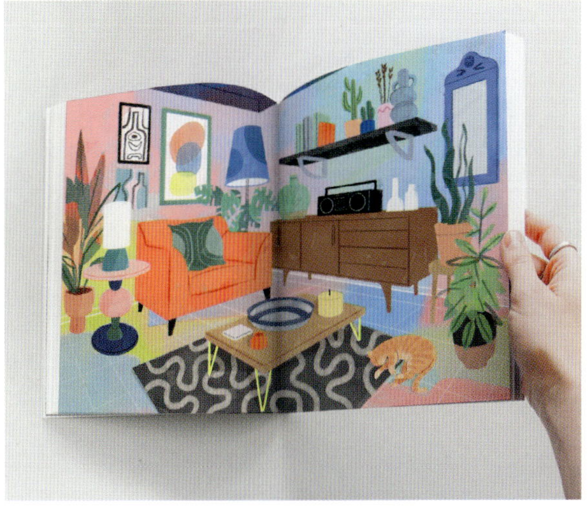

The dimensional presentation brings the spread to life!

NEXT STEPS

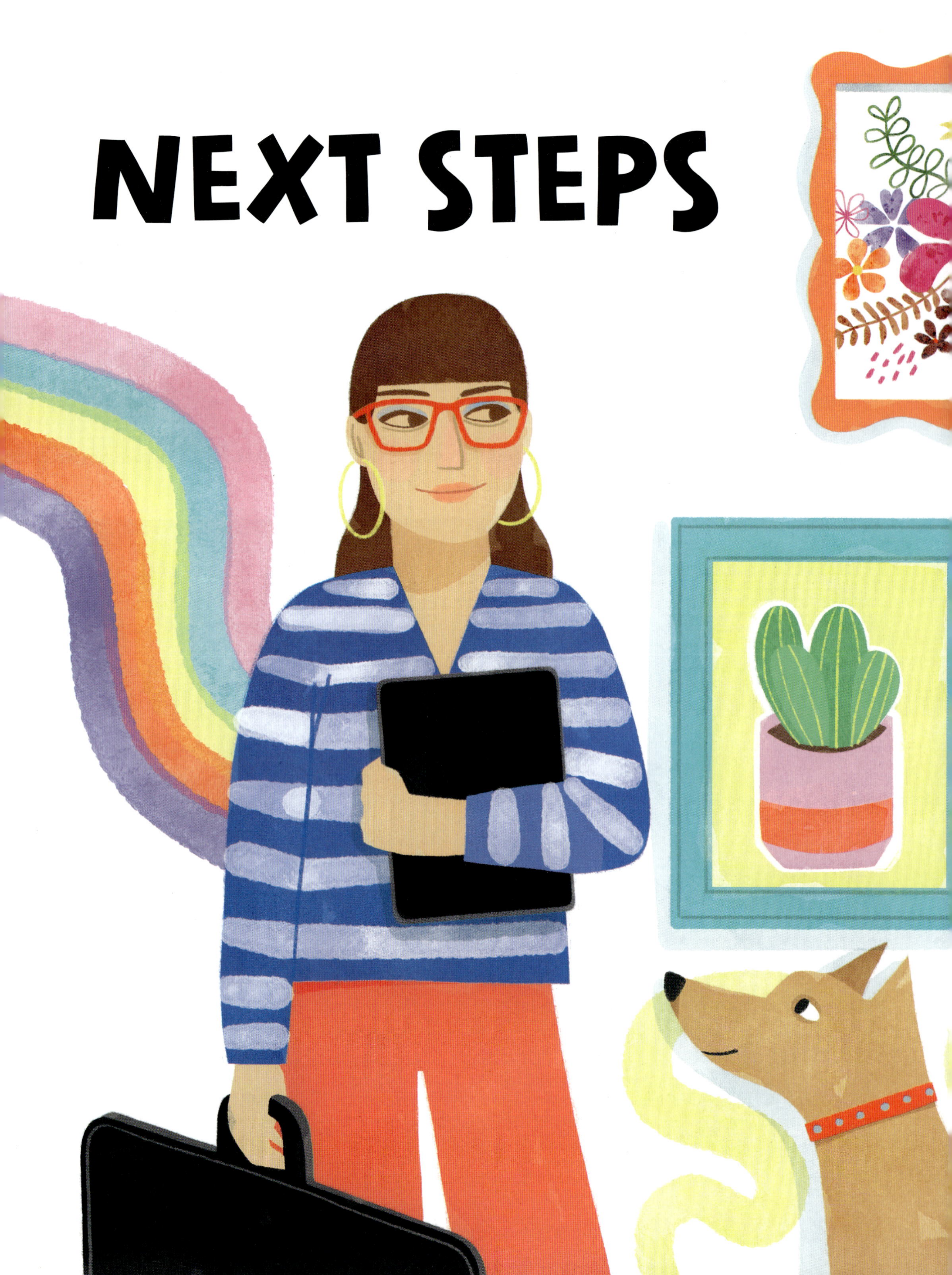

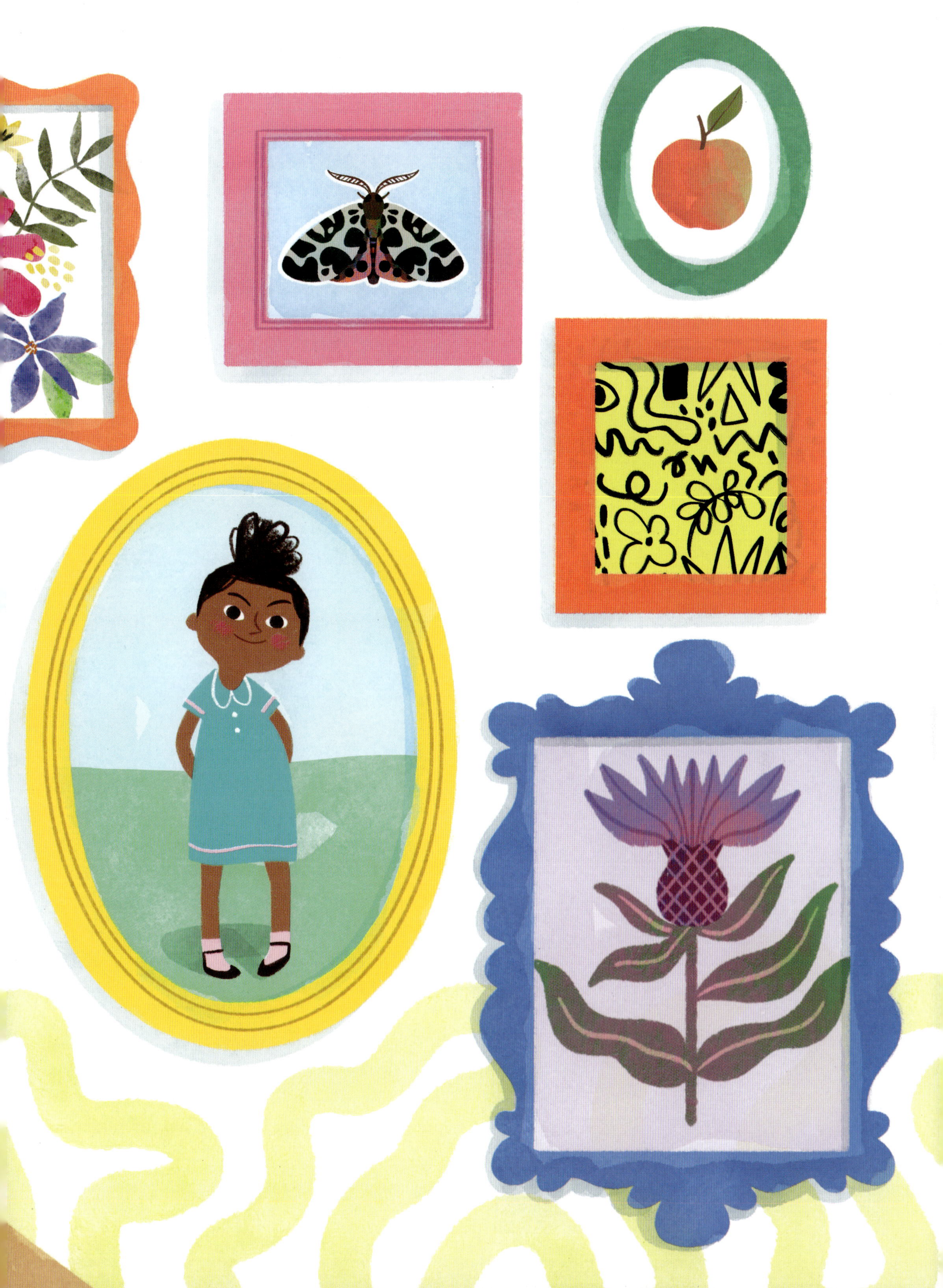

GOING ABOVE & BEYOND

Throughout this book, I have tried to show you how Procreate can be a constant companion on your art-making journey. I wanted to include a variety of projects and themes to showcase the app for drawing and painting, pattern making, design and illustration. Of course, we have only scratched the surface, but hopefully you can see the full potential of using Procreate as one of the main tools in your studio.

Mix your mediums

I know for many readers of this book, working digitally will not be a permanent replacement for your usual art-making practice. You'll continue to draw and paint traditionally. Nothing beats a quick sketch with a pencil or mark making with a dip pen and ink. Mixing gouache or building up layers of acrylic paint on a canvas allows your artistic spirit to be free – I would never try to convince anyone to give that up to sit in front of an iPad!

I would, however, encourage you to use Procreate to extend and enhance the skills you already have or, if you're a complete beginner, develop a process that includes traditional media alongside digital art making.

Enjoy your mistakes

There is a freedom in using Procreate too. Starting a piece of work knowing that everything can be edited, modified and refined is like walking a high wire with a safety net underneath. You can push yourself and take risks because every mark you make can be undone! Along the way, some of those mistakes will turn into happy accidents – you may unintentionally learn a new technique and start to incorporate that into your work.

Maximize your workflow

It's worth looking at ways to improve your workflow. I've tried to pass on gestures and shortcuts that I know and use day to day, but there are alternative ways of working and you'll find your own way of navigating the tools, layers and effects. Be open to implementing new habits. When you find a new way to do something, practise until it becomes second nature.

Join your tribe

You'll also want to expand your knowledge beyond this book. Take a look online at all the talented artists who are sharing their skills and know-how in videos and tutorials, many for free. Watching Procreate Time-lapse videos of artists' work will give you a real insight into how they put everything together.

In my experience, being part of an online community of like-minded creatives is a good thing. If you join a course for example, there may be a Facebook group for participants. Artists love to share tips and tricks; they'll help you out and encourage you to share your work. They will be kind critics and suggest ways to improve.

Discover your style

As previously mentioned in this book, finding your own style is important. If you're thinking about illustration as a career, you must develop your work in a way that is personal to you. You can admire other artists, you can be inspired by them, but you must have your own voice.

Creating consistently will help you in this quest. Set aside regular time to work. If you don't know what to draw or paint, think about joining an online drawing challenge. Prompts will be supplied daily or weekly. Sometimes it's just a word or a phrase, but it will get you started. You'll also find yourself part of one of those online tribes!

Procreate is the ideal tool for developing your own personal style. You'll eventually build up a library of favourite brushes and colours. You'll embrace a personal workflow and establish your own ways to create texture and depth. Your skills will evolve and enable you to create work that you're happy to share.

Before

After

PORTRAITS
The journey here is really about finding my style and not being afraid to draw facial features in different ways. I'm also starting to bring in hand-painted textures and signature motifs.

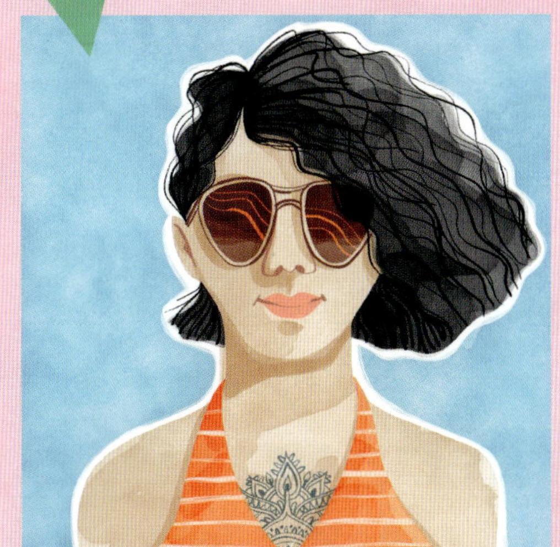

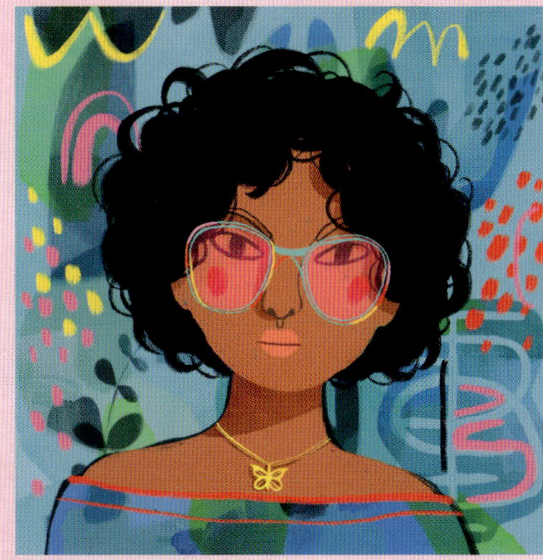

Before

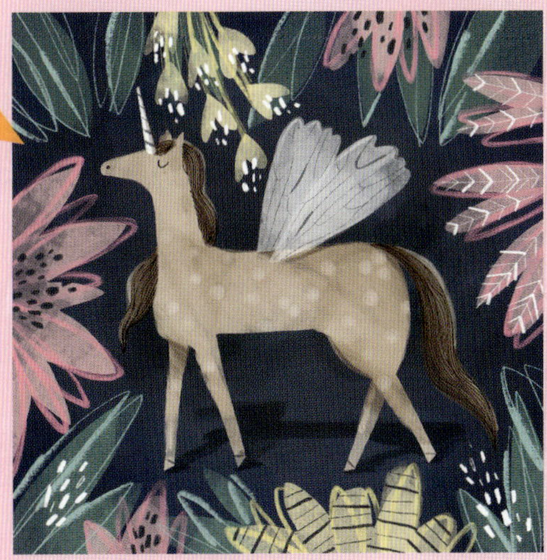

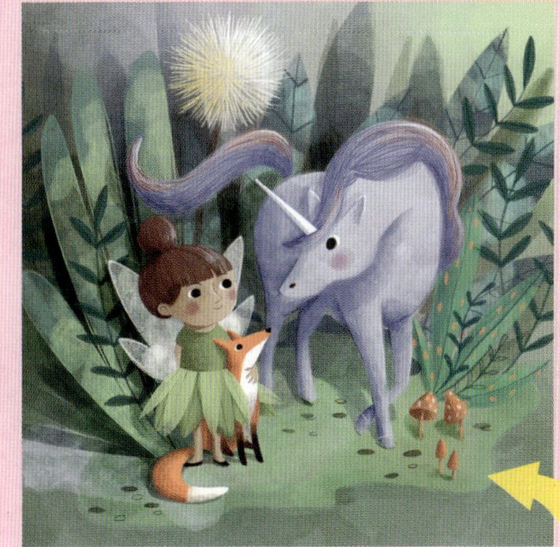

CHARACTERS
The unicorns were drawn only days apart. I distinctly remember thinking I had to up my game if I wanted to get serious about illustration. I threw everything at the second piece to prove to myself I could do it!

After

STILL LIFE
These weren't painted too far apart either, and I still love the earlier version. In fact I may use a similar style now for certain pieces. The "After" is me enjoying Procreate by using multiple brushes, layers and effects, and adding traditional media.

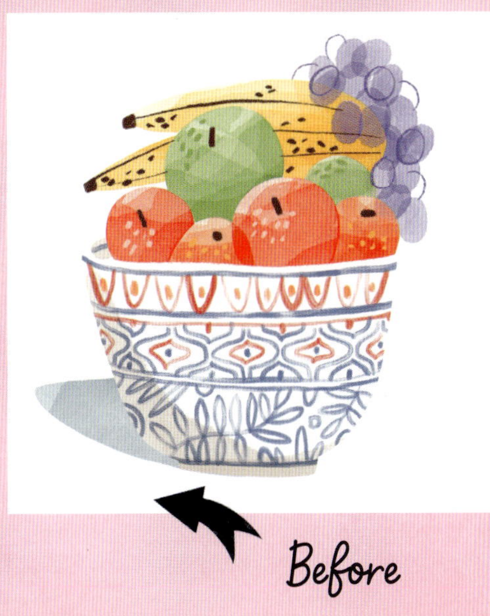

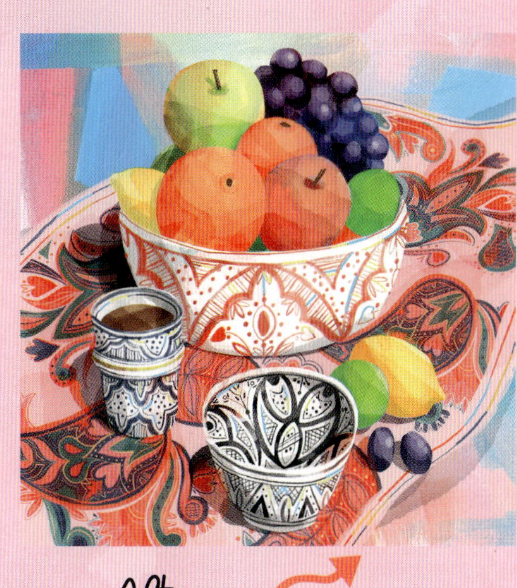

Before

After

MONETIZING YOUR ART

When you feel confident about your work and are ready to share it with the world, you might start to think about ways to make money from it. Being a creative in a world full of "content" can only be an asset. Look around – art appears everywhere. Not just online but in our day-to-day life. Packaging, toys, fabric, stationery and books are just a few of the things that require illustration, art and design. So, how can the art on your iPad find its way onto these products? There are many routes to take and many avenues to explore. Let's have a quick look at how you can monetize your art.

Print-on-demand sites

In the *Abstract Collage Wall Art* project, I touched briefly on the subject of print-on-demand (POD) websites which can be a good place to start. They are very competitive and hold the work of thousands of artists, but as a platform to showcase your work on a variety of products, they are unrivalled. Simply upload your work, then when something is ordered, they will print and ship the items. You have nothing more to do. However, with such a convenient business model, your percentage of the profit from sales will be very low. It is however an income stream, and with a bit of persistence you can make it work.

Another popular way to sell your designs, especially repeat patterns like the one we created in the *Repeat Pattern Fabric Design* project is by uploading to a POD site that specializes in digitally printing on fabric and wallpaper. You can also order fabric for yourself and produce your own items if you love sewing or crafting.

Producing your own product

Making your own products can be very rewarding and more lucrative than POD. You'll have to buy materials and pack and ship everything yourself, but you may be able to generate more profit this way.

In the project *Natural Symmetry Tote Bag*, I printed my design on to a tote bag using a heat press machine. I've used this method successfully in my business for many years. With a bit of investment, you can buy the tools and machinery to apply your designs to bags, t-shirts, mugs and coasters, amongst other things. It requires patience, trial and error, but the end products can be very saleable.

Prints and other paper-based products

Another way I sell my personal work is by making prints. You can use your local printer or search online for a suitable firm. Some artists invest in their own printer, which is great for smaller items such as the cards in the project *Still Life Greetings Card*. Either way, prints are always popular, especially with people who follow your work and want to support you. Ditto for stickers and postcards!

Selling online

If you're tempted by any of the ideas for producing your own items, you may also be thinking about establishing an online shop of your own. Please look into this possibility as it is really quite simple these days. A lot of website platforms are easy to use and have integrated software to set up a shop and take payments. I found www.wix.com especially useful when I set up my own e-commerce site.

Books and magazines

If you want to illustrate for books or magazines, you might want to think about looking for an agency to represent you. You'll need to build up a substantial portfolio of work before an agency will agree to represent you, but if you're successful, you'll have a good chance of securing illustration work in the professional field. The agency will also deal with contracts and payments, so you can concentrate solely on the business of making art!

Whatever you decide to do, Procreate will help. Having digital files of your work is necessary for all the above approaches, making your route to market a little bit easier!

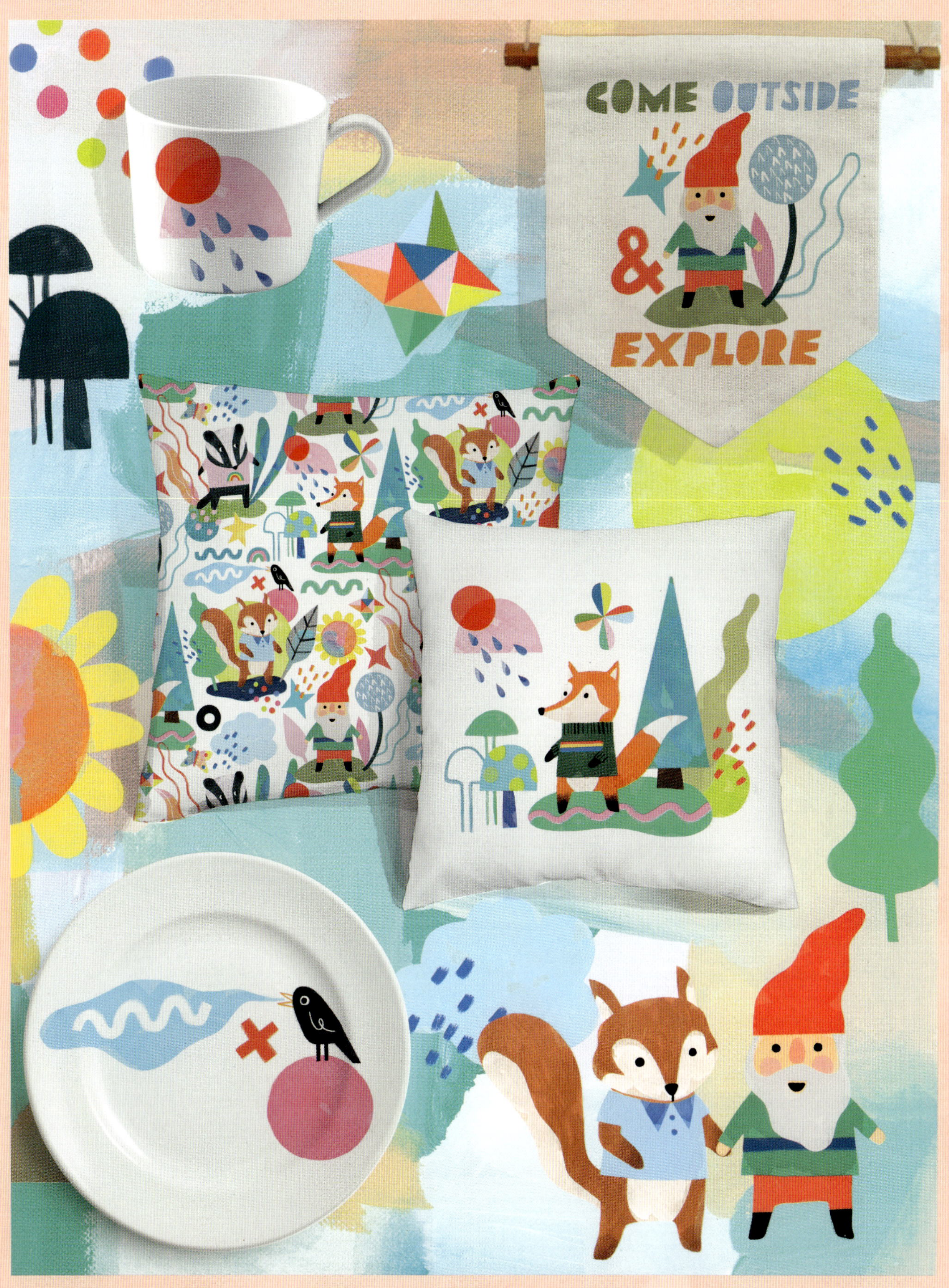

GETTING IT OUT THERE

This pitch board is something I would create for my agent to send out to potential clients. You have to create a lot of work for your portfolio. I'm always learning and trying new things on my illustration journey!

ABOUT THE AUTHOR

I have always loved drawing, painting and making. My nan used to keep empty boxes and a large roll of sticky tape ready for my Saturday visits. I remember making tiny homes and furniture for my dolls, and boats out of old chocolate boxes! I also loved entertaining and always took a lead part in the school play. My two main passions eventually came together when I studied Theatre Design at Nottingham Trent University.

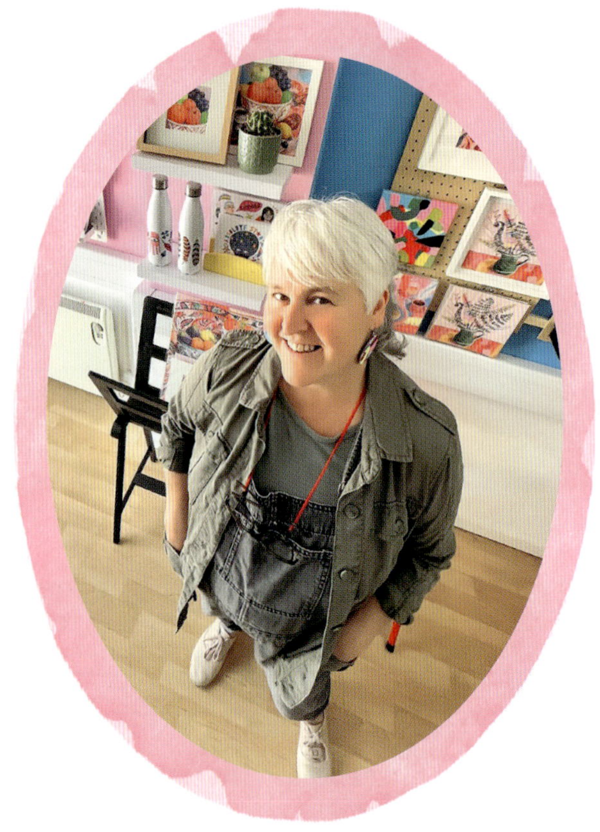

After moving to the United Arab Emirates at the end of the 90s, I started to develop an interest in computers and made my first piece of digital art in CorelDRAW around that time. I also started a long and interesting career in Event Design, designing seasonal decor for the mega malls of Dubai!

During this time, I was able to keep my self-taught digital skills updated by working in Adobe Photoshop and the 3D design software SketchUp to produce visuals for the event industry. I also opened a small gallery in Abu Dhabi and started making art again.

I eventually realized that illustration was the way forward for me. It seemed to combine all my skills learned over the years. It also involved that sense of storytelling and working to a narrative that I had enjoyed in the early days of studying Theatre Design. After dabbling in book illustration for friends who were self-publishing, I eventually found the online community Make Art That Sells and signed up for every class. It was time to get serious!

Fast forward to 2020, when the world slowed down and I found myself in the luxurious position of being able to make art every day and really concentrate on building up my portfolio, ready to send out to agents. I was taken on by Lilla Rogers Studio in 2021 and have since enjoyed working on a variety of dream projects including this book!

I look forward to seeing what you'll do with the projects in this book and would love to see and share what you do. Please post on your social media and use the hashtag #IllustratorsGuidetoProcreate

Thanks

I had never considered writing a book. I always thought I would be the one drawing the pictures and it never really occurred to me that this was a thing I could do.

Thank you to Ame and the team at David & Charles for giving me the idea and trusting that I could make something out of it!

Big thanks to Lilla Rogers and all the team at Lilla Rogers Studio – they find me the most amazing jobs and support me calmly every step of the way with their combined knowledge and vast experience.

Thank you to my family, who put up with my highs and lows, my erratic working hours and my constant neglect of their basic needs. I'll make it up to you when I've completed all my deadlines.

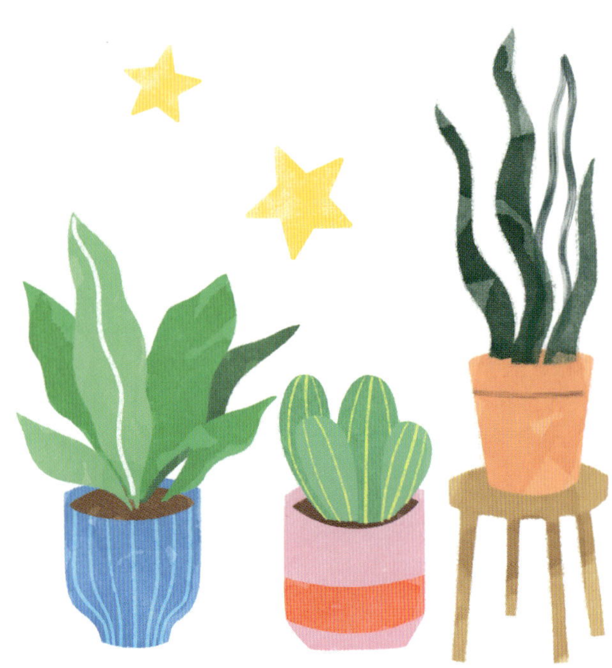

Website: www.ruthburrows.com

Instagram: @ruthburrowsillustration

INDEX

A DAVID AND CHARLES BOOK

David and Charles is an imprint of David and Charles, Ltd
Suite A, Tourism House, Pynes Hill, Exeter, EX2 5WS

First published in the UK and USA in 2023

A catalogue record for this book is available from the British Library.

ISBN-13: 9781446309629 paperback
ISBN-13: 9781446382189 EPUB
ISBN-13: 9781446310427 PDF

This book has been printed on paper from approved suppliers and made from pulp from sustainable sources.

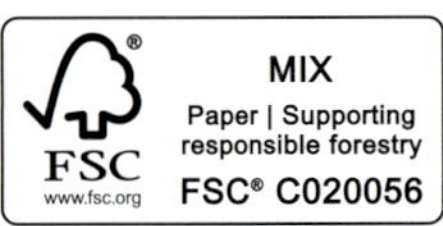

Printed in China by Leo Paper Products Ltd for:
David and Charles, Ltd
Suite A, Tourism House, Pynes Hill, Exeter, EX2 5WS

10 9 8 7 6 5 4 3

Publishing Director: Ame Verso
Managing Editor: Jeni Chown
Editor: Jessica Cropper
Project Editor: Jenny Fox-Proverbs
Head of Design: Anna Wade
Design & Art Direction: Sam Staddon
Pre-press Designer: Ali Stark
Photography: Jason Jenkins
Production Manager: Beverley Richardson

David and Charles publishes high-quality books on a wide range of subjects. For more information visit www.davidandcharles.com.

Share your makes with us on social media using #dandcbooks and follow us on Facebook and Instagram by searching for @dandcbooks.

Layout of the digital edition of this book may vary depending on reader hardware and display settings.

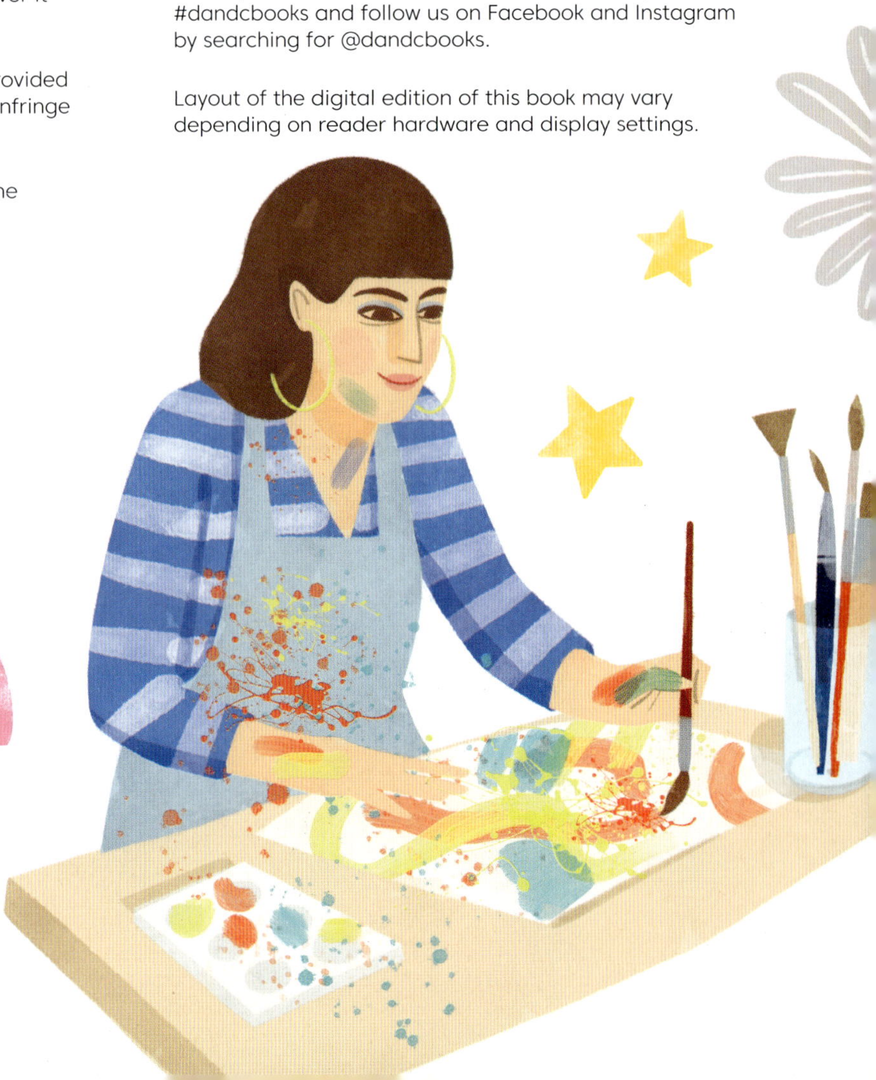

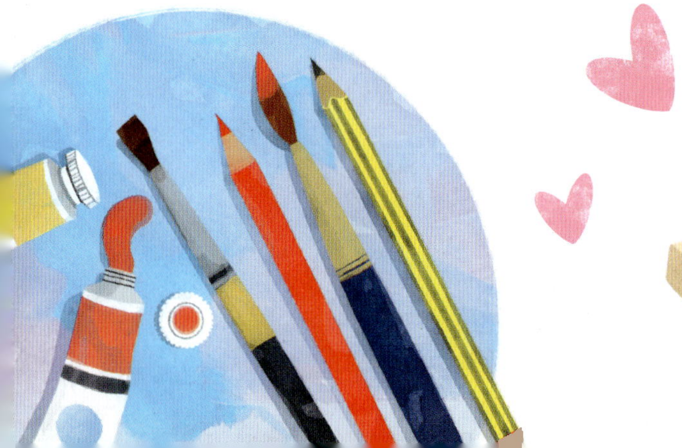